Collected Columns of Nick Clooney

WVXU 91.7 FM
Xavier University
3800 Victory Parkway
Cincinnati, Ohio 45207-7211
(513) 731-9898
Fax (513) 745-1004

Library of Congress Catalog Card Number: 95-60611

First printing March 1995

ISBN: 0-9646064-0-2

Typesetting by Pagemakers, Inc.
Printing by The Merten Co.

Dedication

To Nina
With Love

Introduction

I DON'T REMEMBER the first time I saw him. I don't suppose I was that impressed. I was, after all, six years old. Along about the time he was a year old I figured he wasn't going anyplace else so I took a good look at him.

He was a round kid. You couldn't see his eyes when he smiled. But when he wasn't smiling he looked at you very personally, as though he was regarding you. Not judging, really, but learning what you were all about.

He always wrote things. The songs he composed during World War II — when he was seven or eight — were especially memorable and especially gory. I remember every word of them, too, and sometimes we sing them together, even now.

He picked me up at the airport in Las Vegas when our sister Betty died in 1976. I had been living with my new prescription-drug-free sanity for a couple of years by then, but both of us knew this was a test I could easily fail. We walked through the airport, got into a car and found ourselves in desert sunlight. But neon was ablaze everywhere. Nobody seemed to know it was daytime. Nicky and I still hadn't said anything. I remember thinking I could slip away from all this with one turn of my mind.

Then Nicky's voice — sad, funny, strong, but more than anything, private — the one voice left that I would always hear:

"What a dumb place to die."

He is a writer of importance. He is a fair man. He has our grandfather's temper, I'm afraid. And when I get very scared, the first thing I think and — if I can — the first thing I say is, "Call my brother."

Rosemary Clooney
Beverly Hills, California
December, 1994

Prologue

IT WAS 1989 and Nick was unemployed.

Nick Clooney has had a remarkable string of jobs. About 22. He's not sure. Most of Nick's jobs have been in broadcasting, a business not known for job security. So getting fired or quitting or getting a promotion should have been routine. But this time seemed different.

Nick was king of local TV news in the late '70s and early '80s, before he was lured away to Los Angeles, to the major leagues. In 1986, he came back to Cincinnati, back to WKRC, but it just didn't work out. Maybe you can't go home again.

So in early 1989 he was between jobs, and I saw a golden opportunity. I'd hire Nick Clooney as an editor for The Post.

I wasn't concerned that none of Nick's jobs had been at a newspaper — he had proven that he was just about the best newsman around. He knows the area better than anyone, and he has interviewed nearly every mayor and business leader and police chief. He'd be perfect, I figured, to help direct our news coverage.

So I wrote Nick with a vague offer: let's talk.

I certainly had no intention of hiring Nick Clooney to write a column. The very last thing The Post needed was another columnist. We had columns for every topic, for every hobby, for every political cause, for every form of human endeavor. Ann Landers, David Broder, Sharon Moloney, David Wecker, George Will, Ellen Goodman, Mike Royko. Stamps, coins, politics, pets, investing, sports, fashion, fitness, religion. And for every column we published, there were a dozen budding columnists trying to land a place in the newspaper.

What I needed was a top-notch journalist to help us figure out how to cover the news. And Nick Clooney knows news. I wanted Nick to help us run The Post.

So, of course, we hired him to write a column. It was his idea, and it was, perhaps, the best one he's ever had. Certainly, it was about the smartest thing I've ever done.

Just one thing about Nick's columns. We've published 1,000 of them now, and people love them. They can't wait to read them.

When it was announced that Nick was going to work in Salt Lake City, then in Buffalo, frantic readers called, worried that he'd no longer write for us. Thankfully, he kept writing.

Once, due to misunderstanding, Nick's column didn't appear. The ink wasn't dry on that day's paper when the phone calls started: What happened to Nick?

No other columnist has that loyal a following.

Read on and you'll see why.

Paul Knue
Editor
Cincinnati Post

World War II

THE PUBLICATION DATE of this collection coincides with the 50th anniversary of the end of World War II. Though my age barely got out of single digits before the war was over, I, just as everyone else who has lived in this century, was profoundly influenced by it.

Actually, I didn't know how much the war affected me until I started thumbing through five years worth of columns. It has been a recurrent theme.

Perhaps these will strike a responsive chord with some of you.

Nick.

World War II

London, 50 Years After the War Began

Friday, September 1st, 1989

London —
   As you read these words, I am back in my hotel, going over a memorable day in my mind. It is five hours later here, and there is a lot to remember.
   Not just about today, although heaven knows there is enough about this late summer day in this sprawling, busy gem of a city worth committing to memory.
   Instead, what keeps coming back to me is a little wink of time earlier this afternoon. We stood in front of 10 Downing Street, the traditional residence of Great Britain's Prime Ministers.
   In this city built on layers and centuries of tradition, this moment is a solemn one. Fifty years ago right on this spot, World War II began.
   Hitler had invaded Poland, and inside this very door an ultimatum was formulated. If Hitler did not pull his troops back, a state of war would exist between the Third Reich and His Majesty's government. Neville Chamberlain, heretofore a pussycat, would find the iron his spine required.
   Part of that iron would have a name. Winston Churchill, at this moment fifty years ago less than a year away from succeeding Chamberlain as Prime Minister.
   I suppose no place in the world resonates more of that time than here in front of this unpretentious door. Not one of the great figures of 1939 is still alive, but their presence echoes here as nowhere else.
   What an incredible six years began on that long ago September 1st. What a terrifying cataract of disaster was about to be unleashed. The uneasy Phoney War of the winter of 1939-1940. The fall of Poland in a month. Blitzkrieg came west. The Netherlands, Belgium, Luxembourg swept away. Then, unbelievably, France gone. The Battle of Britain with Spitfire and Hurricane fighters soaring in these very skies held off Goering's

triumphant Luftwaffe. Then the Blitz, sudden death to thousands of men, women and children in these streets.

Then, later, unmanned missiles were turned loose on human beings, and it was these human beings here in this stately city that felt the pitiless, Orwellian sting of the V-1 and the V-2 first. Small parks and smaller placques now dot London, all telling the story of those days. This old church destroyed but rebuilt, that historic home blown to bits but replaced by trees, flowers and benches, another district flattened but resurgent in a different, better form.

The wonderful old walls reverberate with famous words:

"Never...has so much been owed by so many to so few."

"I have nothing to offer you but blood, toil, tears and sweat."

"...let us so conduct ourselves that though the British Empire and her Commonwealth last for a thousand years men will say 'this was their finest hour'."

Well, the British Empire did not last for a thousand years. It did not last ten.

The United Kingdom is no longer a great voice in world affairs, and its adjustment to that fact may prove to be an even finer hour in this city's illustrious story.

London is a remarkably resilient. It has a vitality that belies its decline in influence worldwide.

But if a nation's greatness can be measured by the power of its enemies, Britain is diminished indeed. The ferocity of Hitler and Mussolini is replaced by the dark-hearted terrorism of the IRA. Huge villains who lusted for world conquest replaced by moral pygmies of limited dreams. The V-1 replaced by the cowardly car bomb. It is quite a comedown.

But not today.

This 1st of September 1989 I looked at the famous door at 10 Downing Street and thought of how it brought down the massive Reich Chancellery of Hitler and the grandiose Palazzo of Il Duce, and I feel a surge of admiration for these great people.

In a small, self-conscious gesture, I saluted 10 Downing. It got puzzled looks from a few bystanders, but I am glad I did it.

Pearl

Friday, December 6th, 1991

Last year, I was accused by a reader of being obsessed with December 7th, 1941. On the evidence, I'll have to admit it. Guilty as charged.

Since I began my career in communications, every December in which I had access to a microphone or camera, or had a forum for the product of my typewriter, I have written about some aspect of Pearl Harbor day. This year, because we have reached the benchmark 50th anniversary of the surprise attack, many apparently share my obsession. I'm glad of it, because I believe that the bombing of our naval and air bases on Oahu was the seminal event of the 20th century.

I know that the point is arguable. I realize there are many who believe that the world's turning point occurred at the instant of the explosion of the two nuclear bombs over Hiroshima and Nagasaki. I disagree on the grounds that one led directly to the other as inevitably as lightning leads to thunder, and we all know which is the most important element in that tandem.

I believe that the lesson of Pearl Harbor is the most important in the long march of history. What was the lesson of the Sunday morning in Hawaii? That underestimating your adversary can have potentially fatal consequences.

We underestimated Japan. We will never do that again. Some of our miscalculation was racial. Even up to the highest levels of government, we believed the Japanese to be a near-sighted, obsequious, imitative people who made and exported cheap goods which fell apart when we used them. In spite of increasing evidence to the contrary 50 years ago, we never really believed they would attack the United States. And if they did, we were certain we would brush them off easily and chase them back to their island home in a month or two.

Japan also underestimated us. They will never make that mistake again. Some of their miscalculation was also racial. They believed themselves to be superior to other peoples, particularly Americans. They considered us soft and effete and were certain that one or two hard blows would knock us out of the war before it really started and give them the free hand in Asia they demanded.

Our sin of underestimation cost us dearly. We lost our Pacific fleet, were knocked back on our heels for nearly a year, and left treasure and little white grave-markers all over the South and Central Pacific during the next four years.

But Japan's sin of underestimation was to cost the land of the Rising Sun its national life. The Japan of today bears no resemblance to the Japan of all the years leading up to the first week in December, 1941. It was wiped as clean as a washcloth over a blackboard. The new nation which began in the fall of 1945 was a blank page which was modeled on and shaped by the United States of America.

The nuclear device which we all called the atom bomb was, in the tenor of the times, just a bigger and better bomb. Germany and Japan had introduced the new element of terror bombing of cities in Spain, China, Holland and Britain. Thousands of innocent women and children were blown to bits or burned to death as the rest of the world watched in horror.

After Pearl Harbor, the allies returned the favor with grisly interest. The fire bombings of Hamburg, Berlin and Dresden in Germany and of Tokyo in Japan exacted as many innocent lives as the nuclear devastation of August, 1945. Bombs became more sophisticated and efficient in their deviltry. In that sense, the atom bomb was simply the natural progression of grim technology.

For a time after the war, some historians advanced the theory that we goaded Japan into the war and that we had previous knowledge of their surprise attack. Exhaustive studies have shown both theories to be incorrect. Japan needed no goading. It had an arrogant sense of its own destiny as ruler of Asia. Our leaders were not conspiratorial, they were simply lulled by our own delusions of superiority.

Pearl Harbor ended all of that.

Swept away in the ensuing humiliating defeat was Japan's belief in the military cult. They would win future victories with economics, as they were taught by the Americans. They would learn well.

And we in this country would never again underestimate our major adversaries. With the exception of a few bloody sideshows such as Vietnam, we were more likely to overestimate our enemies than to underestimate them. That was certainly true of our attitude toward the Soviet Union, and our perseverance and vigilance gave us our greatest victory; the Cold War.

That's what those long-ago youngsters paid for in the early hours of a soft Hawaiian morning 50 years ago. That's their real monument as they rest in the hull of the Arizona in the blue harbor they were never to leave.

That's why those of us who were alive on that day seem obsessed. We feel the need to tell everyone how it was and what it meant. We want to make sure that everyone will always Remember Pearl Harbor.

The Tokyo Raid

Friday, April 17th, 1992

I wonder what was going through Tom Griffin's mind exactly 50 years ago today?

April 17th, 1942. In 24 hours, he and 79 other young men would do something that had never been done before, even in practice. They would fly fully-loaded, twin-engine B-25 Billy Mitchell bombers off the pitching deck of an aircraft carrier. Their target was Tokyo.

It's very important for everyone who was not alive then to know how it was. The United States had been kicked all over

the Pacific. Just a few days before, our troops had surrendered
on Bataan Peninsula in the Phillipine Islands and had begun a
terrible ordeal in captivity that only half of them would
survive.

On the little fortress island of Corregidor, Americans and
Filipinos fought on. They would hold out for three weeks more.

The British had been chased out of the Malay Peninsula and
impregnable Singapore had surrendered. So had Hong Kong.
Most of the American Pacific fleet was at the bottom of Pearl
Harbor, and surviving British and American warships were
being picked off one at a time by the triumphant Japanese Navy
and Air Force. There was no victory to cheer. We were losing
the war.

At home, we were angry and scared. We were seriously
planning to defend against an invasion and a few within the
Japanese military were seriously considering it.

That's how it was on April 17th, 1942, when a seasick Tom
Griffin looked out over the Pacific Ocean as the wind freshened
and the "Hornet" sped toward Japan.

Sixteen aircraft. Eighty men. All volunteers.

Tom and the others had trained hard for this moment. He
had seen the war coming and had joined the Air Corps back in
the fall of 1940. He trained as a navigator in Florida and by the
fall of 1941 he was a member of the crew of a B-25 stationed in
Pendleton, Oregon. That's where December 7th found him. Tom
was in the war.

In January, there was a call for volunteers for a dangerous
mission, just like in the movies. Those who were accepted,
including Tom Griffin, were launched on the great adventure of
their lives. First, they gathered in Columbia, South Carolina. In
February, they were in Washington, D.C. for intelligence brief-
ings, but they still weren't told their target. However, they did
meet their commander, the legendary pilot Jimmy Doolittle.

At Eglin Field in Florida they were told to practice getting their
B-25s off the ground in 400 feet rather than the usual 1200 feet
it required. 400 feet! Tom says that not one of the aircraft ever
really accomplished it, though some came close.

The third week of March they flew to Sacramento, California. At least now they knew the direction they would take. West. April 1st they were in San Francisco and their planes were lifted aboard the aircraft carrier "Hornet". Soon they were underway. Tom Griffin found out their target the same time as everyone else. A few had other Japanese cities. His target was Tokyo. Specifically, his crew would hit a factory on Tokyo Bay. They studied it until they knew every brick. They would fly at 50 feet.

The morning of the 18th there was a flurry of activity aboard. Navy Captain Mark Mitscher said a Japanese submarine may have spotted them, so they would take off earlier than planned. Tom and four others clambered into the "Whirling Dervish" and he squeezed into the navigator's spot behind the cockpit. There was a 20-knot wind and the "Hornet" was full-ahead at 30 knots. Perhaps that combined 50-knot headwind would be enough to get the bombers into the air. Perhaps. No one knew.

One after another, the B-25s followed Jimmy Doolittle down the rolling deck into history. Every one of them got into the air. All headed for the target. They were to bomb Tokyo or the other cities, then head for airfields in the Nationalist-held China. Very long odds, indeed, but we were losing the war.

Tom remembers the gray sea and the green coast of Japan, 50 feet below. Then Tokyo Bay. Then the factory, just as it looked in the pictures. They hit it dead center. They swooped over the Imperial Palace of Hirohito. Strict orders not to bomb it.

Surprise was complete. Some Japanese pursuit planes and flak finally got busy, but not one plane was shot down. Still, headwinds and a storm ran the Americans low on fuel. Tom's plane climbed to 10,000 feet. His calculations put them over friendly territory. The tanks were on empty. He and the other four bailed out. After many adventures, they arrived in Chinese hands.

Not all were so lucky. Eight were captured by the Japanese. All were tried and condemned to death. Hirohito intervened for five, but three were executed.

After the war, Tom moved to Cincinnati where he has lived ever since. This weekend he'll be at a reunion. 39 of the 80 are still living, including General Doolittle.

If you run into him next week, how about saying "thanks"? He owns a piece of our first victory of World War II. Some of us remember how important that was.

30 Seconds Over Norfolk

Friday, March 25th, 1994

Let me tell you one of the great untold stories of World War II.

You know the remarkable tale of the young fliers under the command of Jimmy Doolittle who took off from the pitching deck of the USS Hornet and flew their B-25s over Japan, bombing Tokyo and other cities in the early, desperate days after Pearl Harbor.

On the 50th anniversary of that event — almost exactly two years ago, now — there were many stories about the achievement and about the surviving pilots. I wrote one in this space.

A famous movie was made about it all: "30 Seconds Over Tokyo." The all-volunteer crews practiced short-field take-offs on day land, remember? One of the intriguing parts of the story is that they never took off from the deck of a carrier until they actually started their mission a few hundred miles from the Japanese coast.

They believed, and we in America believed, and screenwriters believed and reporters believed that they were they first ones ever to fly a fully-loaded B-25 bomber off the deck of a carrier.

All of us were wrong.

Weeks before these young men headed for Florida to train for their mission, three crews were already practicing to see if it could be done. In command was Captain Jack Fitzgerald, who knew as much about the B-25 as anyone. He had been a test pilot for the "Billy Mitchell", as it was called, at Wright Patterson in Dayton.

The co-pilot of the second plane was Tommy Cline from Augusta, Kentucky, my friend and neighbor. The pilot of Tommy's plane was Oscar Wertz. Both were second lieutenants. Tommy had been in the service since 1940.

In January, 1942, a scant five weeks after Pearl Harbor Day, three B-25s landed at the naval air station at Norfolk, Virginia. The crews were told to practice short-field take-offs. They did. More than 100 take-offs in such small airports as Lynchburg, Virginia.

A Commander Koepke of the Naval air arm was their liaison, so they could guess what was going on, though no one specifically told them.

In the last days of January, 1942, the aircraft carrier Hornet docked at Norfolk after a shakedown cruise of a month. Her captain was Mark Mitscher, later a famous task force commander. Captain Jack Fitzgerald gave Mitscher a letter which explained the project.

Soon, two of the B-25s were lifted onto the deck. The third had to be left behind because of engine trouble. On the night of February first, the Hornet cast off and went to sea, carrying with her the prologue to one of the war's great stories. Everyone knows the story. No one knows the prologue.

One hundred miles off the Virginia coast in sub-infested waters on the second of February, 1942, Mitscher turned the Hornet into the wind.

Jack Fitzgerald and his co-pilot revved up the twin engines. There were enough sandbags aboard to simulate the "gross weight, loaded", about 30,000 pounds. The ship was making 28 knots.

In a heart-stopping moment, the big bomber rolled down the deck. It got off with room to spare. That was the first B-25 ever to fly off a carrier deck.

Moments later, the B-25 flown by Oscar Wertz and Tommy Cline of Augusta, Kentucky, became the second. Tommy, a math whiz, says it took their plane 183 feet to get airborn.

Twenty-eight minutes later, both landed at Norfolk, where then-Colonel Jimmy Doolittle met them and asked many questions. Doolittle then went to Florida to gather his small band together for their great adventure. The two pioneer crews were not invited. They think it was for security reasons. Doolittle didn't want his group to know exactly what they were doing until they did it.

Oscar Wertz didn't survive war. He was shot down over Lae in New Guinea in 1943. But I spoke to both Jack Fitzgerald in San Diego and Tommy Cline in Augusta before writing this.

Tommy had been disappointed not to be part of the raid, but today he has no regrets. His 60 missions in the South Pacific provided enough memories for a lifetime.

Still, both Jack and Tommy wish they had been invited to one of the "30 Seconds Over Tokyo" reunions. They never were. And they wouldn't mind if the record were set straight about who flew a B-25 off the deck of a carrier first. But they're happy to salute their colleagues who made history and gave the country a boost when it needed one. Badly.

They know that without their 30 Seconds Over Norfolk, there might not have been a 30 Seconds Over Tokyo.

Tom and D-Day

Monday, June 6th, 1994

Fifty years ago today, Tom Anderson of East Price Hill was nowhere near Omaha Beach. He was a 19-year-old Ranger stationed for the moment in Camp Shanks, New York, where he heard about the invasion.

"My first thought was, 'Great! That's the answer to Dunkirk.' The Germans kicked the allies off the continent in 1940. Now we were back. I knew I'd be there soon, but I wasn't worried about it. Not yet"

Tom is my cousin. He's always been the good-looking one in the family. He has a kind of sideways smile that women seem to like. He was also one tough kid. He boxed a little down at the Fenwick Club. Nobody in Price Hill messed much with Tom Anderson.

He turned 18 in December of 1942. Three months later, in March of 1943, he joined the service. He thought he was going into the Army Air Force. Instead, he ended up at Ranger school near Little Rock, Arkansas. You know about the Rangers. The training was the toughest the Army had to offer.

"We'd build these toggle rope bridges. Two ropes over a creek or river. We'd cross them under full field pack while cadre threw dynamite in the water under us. It was good training. Sometimes it was too good. We crossed the Arkansas River during an exercise. Seven Rangers drowned. Good swimmers, too, but the conditions were tough.

Forty days after D-Day, Ranger Anderson and thousands of others, "including Winston Churchill, some Royal Marines and bunch of crazy paratroopers" embarked on the Queen Mary for Great Britain. The huge ship sailed alone, without convoy.

"Those paratroopers were something. They'd climb all over the ship, up the rigging, anywhere. I was on guard duty and I'd have to go up and get them."

He arrived at War Minister Barracks near Wells, England, but not for long. He boarded an L-C-I (Landing Craft, Infantry) in Southhampton for Le Havre, France. It was the roughest trip he'd ever taken. It was August, and now he knew he was in the war.

"We boarded trucks in Le Havre and headed toward Belgium. Some of our trucks got taken out by artillery on the way. Six or seven, I think. Those guys never got into the war at all."

Tom got into the war all right. He was with an anti-tank unit. As an "assigned Ranger", his duty was specific. He would disarm mines and booby traps. He would also plant them when necessary. He dealt every day with high explosives.

"The nights were the worst. During the day we'd see German soldiers and very seldom do anything about it. But the night was different. We'd tie cans onto the wire and at night we'd hear them rattle. Then there would be an attack. Nobody slept much."

Tom's 20th birthday found him in the Battle of the Bulge. His unit was assigned to cut the supply lines of the Germans who had surrounded Bastogne. They got the job done, but Tom has never forgotten what he saw.

"The bodies were stacked everywhere. I even saw some up on telephone poles. They were frozen, all of them. Germans and Americans. It must have been below zero."

February, 1945. His unit was in Germany, not far from Cologne. "Every time I disarmed another booby trap, I knew the odds were getting shorter. These German soldiers were smart. They'd come up with something new. They'd booby trap the booby trap." On February 19th at 7 P.M., the odds caught up. "It just blew up. Knocked me ten feet in the air. I landed on my backside. I reached back to check. That's when I found out." What he found out was that one hand was gone and most of the other was gone, too. "I didn't think about that. Not right then. I was scared I might die. Losing all that blood."

He was listed M-I-A for two weeks. Then the doctors in Liege, Belgium patched him up and send him home.

"I was on a plane with other amputees, but all of them had lost either one or both legs. I was the only one who could walk. When the plane landed, there was a band and a red carpet and beautiful girls from Republic Aviation and I was the only one who could march out for the welcome. I had my own parade."

That was about all he had. When he got home, he had trouble sleeping at night for a year or two. He bounced from job to job before landing at the Post Office. After eight years there, he saved enough money to start his own floor covering business, which he operated for 28 years. He's now a sales consultant.

Tom married Joan Broderick in February of 1947. Their daughter Terri has presented them with nine grandchildren, eight of them boys.

Tom has run for Congress and for the state legislature. He gives motivational speeches. He's the most positive person I know. I asked him why.

"Faith," he said, "just blind faith. Some may not think that's much of an answer."

It'll do, cousin Tom. It'll do.

Spiced Ham

July 26th, 1989

All right, so we had a big bash for the nation's bicentennial. Fine.

Okay, a lovely party for the Constitution's 200th, then Cincinnati has a year-long blowout for its 200th, and now we're planning the same for Congress this year. Swell.

We're in the grip of 50th anniversaries for "Gone With The Wind" and "The Wizard Of Oz". That's nice.

But I'm here to tell you that we missed one of the great national celebrations of them all two years ago, and I for one don't understand it. I'm going to ask Tom Luken to institute an investigation.

In 1987, SPAM was 50.

Did you hear of the Tall Ships parading past the packing plant in Austin, Minnesota? Any commemorative pig coins struck? Even one tiny television special with fireworks illuminating a giant SPAM can? Nosiree.

My question is, why not? Surely this is one of the great survivors in business history, and we dearly love the triumph of the underdog. No product ever got off to a rockier start, none was more vilified by more people around the world, and yet it came through and prospered. My wife brought home a can of it last week and it showed no sign of the conflict; not a scratch or dent, no contemptuous graffiti scrawled on it.

It was not always so.

I remember the campaigns to introduce it when I was a little boy and the radio commercials were met first by shock, and then with laughters. The jingle was terrible; I don't remember how it

went, but I do recall the announcer would follow the jingle by
saying "Don't forget the new dance, the can-can full of
SPAM-SPAM". If Gertrude Stein wrote commercial copy, that
would have been it.

I remember a "Life" magazine article that told the story of a
Christmas party at which Mr. Hormel conducted a contest to
name their new canned meat, and the winner got a free drink.
After the verbal pasting the product took in World War II, he
probably needed it.

It was the company's own fault, really. They started it all by
encouraging people to make a "SPAMwich" and to start the day
with "SPAMbled" eggs.

"SPAM" is a pretty funny name, and the G.I.s were merciless.
When they got a steady diet of SPAM, or what they thought was
SPAM, they got on a caustic verbal roll that didn't end until long
after the war was over.

I think it was Bill Mauldin's characters Willy and Joe who prayed
"Now I lay me down to sleep, I pray the Lord the SPAM don't
keep". Brutal. And they didn't let up.

Uncle Sam quickly became Uncle SPAM.

Any group of troop-carrying vessels became a SPAM fleet. Any
sandwich was a SPAMburger. When entertainers went on a
U-S-O tour, they told everyone they were working the SPAM
circuit.

One of Bob Hope's sure-fire lines on his trips to entertain the
troops went like this: "I had a great dinner; fried SPAM. You know
what SPAM is, don't you? It's ham that didn't pass the physical."
Big laugh, much applause.

Only the Russian soldiers didn't join the general derision. They
liked it. They didn't call it SPAM, though; it was "Roosevelt's
sausage" to them.

But the Russians were the exceptions; everyone else, it
seemed, took shots at poor old SPAM. The sarcasm came in
torrents, and never slowed down. It became so pervasive that
there began to be a backlash of newspaper and magazine
stories urging people to let poor SPAM alone, some even
claiming that SPAM won the war.

Well, maybe it didn't win it, but it did survive it, and that seems to me to be reason enough to celebrate, because SPAM's survival was surely against the odds. Returning veterans almost unanimously vowed to boycott the canned meat when they came marching home, and they sounded as if they meant it.

But there it sits on the supermarket shelf, looking much as it did all those years ago; unpretentious, homely, solid, and, ultimately, triumphant.

I thought I'd call the Hormel company to see if they'd had a celebration on the 50th anniversary two years ago, but I decided against it. I was afraid I'd find out that Hormel had been gobbled up by some conglomerate with a taste for SPAM.

It would serve them right if SPAM proved to be as indigestible as all those veterans said it was.

The War Years

March 22nd, 1991

Let's see now, a centennial is 100 years, a sesquicentennial is 150 years, a bi-centennial is 200 years. All right, what is 50 years, a semi-centennial? I don't know, but we'd better find out, because later in the year we'll begin marking the 50th anniversary of our entry into World War II, and it looks as if it's going to be a four-year remember-fest.

We're getting warmed up already. Next month, the Historical Society will open its exhibit on Cincinnati during the Second World War at Union Terminal. A couple of famous vocalists have released albums saluting music of the period, including the "For the Duration" collection by my sister Rosemary about which I wrote a few weeks ago.

All this came to my mind as I was driving through town last weekend, switching the radio across the dial trying to find

When the Clooney sisters started at WLW in 1945,
Rosemary wasn't quite 17 and Betty was not
yet 14.

something both Nina and I would enjoy. I was brought up short
by the sound of my own voice, always an unsettling experience
and usually a reason to hasten on to the next station.

This time, however, I paused. What I was hearing was an
excerpt from WVXU's new compact disc "Cincinnati Radio, the
War Years". I narrate the collection, but my introductions are
mercifully brief. What dominates the album is the actual sound
of Cincinnati from 1941 to 1945. We hear Peter Grant on
December 7th, 1941. We hear young men being sworn into the
service. We hear big bands playing at army bases.

Perhaps more than any book or picture or artifact, these
recordings come closest to letting us know what it was really
like in our part of the world during the four most important
years of this century. What we felt, how we reacted, whom we
cherished, what we believed, what made us laugh, what made
us angry and how we expressed all of this to one another. The
Way We Really Were.

And just at that moment, coming out of the radio, were the Clooney Sisters, Rosemary and Betty, singing on WLW's late-night favorite "Moon River".

The two girls just barely got in under the wire as World War II performers. They began work at the Nation's Station less than a month before V-E Day and had been on the staff fewer than six months when V-J Day brought an end to the cataclysm. When their voices were caught on that long-ago acetate, Betty was not quite 14 and Rosemary had yet to reach 17.

As I listened, I suddenly became aware of where I was driving. Reading Road in Avondale. Right there, behind that statue, was a school where Rosemary, Betty and I spent a year of our lives. The building is gone. It was the war year 1943, and Rosemary and Betty were 11 and 14 and still two years away from starting their professional careers. I was 8, and it would be fully another eight years before I would begin my slow, painstaking march through the mysteries of the communications business. I was always a late bloomer.

At this time, Rosemary and Betty and I lived with our mother in a brand new apartment building on Clinton Springs. It was a very exciting time because we had never lived in a brand new anything before. Our homes in Maysville and Ironton and Evanston and elsewhere had all been built at the turn of the century or before, so we felt thoroughly modern.

Betty, the bravest and most imaginative of us, made by far the biggest splash at Avondale school. For instance, she told several of her schoolmates that she was a personal friend of the then-overwhelmingly popular heartthrob Frank Sinatra. They believed her.

As fate would have it, Frank came to Cincinnati for an appearance at the Albee. Betty didn't back off. She and her friends boarded a streetcar and went down to Fountain Square. She told them to wait while she went over to tell the usher that Frank's good friend Betty Clooney was here to see him. She had an animated conversation with the usher while her anxious friends stood by the Fountain, watching.

When she came back, she was in tears. Real tears. Frank was ill, she told them disconsolately. It was serious. He would probably die. He couldn't see anyone, but he sent his love.

By now, all the fifth-graders were crying, and they cried all the way home. Betty believed the story more than any of them, and helped them make plans for a Cincinnati memorial service for Mr. Sinatra when the inevitable happened. In the meantime, she suggested they all pray for him, and they did, right there on the streetcar.

Fortunately, their prayers were answered. As we all know, Frank made a miraculous recovery, and is still singing. Betty's coterie of Sinatra fans believed her utterly. Probably believe her still.

For a while there, Rosemary and I, who watched the virtuoso performance from the beginning, weren't so sure ourselves.

Train Travel

May 31st, 1993

I was talking to a young couple about to embark on a Memorial Day train trip. Not Amtrak. One of the excursions put together by dedicated people whose hobby it is to preserve the experience of train travel as it was in its heyday.

"It must have been great", enthused the young woman, "to have the time to absorb the sense of distance. It was the best of all worlds. You could get to your destination quickly enough to take care of any reasonable business, but slowly enough to let you adjust to time changes. No jet lag back then!"

That was a remarkably perceptive thing to say, and all of it was true. But it wasn't all of the truth. Still, I decided not to rain on her parade. I'm sure she's having a good time today.

Train travel did have great advantages, but there's no point in romanticizing it beyond reality. For those of modest means, a long train trip was no walk in the park.

Come with me on a journey from Cincinnati to San Francisco in March of 1943. My mother was going to the west coast to join her new husband, a Seabee stationed there. She was taking me with her. My sisters Rosemary and Betty were to join us soon. At least, that was the plan.

I was a very little boy. Union Terminal was a very big place. It was also unimaginably busy. Hundreds of trains left every day. Standing in the huge rotunda, we understood literally nothing of what the man on the loudspeaker was saying.

We traveled coach. It was scheduled to be a four-day trip. Mom had a full fare, which guaranteed a seat. I had a war-time half fare, which did nothing of the kind. The trip to Chicago was relatively quick and easy. I even had a seat of my own, by the window.

In Chicago, where we had to change trains, there was much confusion. The city boasted many train stations and we were directed to the wrong one. We eventually made the connection, but just by the skin of our teeth.

The coach was old. The seats were frayed and sprung. In the days that followed I often had no place to sit, except on a suitcase in the aisle. Other children did the same.

The dining car left us somewhere in Minnesota, but we hadn't used it anyway. Too expensive. A man came through each coach selling box lunches. These were our staple. I can see and taste the contents as I write this. A wizened apple or a brown orange. A cheese sandwich made so long before that the cheese and bread had fused. It was next to impossible to swallow. There was a little carton of milk. On one occasion, the milk was sour, a fact I didn't discover until I took one big swallow with which to dislodge the cheese sandwich. There was a water jug at the head of the coach car with little paper cups. After the first hour, the ice melted and the water was warm the rest of the way. We ran out of the cups on day two.

The weather turned unseasonably hot and the packed railroad car was stifling. Mom wrestled a window open. A mixed blessing. The breeze was welcome but the cinders were not. The steam

engine left its mark on us all with tiny black spots on face, hands
and clothing. Mom used her handkerchief to spit-clean my face.

The bathrooms were untidy from over-use. Sleep was sporadic
and uncomfortable. We were often shuttled to sidings, waiting
for express or troop trains to rush by. Even those who were a
laugh-a-minute when we started had become subdued or surly
by the time we reached the Nevada desert.

There was a highlight. Somewhere along the way a dining car
was re-attached. Mom found enough in the budget for us to have
breakfast. There was a tablecloth and silverware. I carefully
printed my order on the paper provided. RICE KRISPIES. The
snap, crackle and pop were comforting.

But only for a moment. I missed my sisters. We had never been
separated for long. A popular song of the day was "Close to You",
not the same one made famous by the Carpenters. This was a
Frank Sinatra hit, I think. It was suitably melancholy. I hummed
it all the way across the United States, driving Mom and all within
earshot to distraction, I'm sure.

Despite Mom's best efforts to clean us both up and put on our
best clothes in the cramped restroom as we rattled into Oakland,
we arrived stiff, tired, dirty and hungry. To top it off, we were so
ignorant of "sunny California" that we arrived at San Francisco
Bay, Mom in her thinnest summer dress and I in a short-sleeved
polo shirt. We almost froze to death on the platform.

Had we but known, it would have been a great comfort to
realize that at least we didn't have jet lag.

Guadalcanal

Monday, August 3rd, 1992

It's inevitable that over the period of the next three years, we will
continue to read, hear and see a lot about World War II. Every day
between now and August of 1995 will be the 50th anniversary of some
major event in that seminal struggle of the 20th century.

For instance, already on this page we've remembered the 50th Pearl Harbor Day and the 50th reunion of the survivors of Jimmy Doolittle's raid on Tokyo.

I think that's all to the good. I believe it's important that those of us who were children at the time be reminded, and those of us who were not yet on the planet be told, how it was, what it meant and what it means still.

Friday, August 7th, will be another anniversary. 50 years ago Friday, United States Marines waded ashore on Red Beach on Guadalcanal in the Solomon Islands of the South Pacific.

It was eight months after Pearl Harbor to the day, almost to the hour. It was our first major offensive of the Second World War and we at home had not the least notion how narrow were the margins by which our young men were holding on.

How many from Price Hill or Deer Park or Covington or Aurora or Flemingsburg were there on that morning or in the succeeding six months, do you suppose? Old men now in their 70s and 80s. How will they mark the day? Will they lift a glass to absent friends? Or will they choose not to remember at all?

In Washington, D.C., they'll lay a wreath at the Marine Corps Memorial. Simultaneously, on the island of Guadalcanal itself, a new U-S memorial will be officially dedicated. Eventually, there will be eight other obelisks sprinkled around the island marking such famous places as Henderson Field and Bloody Ridge.

Bloody, indeed. It's hard to imagine now the blood tax paid by those young men for every square yard of that steamy jungle. The Marines had been thrown ashore with their First World War Springfield rifles and had so surprised the Japanese that there was little resistance. At first.

The advantage of surprise didn't last long. The Japanese held all the cards. They significantly outnumbered the Marines, they had the defensive positions, they had nearby land-based air power and their naval forces were stronger than ours in the waters around Guadalcanal.

In fact, as soon as the Marines were landed, our naval task force was chased away by superior enemy numbers, leaving long before putting sufficient supplies ashore to sustain our troops.

The battle of Guadalcanal was much more than nasty firefights on obscure ridges, beaches and riverbanks. It was also a desperate struggle at sea, and we lost as many of those battles as we won in the next six months. The same was true in the air where our rag-tag "Cactus Air Force" fought to keep Henderson Field open and protect our ground forces.

The truth is, our success in World War II hung in the balance. We had never beaten the Japanese, nor had anyone else. The struggle was titanic.

Numbers tell a great deal about Guadalcanal. Our death toll on the ground was 1,800. At sea we lost 5,000 young men, including the five Sullivan brothers, on 24 warships. In the air, 420 died. A terrible toll.

But for the Japanese, Guadalcanal was a cataclysm. They lost 25,000 troops killed on the ground, 3,500 sailors and 1,200 airmen. Many grim days were ahead and thousands more would die, but Japan never regained the initiative. Guadalcanal was decisive in the Pacific.

But 50 years have gone by and the world has turned thousands of times. Today, Japanese own much of Henderson Field. They own much of the island's thriving tuna factory. Japanese also own the only first-class hotel.

I have a feeling that somewhere in Elmwood Place or New Richmond there's an older fellow reading those words, shaking his head, alone with his thoughts which we haven't earned the right to share.

I'd like him to know what that marker they're unveiling near Red Beach on Friday will say.

"May this memorial endure the ravages of time until the wind, rain and tropical storms wear away its face, but never its memories."

So long as Americans can feel pride and gratitude, never its memories.

Uncle Chick

Wednesday, June 15th, 1994

The war stories were flying thick and fast and coming from all directions. I was moving in and out of conversations, catching a phrase here or a sentence there. Most of them I'd heard before, so I'd pause just long enough to identify the anecdote before going on to the next group.

I'm sure all of us do that kind of story grazing at our family reunions. On a rare occasion, we might even hear a tale we've never heard before. That happened to me Sunday a week ago at our house in Augusta.

The "war stories" I referred to usually mean any family legend at all from any era. However, because the widespread commemoration of D-Day coincided with our gathering, many of the narratives this year were literally "war" stories. This is one of them, a 50-year-old family yarn I heard for the first time ten days ago.

One paragraph of background. There were four boys born to my Grandmother and Grandfather Guilfoyle. Samuel Cornelius, called "Neal", was the oldest. Next was James Louis, nicknamed "Chick." The third was William Joseph, known as "Choton". The youngest was George Wesley, whose contemporaries called him "Happle."

When World War II broke out, Neal was too old to be accepted in the service. William was the first to join, right after Pearl Harbor Day and he had quite a career in the Army Air Force ending up in such exotic climes as New Guinea and other South Pacific garden spots.

George signed up at about the same time, but he was ordered to wait until there was room in a class of aviation cadets, at which time he would be called. In 1943, when he was 21, he began his primary training. He eventually piloted a B-17 over Germany for the Eighth Air Force.

Chick was a very special case. First of all, he was one of the funniest men I've ever known. He had much natural talent and charm. He also had the worst luck in the family. For instance, when he was a little boy he contracted meningitis. He barely survived the ordeal and it cost him one of his eyes.

He made the best of it, put in a glass eye and got on with his life. In those days, that meant getting a job as soon as possible to help support the family. As a teenager, Chick went to work for a meat packing company in Maysville. On day, he got a large splinter from a wooden cheese box lodged in his finger. It became infected and before the week had gone by doctors were forced to amputate his finger.

Of course, these two handicaps meant he was precluded from active service. Or so he had been told by recruiters and so we all believed. We did not reckon with an angry father. Here's how it happened.

Uncle Chick's bad luck sometimes followed him into the field of romance as well. For instance, in a small southern Ohio town where we lived for a time, Uncle Chick wooed and won the daughter of the town's mayor. However, the union did not work out and the two quickly divorced.

Hizzoner the Father was not amused. Legend has it that he wielded considerable influence with the local Selective Service board. Much to everyone's surprise, Chick was reclassified 1-A, missing eye, missing finger and all.

Actually, Chick was delighted. However, there is no telling what mayhem he might have wrought on a firing range had he ever been required to qualify with a rifle. Fortunately, the Army recognized Chick's other abilities and made him a recruiting sergeant. As a result, Chick spent the rest of the war at the Metropole Hotel in downtown Cincinnati.

When the war ended, William came back from dodging Japanese bombs and George returned from dodging German flak. Both got through it all physically unscathed. They met up with Chick at a Price Hill bar. Chick was still in uniform and the tavern was crowded.

Conversation, of course, got around to the war. William told one of his stories. Then George told one of his. There was only mild interest among the listeners.

Chick had been uncharacteristically silent. Then, he quietly took out his glass eye and polished it. "Yes," he said, "Sherman was right, war is hell." He put the eye back in and reached for his drink. He reached with the hand that was missing a finger. "I suppose you could say there are some things about war that a man will never be able to forget."

There wasn't a dry eye in the house. From that moment, according to Uncle William, none of the three brothers had to shell out a dime for drinks. For a week, they were treated like royalty. Thoughtfully, no one demanded details of Chick's wounds.

Please note that Chick made no false claims. It was the generous imagination of the patriotic patrons which painted him a hero. And, of course, they were right.

They just weren't aware of what specific kind of hero he was.

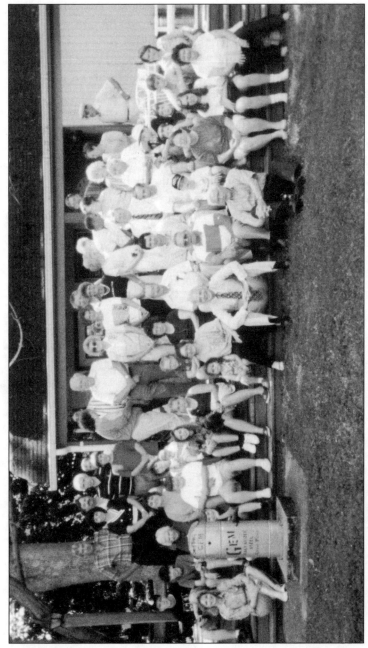

There's a Guilfoyle-Clooney family gathering every year. This is in Augusta, Kentucky, in June of 1994.

Family

My favorite of Papa's columns? I know it seems cliche, but I would have to choose the column about the birth of my daughter Allison.

The popular image of Nick Clooney, that of a calm, reassuring presence, relaxed and well-informed, is not far from the Papa that I knew; but not on this day. In his column, he painted himself as the traditional expectant grandfather, pacing and impatient. I didn't see his demeanor out in the hall, so I carry a different memory from that day.

I had been in labor for more than 24 hours by the time I got to the hospital. When Mama and Papa arrived, I was, of course, exhausted and in pain. Mama immediately hugged me and smiled reassuringly. Papa, wearing his brown camel's hair coat, his scarf wrapped perfectly around his neck and the Sunday paper tucked neatly under his arm, stood absolutely still at the foot of my bed. Only his right arm moved as he patted me tentatively on the foot. I had never seen him so ramrod straight. At the time, I joked to my husband Norman that Papa must have been afraid I'd give birth right then and there.

Looking back, I think that he was just realizing that his little girl was gone forever. So this column marked an irrevocable change in my life and my relationship with my parents. Mama and Papa probably feel the same way.

Ada Clooney Zeidler
Petersburg, Kentucky

Family

Irrefutable proof that Allison is the World's Only Grand-child. I ask you.

Life

Wednesday, February 13th, 1991

I suppose someone out there will try to tell me there have been grandchildren before. I will listen politely, of course. I was raised to be civil, even to those who are obviously misled.

As any fair-minded student of the subject would acknowledge, the history of grandchildren actually began on Sunday night at 10:30.

For some reason, TV did not interrupt the latest Middle East briefing nor the network prime-time schedule to bring you this news, though I, as a veteran reporter, dutifully called in the tip. This new crop of editors obviously wouldn't know a real story if they tripped over it. You'll find this hard to believe, but they didn't use it!

Fortunately, you know where to come for the real news of the world, so I will now fill you in.

The world's first grandchild is a beautiful, strong, loud and brilliant baby named Allison Jennifer Zeidler. She was quite reluctant to assume her responsibilities and fought for more than 24 hours to stay where she was. For a time I thought she would prevail, and so did her mother.

Nonetheless, in her own good time she made her appearance and announced it in a distinct and extended call that bounced off the walls of the St. Luke East Birthing Center for quite some time. I'm told some echoes are still reverberating. What a Girl.

Let me say that I understand and sympathize with those of you who have harbored the misapprehension that you, too, have grandchildren. For years I have looked at the pictures you carry in your wallets and purses. I have made appropriate remarks. But it was always clear to me that you had been hoodwinked. Now that the world's first real grandchild has come along, I can tell you the truth.

All those pictures looked alike! Someone long ago took a picture of a baby — one baby — and ever since then photographers have simply been making copies from the same negative. Yes, they've been clever enough to change the coloring and brush in different clothes, but it's the same child, and you know it. Come on, take it out and look at it. Be honest. Doesn't it look just like the neighbor's picture of his "grandchild", and your cousin's in Goshen and your aunt's who moved to Phoenix? Sure it does.

You'll be happy to know that a large number of the pictures of the first real grandchild have been made and will soon be available for you to look at. In fact, I plan to publish a different pose here in this space each day for the next three weeks. I haven't mentioned this to my editors yet, but I'm sure they'll approve. The pictures will, of course, be suitable for framing.

I must admit that this new event requires some adjustment. In order to have the first grandchild, there is a parallel requirement that one becomes the first grandfather. There doesn't appear to be any way out of it. I have checked with some of the best legal minds in the city.

Actually, when I look in the mirror it's not all that hard to picture myself as grandfather. Perhaps even a great-grandfather. On the other hand, it's absolutely impossible to picture my wife Nina as a grandmother. Those of you who have seen her know what I mean.

Actually, I believe that the world's first grandchild is well served in her choice of grandparents. Bob and Elsie Zeidler and Nina and I are not unaware of the honor bestowed on us and we intend to comport ourselves with the dignity required by our new station in life.

I'm sorry to report that Nina, Elsie and Bob were quite nervous through the entire process. I, of course, was my usual calm self, in perfect control of the situation as anyone at the hospital will tell you. It was occasionally necessary for me to pretend a certain unease with the process as the hours stretched out, just to make the others feel more comfortable. I'm sure a couple of hundred dollars will repair the waiting room, and it won't take much to replace the few worn tiles in the hallway.

The co-stars of the event were our son-in-law Norman who stood by his wife through the birth, a commitment that would have landed me in the coronary care unit.

And Ada. Ada who coaxed her tiny charge into the world through hour after exhausting hour. "Labor" is the most appropriately named activity in the universe. Ada, our little girl. No, a little girl no longer. A mother, courageous and hopeful like young mothers everywhere. Ada, the champ.

I'm happy to report that Allison Jennifer Zeidler, the world's first grandchild, is the second most beautiful baby ever born. A very close second.

To her mother.

Aunt Madeline, the unexpected passenger, finally comes home.

Aunt Madeline

December 4th, 1989

This is a tale of two aunts. One of them is no longer with us, the other most definitely is. Together, they combined to create quite a trauma for Nina and me a while back.

First, say hello to Aunt Madeline. She was my grandmother's sister, so she was either my grand-aunt or my great-aunt, depending on which dictionary you believe. It doesn't matter, because as an aunt she was both great and grand, so either prefix is appropriate.

Born Madeline Farrow in Maysville, she came to the Queen City as a young girl and became a dyed-in-the-wool west side Cincinnatian. She was in the work force all of her adult life, married late and had no children. Perhaps for that reason, she was a wonderful resource for her nieces and nephews and, later, for her grand- or great- nieces and nephews, none of whom deserved the prefix as much as she did.

Aunt Madeline was always good for a couple of bucks in the Christmas card and again in the birthday card. If someone in the family hit a low spot, Aunt Madeline was also always good for a bite to get him or her through.

In other words, she was a nice person to have around. We were all sorry when, several years ago, after a long and useful life she, in the parlance of her generation, "passed away."

Her husband Joe wasn't from the Ohio Valley. He was a native of the beautiful Shenandoah in Virginia and when Aunt Madeline died he wanted her buried up there. Her remains were duly cremated and she was transported to the Old Dominion for a final resting place.

Enter aunt number two. Aunt Christine is my mother's sister, the youngest of a family of nine and a major-league expert in the etiquette and protocol of "passing away".

More than that, she is the essential glue which ties our large and far-flung family together. She spends most of her money and all of her time on the telephone contacting family members, keeping one branch up to date with the latest gossip on the other, patching up spats, mending misunderstandings and generally reminding each of us that we belong to something that is more than just the sum of its parts. That we are a family.

There is no place you can go, nowhere you can hide, no name change you can undertake, no remote facility in which you can dry out that Aunt Chris won't find and contact you several times a year, chattering away about the thousand details that make up a life, bringing you into the picture, reconnecting you with your kin.

But now she was outraged. Aunt Madeline buried in Virginia? She hadn't even liked Virginia when she was alive. It was not fitting. Aunt Madeline should be buried in Maysville, among her friends and family, in the shadow of the hills she had loved.

Her pleas were to no avail, but Aunt Christine is patient. She knew time was on her side, and it was. Uncle Joe remarried and his interest in his former life weakened. Christine made her move.

I knew none of this, so when Nina and I went to Aunt Chris's home in Washington, D.C. to take her on a short driving vacation to Williamsburg and Virginia Beach, I was blissfully unaware of the part we were about to play in a family melodrama.

When, after a week or so, we dropped Aunt Chris off, she gave us a few things to take back home with us. Mementos to drop off to various family members. Nothing unusual. She was the distribution center for pictures and books and trinkets that had sentimental value.

We put them in the trunk and continued our journey. Harper's Ferry and a wonderful night at a hilltop hotel. Driving through the clouds in West Virginia mountains. A quick pause at the lovely Greenbrier in White Sulphur Springs. We took the long way home with many stops, leisurely dinners and long walks under trees coming to life in the first week of spring.

Back home we dutifully delivered our packages, including one small but rather heavy cardboard box that was to go to Uncle George.

It had come open while rattling around in the trunk and an official-looking paper peeped out. A "permit to disinter and trans-ship the remains of..."

Good God, it was Aunt Madeline!

We had just taken a vacation with a dear departed! She had taken the best trip of her life after she had "Passed away"! I nearly passed away myself.

I immediately burned up the wires to Washington, but Aunt Chris, with practiced aplomb said, "Oh, did I forget to tell you?" Yeah, right.

A few weeks later, we buried Aunt Madeline again among her kith and kin. Aunt Chris smiled enigmatically. I have pictures.

Nick, Rosemary and Betty moments before Nick stepped out in the fateful parade in Ironton, Ohio. 1941.

I Was Lost!

Friday, December 18th, 1992

My niece Monsita was recently recounting a family drama which, like so many others, doesn't sound like much until it happens to you.

She and her young family had recently moved from Virginia Beach, Virginia to Connecticut. Among the onerous tasks of such a dislocation is changing schools with all the attendant trauma for the children. New teachers, new friends. And new buses.

One bus looks pretty much like another to a first-grader, especially in Connecticut. Within a few days of his arrival,

Monsita's son stormed out of school at the end of the day and hopped on the bus. The wrong bus.

Too shy to ask questions of his peers or the driver and too brave to cry, he picked a random stop on the side of town opposite to his home, got off and started walking.

There was a happy ending. By fortunate chance he saw a schoolmate he recognized whose parents were summoned. They eventually contacted my now-frantic niece who had been waiting for her son at the bus stop and, other than a few more parental gray hairs, no one was the worse for the experience.

When I first heard the story I asked "Why didn't he just tell the bus driver as soon as he knew he had made a mistake?" But right in the middle of that sentence, it all came flooding back to me and I knew exactly why that little boy didn't ask for help. Perhaps for the first time in half a century I understood that within the world of a six-year-old, what he did was perfectly reasonable. I remembered precisely what it felt like, sounded like, even smelled like. For once, I was actually transported back to a moment in my childhood. Not to an adult memory of an event. To the event itself.

I had begun the first grade at St. Patrick's school in Maysville, Kentucky, but within a month or so, the imperatives of family economics dictated a move upriver to the hard-working, blue collar community of Ironton, Ohio.

Grandma Guilfoyle headed the household, Uncle George, 19 years old, opened what we then called a "filling station", Uncle Chick had a job and Rosemary, Betty and I would enter St. Joseph's school.

The good sisters did their best to make us welcome. Within two weeks I was, wonder of wonders, in the school band. It was a full marching band with uniforms and all and I was overwhelmed with my good fortune and my new importance. I was assured my instrument was the bellwether of the organization and without it the marching cadence would fall into instant disarray. I played the triangle.

Thanksgiving week. A parade through downtown Ironton, a huge, forbidding metropolis which I had not yet explored. The morning arrived and I put on my uniform immediately upon getting out of bed. My tall, plumed hat required the addition of half a bale of tissue paper in its crown to keep it from falling down over my eyes and ears, a decided handicap for a triangle virtuoso. I had my picture taken with Rosemary and Betty.

The whole family went to see me off on the parade and await my return. They were no more experienced in parades than I and did not know that the parade wouldn't return. It would disband at the opposite end of town.

I stepped off proudly with the others and concentrated so mightily that not once did the band's marching cadence fall into disarray. That responsibility lifted from my shoulders, I watched as my fellow marchers melted away in all directions with friends and family. I was alone. Times Square, which I have since often visited, was never so large as downtown Ironton, Ohio.

Several people asked if I was all right. I assured them I was fine. To stop their questions, I began to walk purposefully, as if I knew where I was going. I saw a jewelry store like Papa Clooney's back in Maysville, and stopped. The watches and rings and gold strands were familiar. I reluctantly moved on.

I passed by saloons, and the laughter and the smell of stale beer and cigars reminded me of Market Street in Maysville and were comforting, but when someone would yell out the door, "You okay, little boy?" I'd say that I was fine and move on.

Why did I do that? Why was it perfectly clear to me that I would rather wander the terrifying streets of downtown Ironton forever in my band uniform and die of starvation in the privacy of an alley than to admit to a stranger I was lost? I don't know, but the choice was absolutely clear and perfectly reasonable to me at the time. At last I found the river, which was — and in some ways still is — my North Star. I was skipping rocks across its surface, not afraid any more, when Uncle Chick honked his horn. "Where you been, boy? We've been looking all over for you."

I understand that little lost Connecticut boy very well. He was just looking for the river.

Rosemary

Carnegie

October 14th, 1991

I wonder if I can make you understand this. I wonder if I really understand it myself.

It was Saturday night, and the show was over. Rosemary Clooney was standing on that famous stage, and she had just told us all

"...These few precious days I'll spend with you,
These golden days I'll spend with you..."

and the music stopped, and she looked at us for a moment, and began to walk to the wings. The applause, which had been warm and generous all night, began almost tentatively this time as the last note of the last song made its way to the back row and up, way up to the fourth balcony.

Then the applause exploded, thundering and reverberating off the walls. Somewhere off to my right, a woman stood up, then a man. Then a group behind me, and a whole section to my left.

By the time Rosemary took her last bow, everyone was standing, and the applause was an ovation. Everyone was focused on the performer, but I was looking at them, the glittering, glamorous best of a New York audience.

Carnegie Hall, October 12th, 1991.

They were standing and cheering for Rosemary at Carnegie Hall.

Somewhere in the rugged foothills of the Himalayas, a child grew up in the shadow of Mt. Everest. He was told of it from the time he could walk. He would hear of it from his elders who would speak in reverential tones. Eventually, it would be pointed out to him, and on clear days he could see its summit rising heavenward among competing heights.

Someone had actually been there, he was told. Some few brave and talented people had scaled that mountain against all odds, and because they had, their names would live forever. There was no higher place to be on the planet. The little boy understood. One in ten million would stand there; only one.

He couldn't dare believe he might be the one. A faint hope, perhaps a distant dream; it could be no more than that.

On Market Street in Maysville, Kentucky, two little girls sang from the time they could talk. Some relatives swore they sang their first words. By the time other young girls were planning their proms and whispering about their "steadies", Rosemary and Betty Clooney were singing for a living. They would have sung anyway. The salary was a bonus.

From the moment they knew anything at all about their profession, they knew of Carnegie Hall. If the milieu was music, then its holy temple was Carnegie Hall. Only the best were ever invited to walk its hallowed stage. Only the best of the best.

It was Everest looming on New York's 57th Street, a distant, gray-walled, unassailable pinnacle.

Eventually, the Clooney Sisters became Rosemary Clooney. She carried the music gift and its secret hopes on alone.

No, not alone, really. Betty is with her always. So is Grandma Guilfoyle and Poppa Clooney and Mom and Dad and Uncle George. All gently insistent that she remember her gift, and respect it, and do her best with it.

It has carried her far, that gift of hers. It has made her famous. It has denied her a normal life. Sometimes it has dragged her through places she didn't want to be. Occasionally it has taken her to storied places.

But until Saturday, it had never taken her to the ultimate hall.

The night was electric. The orchestra was made up of New York's best. There were arrangers and composers and instrumentalists whose contributions to the evening were incalculable. The magnificent Linda Ronstadt made a stunning cameo appearance which was unforgettable.

But it was Rosemary's evening. She sang as well as she ever has sung, which is a considerable thing to say. She sang the songs of her life, which are the songs of our lives too. She gave each song its due, and a little more. Everything she had learned about the good and bad that life has to offer were in the words she sang.

Pain was there, and humor. Love was there, and courage. If this was to be her moment at the windswept crest, she wouldn't falter. She would do her best for all of us who were part of her long, dangerous, arduous ascent.

And when she was finished, we all stood up, because that's what you do when a person who has earned your respect is leaving the room.

It's a long way from Market Street in Maysville to Mt. Everest. But perhaps not quite as far as Carnegie Hall.

Lt. George Guilfoyle, B-17 Pilot, 8th Air Force, World War II

Uncle George

July 23rd, 1990

The most unforgettable character I've ever met? Easy. Uncle George.

And underline the word <u>character.</u>

I have often in this space paid homage to the women who have shaped my days. I gladly honor my wife Nina, my sisters Rosemary and Betty, my Grandma Guilfoyle, my Mom and assorted aunts, cousins and friends who encouraged and supported me against the weight of the evidence.

It is clear that the dominant influence in my formative years was female, and I proudly acknowledge it.

On the other hand, what was my male influence? Mom and Dad were separated by the time I was four years old, so who was — in the parlance of the '90s — my "male role model"?

Uncle George. George Wesley Guilfoyle.

A columnist in the '50s said his name was the most mellifluous since the fictional Gaylord Ravenal. He didn't know the half of it.

George was a product of the Roaring '20s, born in December of 1921. He often has reminded me that he only got one month of 1921 and by all rights he should be considered a child of 1922, but I have been relentless. 1921 it was and 1921 it stays.

Some individuals are marked from birth to be unique. To be the one others copy, admire, talk about. These are the people who are welcomed when they arrive and missed when they leave. George has always been one of these star-crossed people.

I often wondered how the starkly Protestant "Wesley" showed up as the middle name of an Irish Catholic boy, but when you're the eighth child of nine, it's likely his parents simply ran short of middle names.

George Wesley was a teenager when I came along. His older brothers drifted away to get jobs and get married and he didn't have any younger brothers, so he was stuck with me. In a sense he was stuck with the whole family; at least that part of it left at home.

After he graduated from high school, he gave up his scholarship to Xavier University and went to work to support us. When he got a chance to buy a filling station in Ironton, Ohio, we all moved there. When he got a job at Baldwin Piano, we all moved to Cincinnati.

The war came, and a friend of his who had gone off to college told George how he had flunked the test for aviation cadets. "It's too tough. You couldn't pass it either", he told George. So, of course, George took the test, passed it and became a B-17 pilot. He flew 25 missions over Fortress Europe, including several harrowing trips to "The Big 'B'" — Berlin. He told me how the fliers sat on their flak jackets instead of wearing them so that an errant piece of shrapnel coming up through the fuselage wouldn't preclude a crewmember's chance to have a family.

When he came back from the war he learned that his nieces Rosemary and Betty were singing on WLW radio. Then they got a break. Tony Pastor offered them a job as singers with his band. They'd travel all over the country and have a chance to hit it big. But they were too young. They were going to have to pass their chance by, perhaps forever. Unless...

...Unless a relative could become their legal guardian and manager and travel with them. And that's exactly what Uncle George did, until Rosemary became a solo hit, and then Betty became a solo hit and both got married.

Then Uncle George got hooked on what turned out to be his real passion in life. Horses. Just as he had made himself a pilot and a show-business manager, he made himself a trainer. A very independent trainer and a rugged individualist who seldom trained any horses but his own.

Through all this period, George always dated the most beautiful and brightest women I ever saw, but he never married. The timing was always wrong. There was the Depression, then the War, then the Clooney Sisters, then the horses. So George has no children.

But there are two generations of nieces and nephews who think he is the best thing that ever happened to the planet earth. He tells the best stories, he takes them seriously, he listens to them, he's fun and funny, he has his own language. He is an absolute original. Every niece and nephew has an imitation of or a story about Uncle George.

Well, no wonder he's so good with kids. He used me to train on. I was his first experiment.

Since there were no other men around, he was the one who taught me what it was to be a man. To face up to bullies, but never to pick on anyone weaker. That no one was better than anyone else. Always to stand up for my family and friends. To be there when people needed me.

Old George Wesley isn't feeling so chipper these days. We're none of us getting any younger. I'm not sure I ever thanked him for those years when I was a kid. That's not exactly the kind of thing we talk about when we get together; but I'm pretty sure he knows.

I named my son for him.

Uncle George died the day this was published.

*Jack Warren, visiting us in Pasadena
in 1984, was once a Show Business
Impresario. Almost.*

The Skin of His Teeth

May 30th, 1990

Timing is everything.

We become famous or remain obscure, succeed or fail, based on our ability to catch the brass ring as it goes swiftly by.

The most obvious example of this axiom in my own experience occurred 20 years ago in Perryville, Kentucky.

First I have to tell you about my father-in-law. Breaking with a timed-honored in-law tradition, I liked and admired him. He was, in fact, one of my heroes.

Jackson Warren was born into a farm family in Western Kentucky. To call them a poor farm family would be redundant. There were few rich farm families in those days in Kentucky or anywhere else. The prosperity that fueled the Roaring '20s never really filtered down to the American family farm.

So the Warrens had to go elsewhere for work. Young Jackson went with them from mill town to mill town. His father took what jobs were available and when they dried up, he moved on. Jackson went to seventeen schools by the time he was 15 and there was born in him an insatiable appetite for stability and roots.

He ended up in Boyle County, Kentucky, and there he would stay. He was bright, and his travels had developed in him a warm, outgoing personality. He had something more, too. It was a quality the people of that time would call "character." It drew others to him like a magnet. They knew they could trust his word and his friendship.

He worked for others, and he worked hard. He also took his education seriously. In a time when farm boys seldom finished high school, Jackson was graduated and then took the unprecedented step of entering Centre College in Danville. No one in his family had ever done that before. Even though economic pressure forced him to leave school, the fact that he had walked through that door was a quantum leap forward, and would change forever the scope of the dreams of the children he would have, and their children. He married beautiful little Dica Edwards and they began their lives as tenant farmers. He knew well the inherent instability of that life, so he set one goal. His family would own its own farm.

Banks wouldn't even talk to him, but one of the people he worked for would. Miss Bruce Morgan admired the young family which was so determined to be independent. She loaned them the money and they bought a 50 acre farm with a small frame house. It was "Tara" to them, because it was theirs.

Children arrived. Nina Bruce — named for their benefactress — Jackie and Kenneth. Times were hard on the farm and the work was endless and back-breaking. For a time, Dica had to take a job in town to supplement the family income.

But eventually, the farm was paid for and a neighboring farm was bought. They had roots, stability. They were successful.

In the meantime, their daughter Nina Bruce had been graduated from Perryville High School and had gone off to the University of Kentucky on scholarship money she had earned by winning beauty pageants around the state.

Two years later, she married a young man she had met in Lexington. He was a broadcaster. A *what?*

The Warrens welcomed me to their home. They were solicitous and civil, but they were bewildered that a man could actually make a living by talking into an inanimate object. They tried valiantly to make a connection with a person whose profession produced no product, didn't touch the soil, left no tangible evidence of its impact.

They respected me and my work, but were sincerely puzzled by it. Until one day 20 years ago.

I was telling Mr. Warren about my new talk-variety show on Channel 9. I interviewed interesting people, but I also featured performers who sang, danced or played a musical instrument.

A light came to Mr. Warren's eyes. Performers? People who entertained other people with their talent? Wait a minute. He knew someone like that. We'll call him "Lafe Wilkins." He hadn't seen "Lafe" in years, but "Lafe" could whistle like a bird. Of a summer's night everyone in Parksville and Junction City would gather to listen to him. He could whistle anything. Bird calls, popular music, country songs, even some of those high-toned classical pieces he heard on the radio. Would I be interested in him?

Would I? I didn't really care so much about "Lafe," but here was a chance to make a real connection with my father-in-law; to bridge the gap between his world and mine. He saw it too and got right on the phone. "Lafe Wilkins" trembled on the brink of fame. Mr. Warren found him in Harrodsburg.

He quickly explained who I was and about my Cincinnati TV show. "I told him about you and how you whistled better then anyone, and he wants you to come right up there and do it on the TV. What? I didn't quite make that out. You what? All of them? 10 years ago? Can't even whistle for your dog? Well, if that doesn't beat everything. Too bad. You were certainly the best. Yes, I'd like to see you, too, 'Lafe'. Yes, I'll come by." He hung up.

Lafe had lost all his teeth. It had ruined his pucker. Show business had come calling 10 years late.

Timing is everything.

Miss Energy

Monday, November 4th, 1991

I had every intention of writing an in-depth and persuasive piece telling you how to vote tomorrow, but I'm afraid you're on your own. I'm too pooped.

It seemed to be such a simple, innocent idea. We would take our brilliant and beautiful granddaughter for an autumn visit to the lovely hills of Kentucky.

As I have described in a previous column, one of our favorite haunts has long been Natural Bridge State Resort Park, just 45 minutes or so south of Lexington.

Little Allison is eight months old now, so it was time and past time she got a look at the jagged hills and towering trees of Daniel Boone National Forest.

All unsuspecting, we put our little group together. Allison would be convoyed by her mother Ada, her grandmother Nina and her great-grandmother Dica. Four female steps in the family progression, each the first-born of her generation.

I was the only male along because Allison's father Norman had a military obligation on that particular weekend. At least that's what he told us. Now I'm not so sure.

The five of us headed south. As usual, I felt layers of unacknowledged tension slip away as we crossed and re-crossed

Four generations, each the first-born of her generation:
Dica Warren, Nina Clooney, Ada Zeidler and Allison
Zeidler. Allison wore them all out.

the Red River and approached the stubby hills of our
destination.

Let me make this point before going any further, because it
will help you understand the rest of my tale. Little Allison is the
best, most beautiful and smartest baby in the continental United
States. I have not checked all other countries, so I'll make no
wider claims. Yet.

To continue, there we were at the lodge, four adults
surrounding the curly-haired baby who smiled back calmly in
anticipation.

First, her mother took her for a walk along one of the
park's few level trails. In an hour, I was puzzled to see Ada
return exhausted. Allison seemed refreshed and ready for
more adventure.

Her grandmother then took her to the lobby, a gathering-place for guests of the lodge. Allison met and jabbered at each person in turn, charming them with practiced ease. In one hour, Nina returned wrung out, but Allison was still raring to go.

Contemptuous of the obvious female frailty, I decided to take matters into my own hands and lug Allison for a walk. She's only 20 pounds, after all. What could be so hard about this?

We began our stroll at 4 P.M. Allison's hearing is so acute that she picks up every bird call, every scurrying squirrel, every voice in the distance and, I truly believe, every falling leaf. And each sound requires her instant attention.

She turns in this direction, then abruptly in that direction, leaning in each case toward the interesting sound. Then she spies the sun glinting off my gray hair which she grabs with both hands, only to then lean toward a passing couple who said hello, followed by a sudden twist of 180 degrees as a limb fell in the woods behind us. Not for an instant was she still. She turns, squirms, moves, leans, then turns again, doubling her weight as she moves. Being carried is not a passive event for Allison. She is a full participant.

Well, anyway, I had walked my hour. I checked my watch. It was 4:10!

At long last, I got back to the lodge, turned Allison over to her great-grandmother and collapsed on the nearest horizontal surface. Mind you, this terrific baby had not cried or fussed for a moment. It's just that she never paused for a moment, either.

Dinner with Allison should be added as an event in the 1992 Summer Olympics. Anything within reach on the table is instantly in her hand then in her mouth. She is omnivorous. Place mats, napkins, spoons, salt shakers, iced tea glasses and the table itself all look delicious to her. One adult would distract her while the other three ate furiously. We finished dinner, including dessert, in what I understand is a park record of 9 minutes 15 seconds.

After dinner, I gave her one more walk in the vain hope she would get tired enough to sleep. In my dreams. She talked and laughed, she smiled and talked some more. At midnight, as the four of us hung limply over various pieces of furniture, she favored us with a nap.

At 3 AM, she woke up. She didn't cry, she just talked so loudly that the sleeping birds outside complained, so I went into her room and walked her for an hour. Her gorgeous eyes got bigger with every step. Finally, her mother relieved me and sang her to sleep.

So it went all weekend. By the time we returned, all four adults were ready to check into a rest home. But there sat Allison in the middle of the floor, vitality crackling out of every fingertip, ready for the next shift. So if you're still waiting for my political advice, here it is. Vote for Allison.

Why? Because we'll save billions in energy costs, that's why. Every time she smiles, the sun comes out.

The Homecoming

Monday, April 5th, 1993

Homecomings are not always what you think they're going to be. Just ask my son George.

Since he went to California against my advice ten years ago to pursue a career as an actor, he has worked almost constantly. So much for listening to advice from your father.

George has worked very hard, and continues to work very hard, learning and growing in his profession. He has done theater, television and feature films. He is at this writing the co-star of an hour-long police drama on CBS called "Bodies of Evidence".

In short, he's a very successful working actor. As many of you know, "working" and "actor" are not often words seen in the same sentence.

For several years, Augusta High School, from which George was graduated, has invited him to return for Career Day to talk about the highly unusual path he has taken from the tiny river town in Kentucky to the glitz and glamor capital of the world.

The first several invitations had to be turned down because of his work schedule, but this year George moved heaven and earth to change shooting dates so he could come back and talk to the kids whose older brothers and sisters were his classmates.

While he was at it, George would visit his sister in Petersburg, Kentucky and his best friend, Pete Harpen in Mason, Ohio. Pete and George had known each other since grade school at St. Susanna and never missed a chance to get together. And for good measure, he would drop in at the University of Cincinnati, which he had briefly attended. Ditto Northern Kentucky University.

He carved out two full days in February. He made all the calls, all the arrangements, all the reservations.

It would be a Homecoming.

When the flight landed, the sky was iron-gray. He picked up his rental car and checked his time. He would make it to Augusta High with an hour to spare.

The snow started as he left the airport. By the time he got to Augusta there were two inches on the ground and the snowfall was getting heavier.

The first person he saw was our friend Clark Hennessey. "Hi, George. I guess you heard Career Day was called off."

Called off! George thought of the rescheduling, the shuffling of appointments. The homecoming was not off to a great start.

He had planned to spend the night at home in Augusta, but there looked to be a good chance he might get snowed in, so he headed back to Cincinnati. On the way, he stopped to call U.C. and NKU. Sure enough, the weather was making his meeting with them for the next day shaky.

The heck with it. He'd just go back to California and try all this another time. At the airport he turned in his car and went to the ticket counter. The young woman smiled. No flights. Airport closed.

George retrieved the car and drove through the snow downtown. Not many people on the road. He got to a hotel.

They asked him to wait few minutes before registering. He had a sandwich in the lounge. The snow kept falling.

When he went back to the lobby, the University of Southern California Band and Choir had arrived! All were in line in front of him. An hour later, he wearily got to his room.

He couldn't visit family or friends and they couldn't visit him. The city was paralyzed. Oh, well. The guide showed a movie on cable he had wanted to see. He snapped on the TV. The snow on the screen matched the snow outside. Cable kaput.

Some Homecoming. Four walls and a bed. Swell.

Wait a minute. Wasn't this Wednesday? Sure it was. George put on all the clothes he had brought with him from California and started walking in the snow. Five blocks up and two over. The Blue Wisp. It was big band night.

George had blind faith they would be there. He knew most of them. He had grown up around them and he knew their priorities. Others may not venture out, but the Blue Wisp Big Band would always be there on Wednesday night.

As George walked down the stairs he heard them warming up and laughing at themselves. They were there, every one of them. The audience was not as stalwart. Only four others joined George at the tables. The band outnumbered them five to one. No matter. That incredible band played as if it were a packed house. It's the music, you see. They are there for the music. Nothing else matters.

George sat mesmerized. It was magic. Paul Piller and Jerry Conrad and other musicians called out, "Hey, George," and his history came flooding back. The nearly-empty basement bistro on snow-choked Garfield Place was home.

It was a great Homecoming.

*Nina in Utah, smiling in spite of missing a
meeting with Robert Redford. 1992.*

Robert Redford

Wednesday, July 8th, 1992

I tell you, I don't know what's wrong with Nina. After all, it was
only Robert Redford.

True, I promised I'd introduce her to him, but things got busy
and there was a mixup and I didn't get it done. If you happen to
run into her on the street, will you explain how sometimes things
happen over which a husband has no control?

It all started when Robert Redford agreed to an interview. He
has a beautiful resort up in the Wasatch range of the Rocky
Mountains called Sundance.

The centerpiece of the development is an outdoor summer
theater. This year, there was a grand opening of a children's
theater, also outdoor, with its own stage, its own seating and its
own season.

Redford has worked hard on this complex. There are cabins, there's a good restaurant and skiing facilities. Meeting and rehearsal halls abound.

A clear mountain stream runs through it. A drinking fountain sticks up from the stream, eternally spouting clear, cold, pure water. All the buildings look as though they sprouted from the stones and the dirt and the trees around them.

Overwhelming everything is the startling mass of a mountain. It's a guardian or avenging angel, depending on your point of view. Maybe it's both. Impressive.

Anyway, Robert Redford was so intent on the success of his children's theater that he would even submit to a private interview with a newsman. That's how it came to pass that Nina, our old friend Dante DiPaolo and I drove up into the Rocky Mountains two Saturdays ago.

Robert Redford. He of Barefoot in the Park, Butch Cassidy and the Sundance (remember Sundance?) Kid, The Sting, All the President's Men, The Way We Were and name your favorite. Robert Redford the environmental and sometime political activist.

When we got to the resort, there was confusion about where Robert Redford was. Many of his employees were understandably nervous about the opening and about having the boss on the premises, and some were flustered. Our photographer, Matt Sohn, was up the mountain at the theater site. Was Redford there, too? Nina and Dante hopped into a 4-wheeler to find out.

At the last minute, a youngster with a handy-talkie grabbed me and pointed me toward Redford's cabin. As we walked, he got another call and we retraced out steps to the actor's private office.

And that's where we had our interview. It was interesting. Redford looked great, with some of the cragginess of his beloved mountains in evidence. He talked of his struggle to "leave as much alone as possible and just develop what was necessary" here in the mountains.

He spoke of how "poor the literature for children's theater was generally" and how he hoped this theater and workshop for writers would help make it better.

He told of bucking all the experts 22 years ago when they told him that his outdoor theater in the mountains would fail. "It was too far, too cold, nobody would come and I said the hell with it, let's try it anyway." He wanted to combine "art and nature." It's now a major success.

Because of his interest in the environment, I asked him about the Rio Earth Summit. He largely dismissed it as a "photo-op."

Because of his interest in politics, I asked him for whom he would vote. He was suddenly more alert. Wary. "You mean for president?" "Yes."

He was clearly uneasy. "You're getting pretty heavy there, pal. Who do you vote for? Do you want to die by fire or poison arrow?" I could see him thinking it over. He decided to go ahead.

"You've got a man who has exhibited ignorance and incompetence on the one hand. Then, down in Texas, you've got a man who, you know," he opened his eyes very wide, staring, "doesn't blink very much. You want to see a guy blink occasionally. And I think he probably has a narrower track than is going to be required to run the country. And then Clinton..." He looked out the window and paused for a long moment. "I don't know. All I can say is, I probably share the view of a lot of Americans. I'm pretty depressed about the options."

The interview was over. We talked for a few minutes, and then I remembered. Nina! Were she and Dante still on top of the mountain? By the time we connected again, Robert Redford was on to other things, and she only saw him from the stage as he introduced the performance.

Actually, she took it pretty well. Perhaps that's because she has her two earlier encounters with Paul Newman to fall back on. But that's another story.

George

Wednesday, September 28th, 1994

1982. Listen, George, this is crazy. You can't just go out to California and break into acting. You know better than that. It's the toughest racket in the world.

Yeah, I know, Pop, but it's the only thing I really want to do. I think I can make it.

("E-R launches surgical strike on the emotions that could make it the medical drama of the '90s...Anthony Edwards is the calm in the storm's eye, solidly supported by dreamboat George Clooney..." Matt Roush, U-S-A Today.)

1982, one month later. Now wait a minute. Let's think about this. You've been out there. You know there are thousands of talented kids waiting on tables and parking cars.

Sure, I know, but I also know if I don't do this I'll regret it the rest of my life.

("E-R is an antidote for bad TV." Tom Shales of the Washington Post. "It's my number one pick for the fall.")

1983. Okay, how about this? What if you come back for one more year of school, then, if you want to go back to California, you go?

Pop, if I come back for one year, then it will be one more, then one more and the chance to do this will pass.

("E-R... has a terrific cast that includes Anthony Edwards, George Clooney, John Terry, Sherry Stringfield, Noah Wyle and Eriq Lasalle..." Alan Pergament, Buffalo News.)

1983, one month later. All right, I know you've heard this before, but couldn't you just go back to school until you have a degree? If you have a degree then at least you'll have something to fall back on if it doesn't work.

Pop, I don't want anything to fall back on. If I have something to fall back on, I may quit before I should. If I'm going to be an actor, I have to act.

("Both [Chicago Hope and E-R] are superbly acted. E-R has Anthony Edwards, George Clooney and Sherry Stringfield as its doctors..." Marvin Kittman, New York Newsday.)

1984. Okay, it's been two years. How are you making it?

Well, Pop, it's no walk in the park. I'm still living with our relatives and my friends. I've had odd jobs to earn my keep. I'm working my way through an acting class. I think I'm learning a lot.

("E-R is one of the fall's best." John Kiesewetter, Cincinnati Enquirer.)

1984, three months later. Now let me understand this. You work in these plays for nothing?

Yeah, for almost nothing, Pop. They're called "Equity Waiver" plays and they produce them in tiny theaters on Santa Monica Boulevard and elsewhere in town. Just a few people come, but most of them are agents and writers and directors and producers. So I did a couple of plays and I got an agent and now he has me up for a couple of parts on TV. They're one-shots, but they pay above scale. If I do well, I'll get more work.

("E-R is sensationally entertaining." New York Post.)

1989. I don't get it, George. "Roseanne" is a huge hit. Why in the world would you leave it? It will probably run for years. Did they fire you?

No, they asked me back, but the role wasn't going anywhere. Roseanne and John are the stars and there's really no room for anyone else. I've got to get out there on my own and take a chance and make a place for myself.

("E-R is a program that looks as solid as any that has ever come along." Jeff Plass, TV Data.)

1993. I'm really sorry they cancelled your show "Bodies of Evidence", George. I liked it. I know it must be tough on you. What is this, three or four shows you were on that got cancelled?

Oh, it's not so bad, Pop. I just think back to my childhood. I had a role model. Nobody had as many shows cancelled as you did.

("Chicago Hope has the benefit of scripts by [David E.] Kelley,...But E-R is more solidly connected with the real world and it, too, can deliver powerfully affecting scenes." John J. O'Connor, New York Times.)

1994. George? This is Pop. I just heard the ratings. E-R is first in its time period and the number one new show of the season, huh? Well, you deserve it. The show is great and so are you. Tomorrow night at ten is the one with Rosemary, isn't it? Incidentally, by actual count, I've read 21 reviews of your show from Flint, Michigan to Salt Lake City. Out of the 21, only one was mildly negative. You won't be surprised to learn it came from your home city, Cincinnati. Well, I can't point a finger at the reviewer.

I was once wrong about you, too.

Let's Think About It

OCCASIONALLY, THE GREAT FORCES eddying around our national life penetrate even so isolated a sanctuary as my desk in Augusta, Kentucky. When they can be ignored no longer, I write about them.

These are the pieces that have gotten me into the most trouble. The sampling which follows has earned more than its share of outraged "letters to the editor."

Still, if one of the functions of a columnist is to get a conversation going around the supper table or the water cooler, these apparently qualify.

Nick.

Let's Think About It

The Aging 20th Century

August 8th, 1990

How do you suppose the old 20th Century feels about reaching 90? A little rheumatiz in the joints? Not as quick up and down the stairs? More knowledge than he thought he'd have by now but less wisdom?

Centuries have the advantage over us humans in at least one regard. They know exactly how long they will be around, right down to the second. Old Mr. 20th will be here until midnight, December 31st in the year 2000 and not one instant less nor one instant longer, then he'll be whisked away into the mists of history where humans will try to get a perspective on him.

All people are absolutely certain that the century in which they spent the bulk of their time is the best, the worst, the most momentous, the most dangerous and altogether the most interesting chunk of time in all the millennia for which the earth has been spinning on its axis.

Since a century is nothing more than the accumulation of the ideas, beliefs, accomplishments and perfidies of the people who inhabit it, it occurred to me that each hundred-year unit might personify all those individuals, and therefore take on a specific personality of its own, separate and distinct from every other century.

From that flight of fancy, it was not hard to imagine a sort of Valhalla of Centuries, where each one of them goes when its time span is over.

How do they get along? Is there a pecking order? Is there jealously among them? Would they talk to one another?

Having gone this far, it was not at all difficult to imagine a social gathering of the Centuries, and even a conversation that might ensue.

"Well, brace yourselves everybody. In just ten years, 20th will be joining the Club and I want to say frankly that I, for one, am not looking forward to it."

"Oh, 14th, you take that reputation for cynicism too seriously. You always assume the worst about everyone."

"Maybe so, 4th, but at least I'm not a Pollyanna like you."

"I must say that I'll be glad to see 20th get here. Then at least 19th will stop spouting off about the Industrial Revolution. I don't know about you, but I'm sick of it. Early automobiles, steel mills, trains, coal mines, she's always talking about *things,* for heaven's sake. Inventions, inventions, more and bigger, that's all she ever says."

"Oh, 18th, you're just jealous because no one pays any attention to your 'Age of Reason' speech anymore. Look, you don't have to sell us on Burke and Jefferson and those other fellows, but give us a break, we all have something to crow about if we want to."

"Sure, sure 15th, and I suppose now you're going to bore us to death with the Columbus thing and all that New World propaganda. You know very well my Europeans were there before your Europeans."

"All right, 11th, let's not get into that again. I merely bring up the 'Columbus thing' as you call it to encourage Centuries in case things go slowly for them in the early years. After all, I was 92 when Columbus...."

"...Sailed the ocean blue", they all chorused.

"Well, I don't know what we have to be proud of, any of us. You know a lot of people down there don't even believe in us."

"Oh, you mean the *other* Club."

"Clubs. Plural. More than one."

"Yeah, those guys are putting some pretty big numbers up on the board. What is it in China these days, the 40th? And in Israel it must be 30 something."

"No, that's the TV show."

"Come on now, the point is that it doesn't matter at all. Each one is sure he or she is right. And as for individual Centuries, whatever our numbers are, we all had good times and bad times. Each of us both helped and hurt the human condition. But when it was all over, we each did the best we could."

"Oh, come, come, come 1st, you're always trying to see the good side of things and to do unto others as you would have them do unto you and all that stuff. It gets to be a bit much, you know."

"I can't help it. That's the way I was brought up. You do remember who we were all named after, don't you? Old Anno Domini? A.D. for short? Well, don't forget, I was the only one who knew him personally."

Eventually, the party breaks up and each Century, waving goodbye, returns to its place in history until the next gathering.

The 20th will have some good stories to tell when it joins the group ten years from now. Understandably, it will be a little full of itself at first. But after the initial rush of excitement, it will find there are a lot of good stories to *listen* to as well.

Bring Back The Protestants

August 23rd, 1989

There was a news item in this paper a few weeks ago that disturbed me mightily. It should also be of great concern to every Catholic, Jew, Moslem, Hindu, agnostic and atheist in the country.

The story described what it called the fall of mainstream Protestantism as the dominant religion in the United States. It cited dramatic reductions in the national congregations of Presbyterians, Methodists, Episcopalians and others who have long been the backbone of organized worship in this country.

This is very bad news, indeed.

These stalwart and stern soldiers of God have made this nation what it is, and have allowed those of us of differing faiths, or no faith at all, to thrive as we have done nowhere else on the planet.

After a few false starts in New England, it became a point of pride in mainstream Protestantism that the functions of religion and those of governance should be separated. Long suspicious of a central authority, American Protestants came to the conclusion that presenting civil officials with power over the soul as well as the body was giving them too much by a long shot, and condemned it.

Because most of the men governing us were mainstream Protestants, their actions reflected this separation of the church authority and the civil authority, and when it came time to write laws and constitutions, these tenets became central to our government.

It was mainstream Protestants who wrote and approved the Declaration of Independence (no, Jefferson was not the atheist his opponents claimed; he was a frequent churchgoer and a lifelong believer) and the Constitution of the United States.

It was mainstream Protestants who conceived and sustained the abolition movement, forcing us to face up to the spirit of our Revolution and the thunder of our rhetoric: "All Men Are Created Equal."

It was in mainstream Protestant organizations where women first began to find their strength and their voice.

When we called our public men (historically, *men*) "hypocrites" it was because they did not live up to the mainstream Protestant ethic which they espoused on Sunday.

And how did minority religions fare? Well, individually, there were plenty of problems.

But, because the mainstream Protestant ethic declared that the state could not *establish* a specific religion, it must logically accept that the state could not *forbid* the practice of any specific religion. This was very hard to swallow in the religious atmosphere of the 18th century, but swallow it our founding fathers did, and what they put down on paper they would eventually have to live up to.

Decency was validated. Tolerance was given a name:

America.

Waves of immigrants took full advantage of it, and continue to do so today. Escaping the church-states of Europe, the Middle Each and the Orient, they came, and come, by the boatload and planeload to the state that had no established religion, and in doing so lifted both their eternal faiths and their temporal lives to unimagined heights.

The Catholic church in America quickly became the most prosperous and slowly became the most powerful Catholic voice in the world.

American Jews invested this nation's culture with their rich heritage and prospered so much that they could finance and support their two-millennia dream; Israel.

More recently, Moslems have found the ground plowed by mainstream Protestants fertile to their own aspirations, and have begun to establish their own power base.

Those who do not believe anything or who don't know what to believe have their own important place in the tapestry woven on the loom of mainstream Protestantism.

If the news story I read is correct, the erosion has not come from outside, but from within. Fundamentalist splinter groups, seeing in the established church's tolerance a despised "liberalism" have defected, taking much energy, youth and money with them.

The phenomenon of televised religion has apparently hurt twice; first by its success in taking people out of pews and putting them in front of a sterile, flickering television tube, and second by its spectacular, scandalous failure, disillusioning millions who identify the flawed messenger with the timeless message.

Now, they tell us it's over?

Say it ain't so. Surely it's just another glitch in a long, tough journey. Those good, solid citizens will come back to the familiar, well-worn Methodist pews and bring their children.

Those of us who are Catholic, Jewish, Shinto, or nothing at all had better hope so.

Mainstream Protestantism is the best friend we ever had.

Dr. Sass

January 7th, 1991

Most controversies have a limited shelf life. We either resolve them or forget them and that's that.

Some seem to go on forever, always bubbling and roiling at or near the surface, occasionally bursting out to burn us all again.

They demand attention.

They force us into separate camps where some of us hunker down, taking positions which no longer require reason, just emotion. We manufacture slogans, develop "buzz" words. Anyone who agrees with us is a friend. Anyone who disagrees is a mortal enemy. Anyone who tries to find a middle ground is a wimp, despised by both sides.

And yet the life blood of a democracy is consensus. We strive to reach an understanding with one another. We seek middle ground. We tolerate diverse views or our whole experiment in self-government fragments and goes spinning off into the deep space of failed dreams.

Abortion has become such an issue.

There are two camps shouting at each other. One screams "murderer", the other yells "neanderthal". One demands to be called pro-life, and who in a free society could be against life? The other demands to be called pro-choice, and who in a democracy could be against choice?

The arguments on both sides are so well-known that they need no rehashing here. Both have their horror stories and worst-case scenarios which they parade before us in now-familiar packages.

Both are utterly, stubbornly convinced they hold the moral and ethical high ground. They will brook no argument, accept no dissent, join in no discussion. I have personally attempted to moderate conversations between representatives of opposing views on this issue, but they adamantly refuse to participate in a real dialogue. It is always two monologues, both conducted with practiced fervor, neither advocate listening to the other.

Into this seething cauldron steps Dr. Hans-Martin Sass.

I heard him on the public radio program "All Things Considered", and in spite of the tough, skeptical questioning of an expert interviewer, I thought I caught a glimpse of a light at the end of our ideological tunnel.

Dr. Sass is a Professor of Philosophy at the Kennedy Institute of Ethics at Georgetown University, the distinguished Jesuit institution of Catholic higher learning in Washington, D.C., and basically, this is his point:

For twenty years and more, most developed countries have reached a consensus on when life ends. It occurs when whole-brain activity ceases. "Brain death". Even though the heart may beat for a while and respiration continue for a while, the end of brain activity means the end of life.

Actually, the Catholic Church took the lead in this position when, in 1957, Pope Pius XII said in a letter that in cases of "prolonged coma", the soul might already have left the body and that the determination of actual death should be left to physicians.

Dr. Sass says, if life ends when brain activity ends, might not life begin when brain activity begins? And when is that? There is some disagreement, but the most conservative estimate is at 70 days. Prior to 70 days, there can be no brain activity because there is no connection between brain cells.

Brain life. Brain death.

We accept one. Dr. Sass asks, wouldn't there be a symmetry, a rationality, a morality, in accepting the other?

Dr. Sass is aware that both sides will attack his position. Those who believe in abortion-on-demand will maintain that the women's choice supersedes all and any tampering with that absolute right is a return to the Stone Age. Those who believe life begins at conception will accept no abridgement of their dogma.

Yet, on the one hand, isn't there some point in the pregnancy process that the little developing human accrues rights of its own? And on the other hand, the Catholic Church itself only articulated the life-at-conception dogma in 1854, just a wink of time ago for a religion that goes back 2000 years.

And most of all, isn't this, finally, a basis for a rational discussion of the deeply-held moral convictions of both sides? Don't we have here at least the beginning step in a quest for consensus?

Brain life. Brain death.

The "Uniform Determination of Death Act" provides brain death as a criterion. This allows, among other things, for organ transplantation without moral strictures for most religions.

Dr. Sass sent me his 8000-word argument on the subject. Through the necessarily opaque technical language shines his conclusion. He believes there should be a "Uniform Determination of Life Protection Act".

Isn't this an idea which deserves serious discussion? Not separate monologues. Not a Tower of Babel. Serious discussion within each camp and, at long last, between the two.

Racism and The Military

Wednesday, May 20th, 1992

The columnist who hesitates is lost. Or, at least, scooped. Doggone it, I've been making notes on this idea for a column for about a year now and just because I was too disorganized to collate them in a timely fashion, two or three syndicated writers have done it first. No fair.

Well, I'm going to write it anyway. There is no point in wasting five long-distance phone calls and one lengthy conversation with a guy at a bar who obviously knew what he was talking about. I forgot to get his name.

The subject is black-white racism.

There are some very intelligent people in this country who have given up on integration as a goal. There is an entirely new "separate but equal" mentality making the rounds and being given political legitimacy by people who should know better.

Some black intellectuals, hiding their rage behind three-dollar words and two-bit theories, have given up on the American idea. They urge other African-Americans to retreat into tiny pockets of racially homogeneous ghettoes, speaking only to one another, associating only with one another, building enclaves of permanent minorities, ignoring clear evidence that remaining permanently separate means remaining permanently subordinate to the majority.

Some white intellectuals agree, but for reasons of their own. Hiding their prejudice behind three-dollar words and two-bit theories, they hint darkly that African-Americans are ineducable. They use pseudo-statistics to "prove" that black family structure is shattered beyond recall. They whisper that massive infusions of money have done nothing to change life for the better for black Americans, which "proves" they don't wish to be part of the wider American experience.

Now, let me prove — really *prove* — that both of these positions are not just wrong, they are wrong-headed. We have before us the largest, most in-depth, most complete lab experiment in integration in history, if we choose to study it. Millions have participated and the experiment has spanned 45 years.

It is that often-maligned American institution, the military.

Not long after World War II, a president from Missouri with all the superficial racist trappings of his time and place signed an executive order which forever wiped out segregation in the United States armed forces, which, prior to that moment had been among the most racist of our institutions. Southern lawmakers squealed like stuck pigs and withdrew support for him in subsequent elections, but Harry Truman told them to go to hell and demonstrated something which few of us would recognize in national politics; leadership.

A lot has happened in this country since the mid-1940s and the integration of the services. Full-fledged wars and brush-fire confrontations. Affluence and assassinations. Patriotism and disillusion.

Through all those cycles, integration has been working in the military. Under the strictest, by-the-numbers conditions of regulated equality, blacks have flourished alongside their white counterparts. They have proved what logic told us all the time. They are just as smart, just as stable, just as brave, just as tenacious as any other group of Americans.

Is there still racism in the military? Of course there is. No one can mandate an end to ignorance. But it is the personal variety, and cannot by law infringe on the structure of military society. It can't keep blacks out of OCS, or Command School, or the NCO or Officers' clubs. And so, African-Americans in the military are succeeding in ways they can't even dream of in South Central LA, or other civilian venues.

Why? Because there has *never* been a consistent policy to redress the original, structural inequality of their opportunity in our society at large.

President Bush says the policies of the Great Society failed. He can say what he wishes, but nobody can prove that they failed because they were never tried. Lyndon Johnson's failure was that he created programs which might have worked, then took the money meant to fund them and paid for the Vietnam War. Only a shell of most of the urban programs was ever established and most of the underfunding went to the bureaucrats who administered them.

Would they have worked? Who knows? Would Jack Kemp's "enterprise zones" work? Who knows? We'll never find out.

Until there is bipartisan, national effort to make the structure of our society equal in opportunity, as it has been made in the military, and until we leave it alone without politicizing it for two generations, as we have done in the military, we'll never see a civilian Colin Powell rise to the top and prove to us once again that the great American idea works. For everyone.

McMartin

January 9th, 1990

This is a painful column to write.

For nearly two years, I was one of the dozens of reporters in southern California covering the McMartin Pre-School child molestation case. As you know, it eventually became the longest preliminary hearing and the longest criminal trial in American history.

When I arrived at KNBC-TV in April of 1984, the story was just over two months old. An investigative reporter on a competing station had broken a story of horrifying allegations in a series of lurid reports just in time for the important "sweeps" February rating period.

There is nothing more heinous to any of us than the mental, physical or sexual abuse of helpless children. It is the ultimate betrayal of those who most need and trust us. We reserve a very special revulsion for those among us who are guilty of this terrible crime. Even those just accused of it bear an indelible stigma.

Now here were seven staff members of one of the best known and most respected preschools in Southern California accused of unspeakable acts.

It all started when a two-and-a-half year old boy dropped a few remarks to his troubled mother that made her suspicious. Enter perhaps the most controversial personality. A young woman, a therapist, was called in by police and began questioning the little boy. As she often said later, she operated on the theory that small children *never* lie about things of which they have no personal experience. They can't, she said.

Based on that presumption she asked a series of leading questions guiding the child through a maze of sexual aberrations and eliciting a chilling tale. The police and others were caught up in the increasing urgency. More therapists who shared the first young woman's philosophy were brought in and dozens of children at the school were questioned in the same manner.

The story that appeared to emerge was both nauseating and sensational and, in a manner yet unclear, was leaked to the KABC-TV reporter, who put it on the air. All the other television stations and newspapers, even the august Los Angeles Times, chose to chase him around the Manhattan Beach landscape trying to catch up.

I had the advantage of coming to the story late. I had not been caught up in that first "feeding frenzy' of coverage. From the first week I was skeptical. You would have been, too.,

Satanic rituals? Animals and perhaps even children slaughtered? Airplane rides to terrify children into silence? Animals and perhaps even children hung on meathooks in local groceries? Thousands of pornographic pictures taken in "naked movie star" games? A horse killed with a baseball bat? Group sex with teachers? And in six years not one adult — parent, passerby, delivery person, mailman — not one had seen any evidence of any of this activity?

There was something else. Six of the seven originally charged were women. In my own reporting experience, sexual abuse of children by women is as rare as snow at the equator. Physical and mental abuse, yes. Sexual abuse, almost never.

I said all this in the newsroom to reporters, writers, producers, the assistant news director and the news director. I got blank stares. Did I really think the District Attorney would bring these kinds of charges if he didn't have the evidence? Don't be ridiculous.

The weeks went on. I accumulated a file. No pornographic photos showed up. I watched men in three-piece suits solemnly digging up vacant lots, crawling over nearby churches and groceries, examining air charter records. No evidence. Medical evidence, inconclusive.

Only testimony elicited from children by admittedly leading questions. I called a number of child psychologists and found that by no means all agreed that children don't lie about those things which they don't experience first hand, but to show you how hot the subject was then, they wouldn't be interviewed on camera.

By the time several months had passed I had gathered enough material for a hard story questioning whether anything at all had happened at McMartin. Once more, I went to my fellow workers. After all, it was their town. Almost unanimously they thought I was wrong. I began to second guess myself. These were children. I waited a day or two, and then I folded. I put the file in my desk and didn't take it out again.

It was a major mistake and it is the reason I'm writing this now. I hope that some present or future journalists will learn from it. Never drop your honest skepticism no matter what the price. It is the linchpin of your profession.

The story I could have written in late 1984 might have meant nothing. On the other hand it could have been the beginning of some hard questioning; questioning which never really began until the trial was underway three years later. The process rumbled to its drawn-out conclusion and nobody won.

McMartin parents and children will forever believe there was molestation because they now have too much of themselves invested not to believe. The therapists are seen by many as foolish acolytes of a failed philosophy. The District Attorney has lost a high profile case which may cost him politically. Peggy and Raymond Buckey have lost everything.

Raymond Buckey, in fact, will now be tried again on the thirteen counts which some jurors did not agree deserved a "not guilty" verdict in his case. The outcome of the next trial doesn't really matter much. His life is ruined in any case.

But in all of this, there is one person who may lose the most, and it's that individual who leaves me uneasy. The babble of voices in the McMartin debacle may drown out the single, despairing voice of one tiny, lonely victim. We must listen closely.

Finally, the press lost a lot too. We stated as facts things that were untrue. We ignored fairness. We scoffed at "innocent until proved guilty", a pillar of our legal system and society.

And those of us who knew better and did nothing were the worst of all. We did nothing for fear of appearing to support child molesters. We courted popularity, not news.

Most of those I talk to believe Peggy McMartin Buckey and her son Raymond Buckey are guilty and somehow beat the system. The only juror to appear on the big-time talk shows is the woman who says "I didn't find Ray Buckey innocent, I found him not guilty." We don't want to hear from the jurors who feel otherwise. We readers and viewers invested something in this sordid case, too.

Two former co-workers of mine from California called when the verdict was in to congratulate me for being right all along. At least I had the grace not to accept their congratulations. I had none coming.

For the first — and, I hope, only — time in my career, I didn't do what a journalist must do if he or she is to earn the name. I didn't follow truth wherever it might lead.

The emperor had no clothes, and I stood on the sidelines, silent.

The Language Barrier

November 26th, 1990

There has always been a generation gap. I'm sure conversations between Adam and Eve about Cain and Abel — and vice versa — would be perfectly familiar to parents and children at this morning's breakfast table. Except, of course, that no one sits at the breakfast table anymore.

Anyway, this is going to be a piece about the generation gap, 1990 style, and I didn't want the reader to have any misconception that I believe this phenomenon to be an invention of this decade, or even this century. No way. It is as old as humankind.

What changes is the form it takes.

In 1990, it is a language barrier as impenetrable as the sound barrier was once thought to be.

Language has always been a part of the separation between young and old. Each generation invents its own jargon to differentiate it from all that went before and all that will follow. "Twenty-three skidoo" gave way to "Oh, you kid" which surrendered to the "cat's whiskers" superseded by "hep" which became "hip" accompanied by "groovy" which actually survived two generations which is more than can be said for "gear" or "boss" or "excellent" or on and on.

The specific mark of the language barrier in the last ten years, however, has been its profanity and vulgarity. Because this is a family newspaper still governed by the norms of the older generation and by what we used to call "polite society", I won't be using the specific words to illustrate my point, but I don't have to. You know them all.

In fact, we all do, and have known them since we were children. But we didn't use them often and almost never in "mixed company".

Apparently, our very reticence to use the words openly was the reason the younger generation pounced on them and shouted them from the rooftops.

Movies and music had a hand in it, certainly, but as usual they were not leading, they were following the trend. Pandering to it, fanning it, extending it, intensifying it, but never leading it.

Thus was born the flood of motion pictures and songs which, in addition to violence, bigotry and explicit sex, bludgeon the ear with an unremitting barrage of profanity.

Now, before you start thinking that I'm trying to defend the virgin ears of the older American, let me point out that there are twenty million or so of middle age and above who spent time in the service. From basic training on, we were exposed to — and usually participated in — the most concentrated period of profanity possible to imagine. Not one more vulgarity could have been squeezed in, even with a shoe horn. It outstripped Robert DeNiro films. For instance, our field first sergeant at Fort Knox once uttered 41 profanities, vulgarities and blasphemies in 60 seconds. I know it sounds impossible, but it happened, and I don't even know if it was a record, because it was the only time we counted.

But after the two- or three- year laboratory for cussing, we relegated the words to special occasion use as we returned to the "real" world.

The "real" world was then, as it is now, an amalgam of all ages, from infants to retirees, of all attitudes and religions, of all ethnic and national backgrounds, of all regions of the country. Our speech was an amalgam, too. A more or less respectful attempt to communicate without being selfish enough to force our own method of communication on everyone else.

We reserved jargon and regionalisms — and profanities — for their own time and place. That time and place was never public discourse.

Men cussed in the locker room. Women cussed in the powder room. We seldom cussed when together in public. Was that hypocrisy? I don't think so. I believe it was a sensitivity to others around us who might be offended.

No such problem now. You can hear any profanity you want at any restaurant. Going to a Bengals' football game is precisely the same as going to the Bengals' locker room. The foulest epithets pour from the mouths of a substantial fraction of our fans. When we disagree with a referee's decision, it is now standard practice to stand and shout in unison "Bull____! Bull____!" while a national audience listens, no doubt enthralled at our culture.

At the soggy and delirious World Series celebration on Fountain Square, several of the young ballplayers in their enthusiasm shouted vulgarities over the microphone. Young people cheered. Older fans winced.

A small but steady stream of movie customers walk out on films and ask for their money back, usually because of language. Profanity clouds and distracts from normal exchanges at the grocery, the garage, the school, everywhere.

One interesting result is that profanity is in the process of losing its purpose. It has been utilized through the ages for its shock value. The rarity of its use in public added to its exotic quality and its impact. It was very effective.

Now it no longer shocks, it just irritates. Soon, it won't even do that. I'm now trying to invent a new word to use when I hit my thumb with a hammer.

Three Lifetimes

Wednesday, April 3rd, 1991

I've always heard what a young country we are, but I guess I never really believed it.

What's so young about the United States of America? We've been around long enough to change the world almost as much as we have changed ourselves. Sure, the tradition-bound kingdoms of Europe and the ancient civilizations of Asia might be a few centuries older, but aren't we the oldest major working democracy? Sure we are. Young, my eye.

Let's face it, the bewigged Founding Fathers are dim, distant memories getting hazier, more legendary and less flesh-and-blood with each year that goes by. They're separated from us by, what, ten generations or more? We have trouble enough coping with a one-generation gap, let alone ten.

The further those hardy souls recede into the mists of antiquity, the easier it is for us to dismiss them as the bucolic beneficiaries of a simpler time, able to apply a strict code of morality to their public and private affairs because of the lack of the kind of stress and complexity and ambiguity modern life imposes on us.

Besides, who's to know how they really felt about anything? You have to peel off layer after layer of great-great-great-great grandmother before you get to a real person, and that is a task that is simply beyond us.

Isn't it?

Well, maybe not. Some friends and I were talking about it a few days ago, and the conversation gave me an entirely new way of looking at things. Let's see if I can reconstruct it for you.

We'll have to use our imaginations. Let's invent a fictional person. We'll make him a man born in Massachusetts Bay Colony in 1775, the year before Tom Jefferson wrote our Declaration of Independence. Our little figment was eight years old by the time we won the Revolutionary War, and a teenager by the time the Constitution was ratified.

When he was old enough to vote, he cast his first ballot for a man from his own state, John Adams, as president. Shortly thereafter, he decided to try his luck in the West. Down the Ohio River he came, pausing at Limestone for a month before taking two more days to work his way down to Cincinnati. He stayed and was part of the city as it became the fastest-growing region of the new nation. He married, went into business, and was 37 by the time we again went to war with Great Britain. He rejoiced when that one ended, because it marked the beginning of the Ohio River boom. The steamboat made the River a veritable thoroughfare. Nobody had ever seen anything like it.

When our friend was deep into middle age, he worried over the nation's great political and moral dilemma. Half slave, half free. When he died at age 75 in 1850, he hoped that the great compromise being prepared by Henry Clay would solve the looming crisis.

The year he died, a little girl was born in Clifton. By the time she was ten, she knew Mr. Clay's compromise wouldn't hold. Her early teen years would see the greatest cataclysm in our history. Cincinnati was in the forefront of the Civil War effort, and she was swept up in it, too.

At the end of the war she saw accelerated immigration, explosive industry growth, and much dislocation. She saw Ohio dominate the White House for the better part of her lifetime. She read of our battles against native Americans in the West. She watched the nation's Centennial as a 26 year old matron, saw a son go off to the Spanish-American War, and was a fifty-year-old grandmother at the turn of the century. She lived to experience the movies and the Great War. At seventy, women got the vote and she proudly cast her first ballot for Ohioan Warren Harding.

She lived just long enough to regret it before dying at seventy-five in 1925.

That very year, a little boy was born in Price Hill. He was ten by the time the Great Depression affected his family, and he went to work delivering groceries. He didn't get in the Army until 1944 when he was nineteen, and was just about to be shipped overseas when the atom bomb ended World War II. He came home, married his high school sweetheart and got a job with the city. His first son was born in 1948. Korea didn't touch him very much personally, and neither did Vietnam until his son dropped out in 1968 and took to the streets to protest the war. They didn't speak until eight years later, when they reconciled at a Bicentennial Celebration in 1976. Last year he retired, and this year, he and his wife welcomed home their granddaughter from the Persian Gulf War. He was very proud.

Look at that. Three lifetimes. Only three. Not ten or twelve generations. Just three lifetimes can tell the whole story of the United States of America.

I had it all wrong. We really are a young country.

Polygamy I

Wednesday, May 13th, 1992

I just had quite a weekend. I want to tell you all about it, and it may take two columns. It's a subject that's not anywhere close to the front burner in the Ohio Valley, but I believe you'll find it intriguing nonetheless.

Polygamy.

I thought I'd get your attention. The western mountain states have some of the most beautiful vistas on the continent. They have dramatic weather. They have incomparable skiing, a strong work ethic and great family values.

They also have plural marriages. In fact, there are said to be more polygamous relationships now than when the practice was an approved and basic tenet of the Church of Jesus Christ of Latter Day Saints, and that was a hundred years ago.

In the interest of accuracy and fairness, let me be clear on this point at the outset. The Mormon Church does not believe in, condone, practice or allow multiple marriages. If someone in the church does so he or she is summarily excommunicated.

The L.D.S.'s connection with polygamy is purely historical, but very important in that narrow sense. It was, after all, the early Mormons who introduced the concept to the region and many who now practice it claim they are merely fundamentalist Mormons, going back to the teachings of Joseph Smith and the old church, before the Elders renounced plural marriage in 1890.

Last Saturday, I visited what must be the most unusual community in our nation. Actually, it's two small towns straddling the Utah-Arizona border. Hilldale in Utah and Colorado City in Arizona. Together, they comprise a town of about 4,000 people. Virtually all are polygamists. If estimates are to be believed, they comprise less than 10% of the practicing polygamists in Utah, Arizona, Idaho, Nevada, Wyoming and Colorado.

I was preparing a TV news series on the subject, and our crew consisted of producer Bob Melisso, photographer Matt Sohn, both of whom did most of the work, and me. Newspeople are not welcome to roam through this small town. If we call ahead, someone will talk to us under strictly controlled conditions. On the other hand, if we just walk the streets trying to strike up conversations, we are met with nothing but a superficial smile and a "hello". Literally nothing else.

There is a deep suspicion of outsiders here and there is an iron-fisted, patriarchal discipline.

The mayor is Dan Barlow. He meets us cordially. He will not tell us how many wives he has. It is "undignified" to discuss it. He will answer other questions.

We had been told by "dissidents" who used to live in Colorado City that there are "arranged" marriages, sometimes involving teenage girls being given to 70-year-old men. The mayor denies it and says no one marries without the consent of both parties.

We were told women are oppressed, given menial tasks, no role in decisions and are expected to be "baby factories". He indignantly denies it, saying women in his community are happy and fulfilled. We do not speak to a woman on the subject.

We were told there is much sexual abuse and incest in they very large extended families resulting from plural marriage. He says there is no more such activity than elsewhere and probably less. He reminds us that theirs is an entirely religious-based community of believers in the old moral code. There is no dating before marriage, no drinking, no smoking.

He drives us around town. It appears very prosperous. New homes are going up everywhere. They are owned by the church trust, not by the polygamous families.

Women are dressed in fashions frozen in time in the rural 1920s. Long gingham dresses. Long hair. No makeup. The men look marginally more contemporary. Perhaps 1953.

That was the year the National Guard invaded the town at night, arresting all the women and men, including Dan Barlow, putting the men in jail, carting off all the children and sending them to foster homes for two years.

"Is it any wonder we're suspicious?" asks Dan Barlow.

We respond that the only reason for the isolation, for the outrage and disapproval of outsiders is this one aspect of their belief; that a man should take more than one wife. Can it possibly be worth all the grief and calumny and the burden placed on their children?

"It is God's law." His tone said the case was closed.

We left his office into the bright sun and backdrop of the mountains of the Canaan Wilderness sawing a jagged pattern in the blue of the sky.

A little girl on a bicycle was weaving down the sidewalk. She wore jeans and sneakers, over which was an ungainly long red and white checked dress with a high collar and long sleeves. She was trying to keep the dress down over her knees against the wind and still not get it tangled in the bike chain. Her face showed exasperation. She sensed me watching, and looked up. There was a hesitation, then she grinned at me and shrugged.

Oh, pretty little girl, this is only the beginning of the complications in your life.

More Friday.

Polygamy II

Friday, May 15th, 1992

We bounced along a gravel road searching for the compound of the most flamboyant and unembarrassed polygamist in all the land. It was Mothers' Day, appropriate enough for a visit to a family with 20 children. We were about to meet Alex Joseph and his nine wives.

A little boy greeted us and took us into a small courtyard. Alex was sitting at a bench. Stocky, 56 years old, a good face etched by life and the dry winds of the Southwest desert.

We're in Big Water, Utah, exactly 61 miles as the crow flies from no place at all. Mountains over there, desert over here, desolately beautiful, the little town is home to 300 people, more or less, most of them monogamous, and Alex Joseph is the mayor.

His hair is a bit long and he has a beard, both of them mild outward signs of nonconformity. He needn't have bothered. His life is a symphony of nonconformity.

For over 20 years he has had more than one wife in the only state in the union which specifically forbids polygamy. I pointed that out to him.

"Call a cop", he responds with equanimity.

A lot of his answers are like that; epigrammatic punch lines.

Is his life-style religion-based? "I'm no fundamentalist. I'm a political activist. Like Moses. On his death bed, he said 'Proclaim liberty throughout the land.' We put that on a bell and the bell broke. I work for liberty. Mine and yours."

How about the perception that plural marriage is all about sex? "I don't apologize for my hormones. I like women. But this is really about family and children and a life-style we like.

I probably have the most boring sex life in Utah. I sleep with the same nine women all the time."

That's all right for you, but what about the women? "Ask my wife." He always says "wife", singular. So I ask his wife.

Dawn is the youngest. She is very blond and pretty. At 21, she looks younger. She works at a restaurant in the next town. "I knew I wanted to marry Alex when I was eight. I came to live with the family when I was nine, but I didn't marry Alex until four years ago. He's so interesting and smart."

A little boy interrupts. The children here run freely, pull and tug and jabber at mothers and father indiscriminately and, unlike Colorado City which we visited yesterday, have no apprehension about speaking to strangers.

Three women are sitting at a picnic bench. They are very attractive. Boudicca is a real-estate agent. Lindy was a legal secretary and now freelances at many jobs. Elizabeth is an attorney. They wait for me, wise to the way of interviewers. They've talked to them all; Oprah, Phil, Geraldo.

Okay, I say, you know the questions better than I, what should I ask? Lindy starts the litany, and the others chime in. "How often do you sleep with him Aren't you jealous Do you fight with each other Who takes care of the money Do you have group sex Why settle for 1/9th of a guy Are you crazy What about the kids...???"

These are very bright, in-charge women. They have careers. They have control. Some had thought of plural marriage as an intellectual concept before meeting Alex. Boudicca says, "My college roommate married Alex, and I thought, hey, why let a marriage break up a beautiful friendship? So, I married him too."

Elizabeth is lawyer-quick. I ask about the polygamist stigma. "Wait a minute. I'm not a polygamist. I'm monogamous. *Alex* is polygamous."

They speak of Alex with great affection. All agree he is very smart. They emphasize that word. Most say they couldn't imagine being in such a relationship with anyone else. All say the greatest part of the arrangement is the extended family, the children, the friendship with other women.

As they speak, something emerges. It is the women who decide when they will have sex. They make the appointments with Alex. They decide if and when they will have children. They decide when and where they will work. They make the decisions about the compound, the children, the future. They tell Alex how smart he is.

Alex, sitting at his state-of-the-art computer, works on Egyptology. His wives are right. He is smart.

But they are smarter.

As we drive away, I'm struck by the enormity of the difference in the two faces of polygamy we have seen. In Colorado City, the growing polygamous community 100 miles from here, the overwhelming impression is that of men using women, not just sexually, but intellectually and spiritually. To an outsider, it is closed, oppressive.

In Big Water, it's the opposite. To outsiders, the compound is open and welcoming. Here, very attractive and intelligent women are using a man for their own purposes. Benevolently, to be sure, but no less competently.

Alex Joseph seems content not to examine too closely the feet of his patriarchy. He might find traces of clay.

Gun Culture

Wednesday, June 2nd, 1993

There will come a time, a hundred years or so from now, when Americans will look back on one aspect of our life in the 20th century and wonder how we could have been so blind.

Much as *we* now wonder how 18th and 19th century country-men who were so advanced in many ways could accept "bleeding" as a treatment for disease, snake pits as treatment for mental instability, ten-hour days in garment factories for ten-year-old girls and ownership of other human beings for hard labor as normal civilized behavior.

Well, we've addressed those aberrations. Now we have an even more intransigent one. The gun culture.

There are good people with high motives on both sides of this issue. There are also wild-eyed nuts in each corner. Any attempt to enter into rational discussion on the matter is invariably sabotaged by the latter.

I have written or otherwise commented on the subject a half-dozen times or so in the last four years. Each time, I have elicited a relative storm of protest from those who disagree. For instance, not long ago I wrote what was perceived as a satire. A supporter of unlimited access to weaponry called a conservative talk-show host. What those who were enraged by my "vulgar", "uninformed" and "low-blow" piece didn't know was that it was a virtual word-for-word transcript of a conversation I had heard a few weeks before.

So why go into this all again as readers' eyes glaze over? It's the acquittal of the Louisiana man in the killing of the Japanese teenager who didn't speak much English and committed the mortal error of knocking on the wrong door.

In fairness, the Louisiana man seemed genuinely devastated by the tragedy and vowed to eliminate guns from his life.

Still, it's understandable why the Japanese people are bewildered and angered by our love affair with guns. In Japan in 1991, *74 people were killed with guns. All but seven of those were organized crime figures. So in a nation of 120 million people, *seven* private citizens were killed by gunfire.

In the same year, nearly *20,000 Americans died from handgun wounds, the vast majority of them private citizens not connected to organized crime.

Japanese laws do not allow individual handgun ownership. Our laws do.

In this country, the question is constitutional and sincere people disagree on it. Actually, the Founding Fathers served us ill in the Second Amendment, not because they endorsed gun

Salt Lake Tribune, May 27th, 1993
Congressional Quarterly, April 24, 1993

96 NICK

ownership, but because they were ambivalent about it. If the words simply read, "The right of the people to keep and bear arms shall not be infringed", the matter would be clear-cut. The nation could accept it or repeal it, as the people have done with other articles and amendments that became outmoded. But our forebears added the clause "A well-regulated militia, being necessary to the security of a free state...", which left open a dozen interpretations of their intent. Too bad.

For a century or so, it didn't matter much. But then technology outstripped rhetoric and the result has been slaughter. Particularly in the last 25 years, the availability of automatic weapons with fearful potential for mass murder has exploded exponentially, especially among young males. Very young. Today we have nearly as many private weapons as private citizens.

We have always paid a price for certain of our freedoms. The convenience and mobility of the automobile costs us 40,000 lives a year. We try to control that number with laws, and it is diminishing, but we accept it for the overwhelming array of positives personal transportation brings to our lives.

What do we get for the 20,000 lives we spend on guns? It's a crucial question.

Safety? The results prove that to be ludicrous on its face. Some say personal weapons are guarantees against government tyranny and point to China, an oppressed nation where gun ownership is forbidden.

But what about East Germany, Czechoslovakia, Hungary, Russia and others where guns were outlawed? They found their democratic voice without them.

Most Americans agree that there should be limits on gun ownership and use, at least as many restrictions as on automobiles. But the minority who disagree do so much more passionately and therefore prevail in the halls of power.

Until and unless the majority finds its own passion on the issue, the question will never even seriously be addressed.

And 20,000 people who are alive as I write these words will be dead before their time by June 2nd, 1994.

The Death Penalty

Monday, April 27th, 1992

Look, I know most of you don't agree with me on this one, but I'll say my piece anyway and maybe it will get a few of us talking over the dinner table.

I'm against the death penalty.

If you got past that sentence, you have probably decided that I am some bleeding heart, itching to take a serial killer to lunch or turn mass murderers out on the street.

No such thing. I personally couldn't care less what happens to these cold, whining ciphers with the dead eyes who cut short innocent lives with no more thought than they would give to swatting a fly. I'm not particularly proud to admit it, but I could watch many of these killers twist in the wind at the end of a rope without a qualm.

Moreover, I can't guarantee that if one of these monsters did hurt to someone I loved, I wouldn't search him out and send him by the quickest means to the next world, accepting the consequences for my action.

No, I have no sympathy for murderers. They are the lowest rung of humankind and they have earned no place in civilized society, ever.

Not only that, I don't buy into any of this "society is to blame" malarkey. The murderer is to blame for the murder, period. Taking another life is a willful act and deserves the severest punishment.

Then why am I against the death penalty?

Because I love my country.

The murderer is the worst of the worst in this world. The act of murder is the most egregious of crimes. Should the government of the greatest nation in the long march of history put itself on the same plane as the dregs of society? Should it let a cold-eyed, ignorant sociopath pull the highest expression of a free people down to his own level?

I say, never.

The government is you and I, not some anonymous function-ary we pay to press a button. It is we who threaten a victim with death, just like the murderer. It is we who taunt the victim with what we are going to do, just like the murderer. It is we who deliberately drop the pellets into the acid and watch the victim squirm and gasp and spit and twitch his life away, just like the murderer.

What a triumph for the cruel killers among us who can laugh at our pretended superiority. We're no better than they, after all.

What reasons do we give for the death penalty? Deterrence? But isn't that a grim joke? There is no credible study nor any empirical evidence that it deters murders.

Justice? Not all states have the death penalty and not all that have it enforce it. Most of those put to death since the Supreme Court lifted the moratorium have been killed in the South with its long history of violence and blood sports. Lynchings are now frowned upon, so Texas and Florida take the lead in legal killings. So much for equal justice.

Vengeance? Surely not. A government has to be above revenge. That's an emotion understandable in one distraught individual caught up in the agony of a personal tragedy, but vengeance as an expression of the deliberate and collective will of a great people? It's not worthy of us.

The death penalty is against the march of history. In the Middle Ages, governments hanged people for picking pockets and poaching rabbits. Families packed lunches to watch the executions. It was a party. A Festival of Death.

A few days back, we took 15 minutes to choke a killer to death in California, then 45 minutes to poison another one in Texas. We listened avidly as witnesses, surrogates for all of us, described their last agonies.

That's not how a great state or a great nation conducts itself on the threshold of the 21st century. Of course it removes dangerous elements from its midst and it puts them away, forever. If the law doesn't allow for that, it fixes the law.

As a footnote, that prison option allows government, if it learns it has made a mistake in its judgement, as it has in at least a hundred documented capital cases this century, to reach into a cell and restore the wrongly accused to society.

Killing, whether by the individual or by the government, leaves no margin for error.

Public Figure Math

Monday, January 3rd, 1994

We always seem to find the beginning of a new year a convenient milepost for reassessment. For the most part, the reassessment is personal. Very occasionally, we think beyond our individual concerns to look at where we are as a neighborhood, a city, a state, a nation.

In my own case, I've been thinking about mathematics. Not the kind with numbers. The more complicated mathematical computations by which we arrive at conclusions about the public figures in our midst.

It is widely accepted that we in this country are faring worse in our pure math skills than we once did. I submit that we have also lost the knack of assessing the success or failure of those we lift above the crowd.

Every man and woman to whom we grant power or celebrity has a personal life. No one arrives at maturity unscathed. Indeed, those with the charisma to catch our attention in the first place are more likely than the rest of us to have had adventures which might embarrass under later — and closer — scrutiny.

For instance, on a dare, a little boy might have shoplifted a toy pistol. A teenage girl may have gone further than she should in the back seat of a 1963 Chevy. A young husband might conveniently have forgotten to report some cash earnings. A young wife might have forged a letter of recommendation to better her chances for a job.

No one get through life pristine. Think of your own experience. Which ten moments would you least like to have exposed to the hot light of publicity? Right. There was a time we understood this. That was where the mathematics of performance came in. If, on balance, the person had done substantially more good things than bad things, we counted him or her a success.

This was true in all categories of public life, including politics. For instance, constituents understood that the person they elected to Congress might not be a Rhodes scholar, but he had common sense and a good heart. Perhaps he would drink a little too much at the American Legion dance on Saturday night, but on Monday he'd be back at his desk, doing the best he could.

It was a compact between human beings, not between voters on the one hand — who were allowed to be as fallible and greedy and prurient and shallow as they wished — and a plaster saint on the other — who must be 100% correct on everything all the time. Life and democracy don't work that way.

We used to know that.

The personal lives of the Founding Fathers and, for that matter, the Founding Mothers, would never had stood such close examination. Benjamin Franklin's encounters with the opposite sex would have eliminated him from any role in today's public arena. Would the country have been better for it?

I must ask of my fellow citizens, what's the point? We may accuse sleaze journalists and opportunistic campaign managers of being the villains in our current feeding frenzy of voyeurism, but they aren't the villains. They are the ethically retarded spawn of a system that justifies any act which results in "victory". They have always been with us.

But there was a time when very few of us listened. We took these revelations for what they were: irrelevant gossip. Now we listen and demand more and more. We are the villains.

We pay football players to play football. If they conspire to shave points we have every right to expose them and put them in jail. If they cheat on their wives, that's none of our business. That's a painful personal matter between them and their wives.

We hire politicians to run our government. If they take bribes or in any other way subvert the process, we should make them publicly pay the price. But if we learn they cheated on a college exam 20 years before, that's none of our business. That's a matter between them and their colleges.

We justify all these invasions of privacy as exposing the "character" of the public figure. But now we're back to that inexorable math. No one does everything right all the time. Does any individual failing obliterate all good qualities and besmirch "character" forever?

To borrow from current headlines, should a candidate for office now be required to disclose whether or not he or she has ever had sex with someone other than a spouse? Which of our presidents could have stood such scrutiny? George Bush? Ronald Reagan? Lyndon Johnson? Dwight Eisenhower? Franklin Roosevelt? The faces on Mount Rushmore? Some people history has rated as men and women of great character and strength might not have passed that particular litmus test.

In the complicated calculus of the real world, a person who was, say, 70-30 good used to be considered a success. What's the new math? 100-0? From what I'm told, there's only been one of those in the last 2000 years.

Nick and Nina take to the road whenever other duties permit. These two lanes stretch to Monument Valley on the Arizona-Utah border. 1993.

On The Road

I WANT TO SAY Nick Clooney's columns on the great philosophical issues of the day are my favorites...the defeat of communism, the benign role of Protestants in the U.S....the hot buttons like abortion, euthanasia and capital punishment.

I want to say my favorites are character pieces...sister Rosemary, the family, the friends in Augusta and Maysville, the broadcasters, the entertainers.

I want to say the history columns are most memorable...World War II, the 1950s, Korea, the turbulence of the '60s.

But I would be lying. It's the travel pieces that immediately come to mind when I'm asked about my favorite Nick Clooney columns. It is the Painted Desert, Niagara Falls, New Zealand, the Amish country. It is the QEII, a float plane in Alaska and a parade in Central Park. And one of my all-time favorites, a column first published in September of 1991 about Raffles Hotel in Singapore.

Bob Hendrickson, Publisher
The Maysville Ledger-Independent
Maysville, Kentucky

On The Road

This is the Rudyard Kipling room at "Raffles" in Singapore.
Nick and Nina in 1983.

Raffles

Friday, September 20th, 1991

A friend sent me a wire story about the reopening of the famous "Raffles" hotel in Singapore.

The friend had reason to know I'd be interested. Nina and I once stayed there. It was eight years ago, and we were vacationing with my sister Rosemary in that exotic equatorial city, fulfilling a childhood fantasy.

When we were kids in Maysville and Cincinnati, we'd see movies about languid British ladies in diaphanous summer dresses and wide, floppy hats, escorted by men in white linen suits, and all of them seemed invariably to be staying at Raffles Hotel. Somerset Maugham, Rudyard Kipling, Noel Coward and many other literary figures made it their headquarters in the East, and made frequent references to it in their writings. Joseph Conrad was another habitué.

We had a wonderful time there, so I was anxious to read about its renaissance. First of all, I was surprised to see that the writer believed the hotel had fallen into "disrepair" prior to its closing two years ago for modernizing. If so, the deterioration must have been quick. When we were there in 1983, it was certainly not in disrepair. It did not have the modern amenities of the newer hotels, such as computers and cable television, but we did not find that to be a liability; quite the opposite.

The story went on that the new hotel will have rooms and suites named after the famous people who had stayed there. Well, so did the old one. Nina and I stayed in the Rudyard Kipling room and Rosemary stayed in one named for Somerset Maugham.

In a decided lapse, the writer referred to a famous incident by relating that "tales sprung up about the reported shooting of a lion under its billiard table." A lion? Please!

The story is so well known as to be cliché in Malaysia and, for that matter, in Britain. Just after the turn of the century, a tiger (not a lion, for heaven's sake) wandered from the nearby jungle into Raffles, already the best-known hostelry East of Suez. Without checking in, it stalked through the hallway past the bar where the notorious Singapore Sling would be invented ten years later, checked a few small banquet rooms, then went into the billiard room, where it settled down under one of the tables, with its tail curling out ominously.

This was a full-grown tiger, so a few of the patrons were a bit non-plussed. The tiger wouldn't go away and started making menacing noises, so the management sent for a teacher who was also a well-known hunter. He came over and dispatched the intruder. When we were there, tiger paw prints were etched in the tile floor marking the non-paying visitor's path.

The newspaper account has Rudyard Kipling saying "Feed at Raffles when in Singapore." That's close, but I have a picture of a sign in the dining room which has the quote a more pithy "When in the East, feed at Raffles." Perhaps he said both. Or neither.

When we were there, the now-independent state of Singapore didn't think much of Raffles. They did their best to steer us to their brand-new gleaming and glitzy Hiltons, Sheratons and Westins, some of which went to fifty stories and more. The new government wanted to wipe out their history, and with some reason. The memory of the colonial years cannot have been all pleasant by any means, nor can another memory about which few there speak publicly.

In the early days, a great attraction for tourists in Singapore was its thriving opium trade. The drug and its derivatives were openly available on every street corner, and the helpless addicts they produced were a British Empire scandal. Small wonder this industrious, authoritarian and very successful small country would like to sweep those memories under a rug.

But Raffles — which, incidentally, was named after the British founder of Singapore — wouldn't go away. The article says it has been completely renovated, but efforts were made to keep its original charm.

I hope so. The memories of those lazy ceiling fans, the dignified, turbaned Sikhs guarding the front door, the huge fan palms in the courtyard, the leisurely high tea at four o'clock and, yes, the filmy chiffon dresses on the ladies and the occasional white linen suites on the gentlemen even now, comprise one of our great travel memories.

They spent nearly a hundred million dollars on the renovation, and their new prices reflect that. According to the story, the rooms will run $350 a night, about three times what we paid.

But there will probably be some deals or tour packages which will knock that published price down considerably. If so, travelers of a certain age who saw the same movies we did can visit some day, down a Singapore Sling and trace the trail of the tale of the tail of the tiger.

Then, if you can still say that, you get one more Singapore Sling.

Nick and Nina aboard the "Concorde", 10 miles above the Atlantic. 1989.

The Concorde

September 6th, 1989

We raced the sun across the Atlantic and beat it by an hour.

We left Heathrow airport in London at 9:25 A.M. local time and arrived at Kennedy airport in New York at 8:07 A.M. local time, the sun limping along one hour and eighteen minutes behind us, an embarassed Natchez to our triumphant Robert E. Lee.

One hundred adventurers huddled together in a ship no larger than the "Nina" or the "Pinta" or the "Santa Maria" hurtling through the air faster than the earth was turning on its axis.

We were aboard the graceful, needle-nosed "Concorde" returning from our wondrous week on the QE2 and in London's Ritz Hotel, capping it off now with another top-of-the-line experience. There are fifty of us, Greater Cincinnatians all. This group venture is the only way we average people can visit these playgrounds of the super-rich. Individually, only plutocrats can afford the luxury of the accommodations and service we've had in these eight days.

Now a climactic return journey and I want you to come along with us.

First, you should know that security is very tight at Heathrow. Ghosts from the tragic Pan-Am flight that left this very airport last year and was blown out of the sky a few minutes later still haunt the British.

Every piece of luggage is banded with a strip of strong tape and may not be opened again. Each passenger must stand by his or her baggage and identify it as it is checked through. Carry-on luggage is not only X-rayed, but is gone through individually by security personnel.

It is inconvenient and it slows our check-in considerably, but few complain. My wife Nina is, however, mildly mortified in the process. Elegant, stylishly dressed, beautiful, she has her most expensive purse out for the journey on the "Concorde". In the midst of the crowd at the counter, a security man going through her purse is loudly curious about one item.

"What's this, lady?" Nina tries to whisper a reply. "It's what ma'am? Oh, it's biscuits, is it?" It's three cookies Nina saved from the breakfast tray at the hotel, wrapped in a napkin and squirreled away in her purse against a potential hunger pang.

Nina the smuggler.

There was a British Airways waiting room and we knew immediately that our trip was to be different from any air journey we'd made before. We were greeted by attendants who offered us fruit juice or anything else we wanted to drink, including champagne, even before we boarded. As we made our way through the passageway to the aircraft, we each were handed models of the "Concorde" to take home.

We had been warned by previous travellers about three things; the cabin space would be cramped, the windows would be tiny, and the flight would be noisy. All three concerns were exaggerated. The cabin is narrow, but the seats are very comfortable; the windows are tiny, but you can see the spectacular view quite easily; the flight is a little noisier than most domestic, lower level trips, but not uncomfortably so.

In the waiting room, a languid young British passenger contemptuously described the technology of the plane as "outdated" and "old". It's true that these aircraft have been in service for twenty years, and that soon these classic beauties will and should be retired before a metal fatigue accident mars their near-perfect record. Still, to decribe the "Concorde" as "old technology" is like describing the "Mona Lisa" as an "old painting". To this day, no commercial jet does what the "Concorde" does.

As we would now discover for ourselves.

Because of its streamlined shape, "V" wings and lack of flaps, the "Concorde" must go down the runway twice as fast as a standard airplane to get off the ground. We're at 250 miles per hour before the wheels leave the concrete.

A read-out on a large panel in front of us keeps us informed about basic information. We aren't allowed to break the sound barrier ("Mach") until we are out over the ocean because the sonic boom would shatter windows.

But we're over the ocean soon enough and the pilot kicks in the after-burners. It's almost as if we're taking off again, down some invisible runway in the sky.

We break the sound barrier and leave Mach 1 far behind. I think of Colonel Chuck Yeager, the first fellow to do that and live. Our information panel tells us we're speeding up and soaring. 40,000 feet, 900 mph; 50,000 feet, 1100 mph; 57,500 feet, 1350 mph. Eleven miles up, twice the speed of sound.

I look down and see the curve of the earth. I look up and see a sky of deep navy blue. I look at my wife and my sister and my new friends from Cincinnati and I think we're all moved by the Buck Rogers miracle we're experiencing.

Back on the ground we chatter about it, trying to find words so that we can lock those 3 hours and 22 minutes away in our diary and dust them off on a rainy day. We've been higher and faster than we have ever been or would ever be again.

We have raced the sun, and won.

Berlin

Wednesday, January 6th, 1993

I was eavesdropping on a conversation at a nearby table in a crowded restaurant last week. It went something like this.

"Go figure the Germans. They knock off a couple dozen immigrants — legal immigrants, mind you — then they march through Berlin by the thousands saying how maybe they shouldn't have done it." "Yeah, but why are you suprised? Those Germans are all alike."

No, they aren't. Not by a long shot. Berliners are a different breed. Not just from other Germans. From everyone else, too.

This is in no way a defense of Germany, today or yesterday. I have already written my opinion on that score. The amalgam of brilliant cultures and restless ambitions which comprise 20th century Germany have caused mankind enough grief for several millenia.

No, there's plenty to worry about with the rise of neo-Nazi bullies of East Germany. The combination of a sense of inferiority to the West, economic hardships and high unemployment is a dangerous brew.

My disagreement with the conversation at the next table had to do with their inclusion of Berlin in the mix. This ancient capital has a mind of its own. I'm told it was always so. As long as Germany was an Imperial power with a Kaiser and the trappings of monarchy, Berlin was awash in and in thrall to militarism. When all that went away after World War I, Berlin did a turnaround and became a European capital of diversity, intellectual ferment, alternative lifestyles, some even said decadence.

As recounted in William Shirer's "Berlin Diary", the residents of the German capital never took to Hitler and were positively morose at the onset of World War II. This is in contrast to the wild enthusiasm for both Hitler and the war in Bavaria and elsewhere in Germany.

I have no personal knowledge of pre-World War II Berlin, of course, but I can attest to post-World War II in that city. I suppose there has never been anything like it, ever. A four-power island in a sea of Red, it was unlike any place I've ever been, before or since. Though it existed on the very edge of the abyss, it was never grim. Quite the opposite.

Berlin was the one place on earth where the nuclear firestorm could begin at a moment's notice, day or night. It was also the leak in the Iron Curtain where East escaped West. Intrigue was common coinage. Spying was a cottage industry. No wonder the nightlife hilarity at the Resi and the Badewanne and the Eiershalle was tinged with hysteria.

Because of the incredible Airlift, Berliners had chosen sides. America was their wave of the future. Besides, in this one spot in the world where the two systems could be seen side-by-side across the Brandenburg Gate, Soviet Communism was a highly visible and humiliating failure.

Hollywood, that acute observer of the straws in the wind of popular history, knew a great story when it saw one and cranked out a dozen Berlin movies. They make fascinating viewing now. If you get a chance to see "Foreign Affair" with Jean Arthur, John Lund and Marlene Dietrich or "Night People" with Gregory Peck and Broderick Crawford or "The Big Lift" with Montgomery Clift and Paul Douglas, or any of the others, they'll provide you with a marvelous glimpse at how the times shaped a people.

Like thousands of other G.I.s, I was in Berlin, too. The American troops stationed there were given liberal leave and three-day pass privileges because of what was called "island fever." You couldn't drive far in any direction without encountering armed Russians. If war came, everyone from the West in Berlin was doomed, and they all knew it.

So when 250,000 Berliners marched on Christmas in the worst weather of the year, lighting their candles against the darkness of bigotry and violence and totalitarianism, we should pay attention.

They know better than most where the deadly trio leads.

Sgt. William Guilfoyle at Wendover Air Force Base in 1943.

Wendover

Friday, February 28th, 1992

I came here to tape a feature story for a television newscast, but I took away much more than I'll be able to tell in two minutes and forty-five seconds.

Have you ever heard of Wendover Air Force Base? I've been hearing about it since I was a little boy. My Uncle William Guilfoyle was stationed here during World War II when the service he joined was still called the Army Air Force.

He enlisted a month after Pearl Harbor Day and following training in Michigan and being promoted to sergeant, he was sent to Wendover.

It was, and is, a desolate place that straddles an invisible desert line between Utah and Nevada. Like many such western border towns, it's now a tawdry amalgam of latter-day cowboy culture and imitation Las Vegas. Its gaudiest features are four or five gambling casinos. Its houses are for the most part modular or mobile homes. There is a temporary quality to it all, as if a year after the last human being walked away from it, there would be no sign man had ever been here.

But if the town is ugly, the area which surrounds it is stunningly beautiful. Mountains guard the west with their snow caps touching the clouds. A picture-perfect desert sweeps away to the south. To the north and east is a salt flat. Just now there is a winter run-off covering the flat with a few inches of water making it a hundred-square-mile mirror, reflecting the mountains and the dramatic sky above it in perfect detail.

I said the casinos were the town's gaudiest feature, but they are by no means its most interesting, or its biggest.

This was once home to 20,000 young American servicemen and women. Wendover was a huge air training base, first as a gunnery range before the war, then as a bombing run for B-24s when Uncle William was there and finally as a major facility for the B-29 Superfortress.

It was here that crews trained for the final assault on Japan. It was here that the "Enola Gay" was readied to drop the bomb heard 'round the world, the first nuclear device used in wartime.

The men and women are gone, but everything else is still here. The enormous hangars are abandoned, glass knocked out of thousands of window panes. The criss-cross runways are here, each a mile long. Taxiways are all here, thousands of yards of concrete, all intact.

The barracks are here, doors flapping, windows staring vacantly. So is the mess hall and the showers and the chapel and the day rooms. How packed they must have been in 1943 and 1944 and 1945, and how noisy. No noise now. Just the wind.

To the east is a gunnery bunker where young men just back from practice over the salt flats would empty their machine guns into a hill of sand before taxiing back to the hangar. Right now, you can dig a few inches into that sand and scoop up a handful of 50-year-old 50-caliber slugs.

The walk-up control tower is there and the firehouse and the hospital and the orderly rooms. All are deserted. The town, a half-mile away, ignores them.

As we go from place to place, Uncle William tells me how it was. "Do you suppose they have hot water here yet?" He tells me what they did and how they felt about it.

He has pictures from 1943 and he shows me exactly where this was and where that happened. He gives me a sense of it, but only a sense. He and a diminishing few know first-hand the feelings at which the rest of us can only guess.

Now he also knows that he was a small part of what history would eventually call the Manhattan Project. He left Wendover before the big Superforts arrived, but the process was already in train. The tests they were conducting, so bewildering to those young men, are now clearly outlined. They were on a track that led directly to Hiroshima and Nagasaki.

The nation is ambivalent about those war-ending explosions now. Perhaps that's one of the reasons this old base is crumbling and ignored.

Uncle William and I waited on the tarmac while the camera was adjusted and watched a storm coming toward us. It was fifteen miles away. It swept the bunkers and the runways clean and when it passed they sparkled in the sunlight. Shiny and new again for a moment, waiting for those earnest youngsters in khaki, unaware they won't be coming back.

Except occasionally, one at a time, disguised as old men.

And, perhaps, after sunset, as ghosts. The thousands of ghosts of Wendover.

Nick wheels his Uncle William Guilfoyle through a deserted Wendover hangar. 1992.

The Float Plane

Monday, August 30th, 1993

All my life I had wanted a ride in what we used to call a "seaplane" when I was growing up.

They were all the rage in the movies of my youth and in the literature of World War Two. The "Catalinas", called the "Big Cats", were workhorses of the Pacific theater and elsewhere. They were slow and could barely defend themselves, but they could fly forever and were as dependable as Old Faithful.

Even before the war, it was seaplanes that made all the transoceanic passenger flights. They even had beds, like Pullman cars on the train.

And the biggest aircraft ever built, though it was airborn only once, was a seaplane. Howard Hughes's "Spruce Goose" lumbered a hundred feet into the air for a mile, then retired forever.

In more recent years, there had been a seaplane up on Lake Erie, near Cleveland, and at one time there were a couple of them taking people from Los Angeles to Santa Catalina Island, but for one reason or another I was never able to find time for a ride on one and when I finally got the time, they were gone.

Some of you may remember there was one on the Ohio River several years back. I recall seeing it fly low, following the course of the river for a while, then turning and heading for home.

Finally, I got my chance. It was on a trip to Alaska. We were in the town of Ketchikan. Great name, isn't it? Sounds like the location of a Jack London novel. To tell you the truth, there's enough excitement in present-day Ketchikan to inspire a couple of books.

It's surrounded by water and forest. If you want to get there you come by sea or by plane. The shore is lined with aircraft on pontoons, almost one to every house, just like the family car.

Not "seaplanes", I learned quickly enough. These are "float planes", and they're as necessary as insulated boots in this part of the world.

When I saw the signs offering flights to the interior on float planes, I didn't hesitate. Nina was tired, so she sat this one out, but my friend Dante DiPaolo and I headed for the dock.

The aircraft was single-engine, but both the plane and the engine were big. It was built by Canada's de Havilland, Incorporated and it looked both sturdy and businesslike. The two floats were larger than I thought they'd be.

There were nine of us aboard when the pilot gave us all something that looked like earphones. I soon learned why. When he fired up the engine, the noise was deafening. With or without the earphones, passengers could only mouth words to one another. We couln't hear anything but the engine.

We took off through choppy water and, actually, it didn't feel much different from a take-off on a runway. I was disappointed.

We headed inland over mountains and glaciers that were spectacular. In about an hour, we saw a lake right in the center of what might have once been a volcano. The water was black. Our plane began slipping sideways in a steep descent and I realized we were going to land on that lake.

Down, down we went. The water seemed even blacker up close. The surface was dead calm. We seemed to be flaring out for a landing. When would we touch down? Where was the splash? Suddenly, I realized we were down already! We had landed with absolutely no sensation whatever and were now taxiing.

This was all I had hoped for, and more. An entirely new experience.

The lake was in wild back country. No facilities. No boats. No people. We drifted toward the shore, 50 yards away. A couple of us got out on the floats to stretch our legs and take pictures.

I looked across the water and couldn't believe my eyes. There was a bear coming down the hill toward the water! I sputtered and pointed. The pilot followed my stare, and then looked startled himself.

"Well I'll be darned," he said, "look at that. It's a coastal brown bear. I've been flying this route nine years and I've never seen one. You'd better get a picture."

I did, and so did everyone else.

I was taking some notes and asked the guide to tell me again what kind of bear that was.

"It's a coastal bear. You know, a Grizzly."

I got back into the plane with all deliberate haste. The takeoff seemed to take forever.

The Park

Wednesday, September 21st, 1994

There are no readily available statistics on this matter, so I will make some up. New Yorkers walk 41.7 per cent more than the residents of any other city in the United States. If that is not true, it ought to be.

If we in Cincinnati or Hamilton or Covington are going two blocks to the grocery we very sensibly get into our cars and drive there. In Manhattan, if locals are going from Carnegie Hall on 57th Street to a restaurant on West 45th Street, they walk. Then, after dinner, they walk to their apartment on East 59th. In the course of one evening, they walk more than a native of Elmwood Place will walk in a month.

Oh, yes, there is the subway and cabs and buses and they all get plenty of use. Still, New Yorkers are the walkingest people in the country. I suppose we shouldn't be surprised. After all, folks originally from Gotham are the ones who walked all the way across the continent in the 19th century and settled the west. Saturday last, Nina and I decided to join the big city strollers. We walked to Central Park and had ourselves quite a day.

All those who have never been to New York cringe when they hear the words "Central Park." They have an image of a war zone. Muggers and murderers behind every bush. That's understandable. Since its earliest days, Central Park has been the butt of New York jokes and there have been enough genuine ugly incidents to fuel the fire of its negative image.

The truth is, Central Park remains a fascinating and entertaining place, doing what it was intended to do. It is providing relaxation for hundreds of thousands of city dwellers whose apartment homes are necessarily small and cramped.

On this warm afternoon, there were children everywhere. I saw three sets of twins and Nina tells me she saw quadruplets in a stroller as wide as an RV. We hadn't been on the pathway five minutes before we were nearly run down by two waves of determined female power walkers. We detoured to a smaller trail which soon led to a reflecting pool where a dozen model sailboats sedately plied the mirror-like surface.

Central Park Lake wasn't far away. When we arrived we saw that a number of couples had rented boats and were rowing all the way around the lake's tiny island, just as couples have done for five generations.

Of course, dogs were everywhere. I will now invent another statistic. Manhattanites have 15.9 per cent more dogs per capita than any other city-dwellers in the nation. Dogs of all shapes, sizes and dispositions. Dogs of lineage royal and dubious. They romp over every square foot of Central Park with surprising discipline and good humor.

On the plaza which borders the lake, a Japanese woman performed a stylized dance while someone video-taped her work. On the other side of the fountain, a film crew sweated through a tedious sequence over and over, actors soaking wet from running up the steps time after time.

The Central Park Zoo is still open. A New York polar bear, six New York sea lions and nine New York monkeys gaped at multi-national visitors while the pricey Essex House hotel loomed over their ersatz environs.

Fortified by a hot dog, Nina and I decided it was time to return to our own hotel. We emerged on Central Park South and walked east to Fifth Avenue.

What we hadn't counted on was the parade. This was a day New Yorkers set aside to salute those of German ancestry. The city does nothing halfway. This was a major-league parade. Our problem was that the parade was using Fifth Avenue and Nina and I had to get across Fifth Avenue to get to our hotel. We asked a policeman if we could cross between units. No dice. We asked how long the parade would last.

"Oh, two or three hours. Maybe more. You could go downtown where the parade starts. They'll let you cross there." How far? "Probably 25 or 30 blocks." Any other choices? "You could try to run and get ahead of the parade. They just got started."

So that's why Nina and I were jogging uptown on the sidewalk, past Austrian dancers, oompah bands and high school drill teams. Suddenly, our sidewalk was blocked. Grandstands had been set up for parade watchers. The stands were packed. We weren't allowed to walk behind them. We still couldn't cross the street.

"The only people allowed on Fifth Avenue today are the ones in the parade", said a policeman.

Then we saw it. Someone had dropped a paper German flag. The black, red and orange stripes were dusty, but I wiped them off, took Nina's hand and stepped out onto Fifth Avenue. Holding the flag high, we marched to the drumbeat past the grandstand for six blocks. Nina got a respectable round of applause. We worked our way to the other side of the Avenue, got off at our street and retreated to our hotel.

Where, in honor of everyone's German ancestors, we had a beer.

Miami Beach

Monday, November 18th, 1991

In a recent fit of adventurism, Nina and I equipped ourselves appropriately and stormed the beach.

Miami Beach.

It took courage. From what we had been told, the sands of Iwo Jima would have been more accommodating and probably safer. Our knowledgeable friends in the Ohio Valley warned us that

Miami was a war zone and that Miami Beach, once the premier attraction of the Florida peninsula, was in severe disarray.

Certainly, they had a point. The Cuban exodus and the out-of-control drug influx from South and Central America had transformed the city to the extent that the title of the '80s TV show "Miami Vice" seemed redundant.

Still, Miami is a large and interesting city and we knew that no trip to Florida would be complete without visiting it, so off we went.

The drive into town seemed to substantiate the worst we had heard. The neighborhood which borders downtown to the north was rundown and dirty, its residents surly or indifferent.

But I remembered that there are neighborhoods in our tri-state cities that wouldn't make it to the pages of "House Beautiful" either. If that was all a visitor saw of our part of the world he would be left with a sorry impression of us, indeed.

So we pressed on.

We decided to stay at a hotel downtown. We often do that. The truth is, most American cities look exactly alike if you only drive around their beltways. Same hotels, same restaurants, same landscaping by the same dull, competent people, same roads, same ramps to the same malls, same cars and trucks, same exhaust fumes.

There is literally no difference between I-275 and its counterparts in Los Angeles, San Francisco, Washington, D.C., Cleveland, Chicago, or Miami.

The only way to learn the character of a city — any city — is to find its heart. Downtowns differ. Each is unique. Each tells you something you didn't know before about the place you're visiting.

Is it friendly? Dirty? Dangerous? Fun? Frenetic? Dying? Elegant? Go straight downtown and you know immediately. If there is no real downtown, then there is no real city.

Miami is a real city, all right. Its downtown is alive and exotic. Like many similar communities, though, it is dangerous after dark. We asked our hotel clerk if we should walk to a restaurant three blocks away and were told "no" before we completed the question.

So we decided to go out to Miami Beach for dinner. Everyone told us how rundown and terrible it had become, but I wanted Nina to get a look at it. I hoped there might be an echo of the charm I had seen there as a teenager.

I thumbed through the phone book and saw a familiar name; the Breakwater. Off we went over the causeway all the way to Ocean Drive.

We turned left to one of the most pleasant surprises in years. The wonderful old Art-Deco section of Miami Beach has recently been rehabbed and gussied up until it approaches the splendor of its glory years. Each of the little hotels competes in charm and neon.

The names rolling by our taxi window evoked the '20s and '30s. The Barbizon, the Park Central, the Majestic, the Avalon, the Pelican, the Waldorf Towers, the Edison, and then the Breakwater, with one part of its front porch a sidewalk cafe and the other part an attractive outdoor bar.

As we enjoyed a good Italian meal, an endless parade of attractive people of all ages strolled up and down the sidewalk, while the surf lapped at the wide beach just across the street.

9 o'clock on a Thursday night in October and the streets were packed. It was a stylish, exotic crowd, and they were enjoying themselves.

Nina remarked that this is what Santa Monica, California should look like and doesn't. There, the militant homeless and an intimidating round-the-clock patrol of aggressive alcoholics dominate the sidewalks and crowd out locals and tourists alike.

Not at Miami Beach. We saw dozens of families with their babies in strollers out enjoying the soft Florida night. Gaggles of well-dressed teenagers added to the pleasant din. Handsome young couples shopped for restaurants. Small groups of mature tourists, dressed to the nines, took their evening constitutionals.

A sudden thunderstorm was a bonus, and made instant friends of total strangers as the walkers crowded onto the porch for some protection from the downpour.

When the rain went away, the night was crystal clear and Nina and I took a walk along the beach. Nina asked what I was whistling. It was "Moon Over Miami." It sounded new.

These are the stark cliffs at the entrance to Hobart Harbor, Tasmania. 1994.

Tasmania

Wednesday, November 2nd, 1994

If there were such a thing as sardonic laughter in heaven or hell, surely we would have heard it today. Here we were, tourists in polyester shorts, gawking at the plain, rectangular stone buildings constructed long ago amidst so much cruelty and anguish. We're snapping pictures and having a leisurely glass of wine and talking among ourselves about how quaint and beautiful it all is. Quaint and beautiful.

This is Tasmania.

Once it was a name whispered only in the same breath with Devil's Island and the Dry Tortugas. It was here that England sent its most violent, incorrigible convicts. The murderers, rapists, the sociopaths of every stripe. And it was here that the British jailers matched their charges' degradation with cruelty hard to imagine at this distance. Twenty percent of the prisoners sent here died before their time, many of them cut down or chewed up by dogs while "trying to escape."

Each of these workmanlike, square buildings which line the lovely harbor at Hobart was constructed by men with tortured backgrounds and hopeless futures. There's a letter in a museum here from one of the inmates to his priest. He was about to be hanged. He was lighthearted, joyful, grateful, he said, to be released from the daily hell inflicted in the name of Victorian justice.

The irony of it is that the tourists are right. Tasmania is quaint and beautiful. There is not even an echo of all that human suffering, except for sterile artifacts under glass and the scrubbed walls of Port Arthur's forbidding buildings.

It was called Van Diemen's Land back then, before being given the name of its discoverer, Abel Tasman. To this day, it is the wildest and most untamed large island in the world. Of its few thousand aboriginal people, not one full descendant remains. Not one. It is the size of Ireland, but no more than 500,000 people live here. We're told that large sections of the west and southwest have not been explored to this day. The notorious and elusive Tasmanian Devil, the tough little carnivorous marsupial with an attitude, still roams these wild hills.

There is every reason for the tourist to come here. The harbor at Hobart is as lovely as any I've ever seen. The weather, which gets a bad rap, is actually quite temperate and more moderate than most of the great cities of Europe or North America. Many of the people are accomplished craftsmen. We saw more crafts produced on the premises by the shopowners themselves than anywhere outside of Asia.

It was quite a contrast to sail into this port after a day-long stay in Melbourne, which, among our stops so far, looks most like a large American city. Subtract the left hand drive and the charming accents and Melbourne could be Chicago. Soaring skyscrapers and the peculiar tension which results when millions of people occupy the same space were immediately apparent. All the virtues and vices of large 20th century cities are present in Melbourne. Sparkling new office buildings next door to older, vacant ones. Imaginatively planned outdoor malls festooned with obscene graffiti. A breathtaking new arts and entertainment complex six blocks from a row of empty, decaying theaters and movie palaces.

The feature we will take away from Melbourne is the tram. Trams efficiently intersect the city. They are cheap and much quicker than the bus or automobile. An interesting offshoot of Melbourne's romance with the tram is a popular dinner attraction. About thirty people board a special tram at 8:30 P.M. It has been decorated in the style of the dining car of the Orient Express with brocades, lamps and mirrors. A gourmet French meal is served, complete with champagne and other appropriate wines, while the tram tours the city, much of which sparkles with festive lighting after dark.

No gourmet trams in Hobart, although the food in a waterfront tavern where we had lunch — the Salamanca Café — was excellent. The waiter took a shine to Nina — not an unusual occurence, may I tell you — so our service was world-class. Our Tasmanian Chardonnay, "Ninth Island Straits Dry" was a perfectly good table wine.

It was Sunday and Hobart is usually closed up tight for the Sabbath. But the arrival of a huge cruise ship is no small event in a city of 150,000, so the stores and many services opened up from 11 to 4 to accommodate us. Local wood and glass crafts were unique and reasonable.

A Tasmanian footnote. My sister Rosemary has a passion for "Payday" candy bars and stocks up on them for each of our vacation trips. She showed me a "Payday" wrapper. It read "Win a Trip to Tasmania — or Other Nutty Stuff". Rosemary sent a note from Hobart to the "Payday" home office in Monticello,

Minnesota. "I'm already in Tasmania. How about a nutty trip back to Beverly Hills?"

Not nutty, not ghostly, beautiful Tasmania is haunted no more. It has excorcised its devils.

I think.

Nina at the Women's Rights National Historical Park, Seneca Falls, New York. 1994.

Seneca Falls

Monday, May 30th, 1994

I closed my eyes for just a moment and tried to imagine what it had looked like back then. No cars on Fall Street, of course. Buggies. No electric lights. Lanterns and candles.

Seneca Falls, New York, is another pretty little town in the western part of the state. The Cayuga and Seneca Canal splits it in half lengthwise. It is attractive, but the casual visitor might be forgiven if he or she missed the town's importance.

For two summer days in the year 1848, Seneca Falls was the epicenter of a coming worldwide earthquake. A brilliant woman named Elizabeth Cady Stanton, only recently arrived in Seneca Falls from Boston, voiced her discontent at the lot of women in society. She was passionate and convincing, though her audience was only four other women who had gathered for tea.

It might not have seemed like much, but it was the beginning of the movement for women's rights in this country.

Nina and I had heard about the Women's Rights National Historical Park in Seneca Falls. I confess I had little idea of its history and significance. That was reason enough for a visit. It was time and past time I found out.

The town is just 15 minutes south of the New York Thruway. There is the standard commercial clutter at its fringes. That disappears when you approach the town center. Much of it has been rehabbed and looks just fine. We drove right past the Women's Rights National Park. It is not a very big park and is quite tastefully understated, all of which makes it easy to miss. However, it is well worth backtracking for. The displays in the building are remarkable. I learned a lot I didn't know before and I was taught in a quite interesting and entertaining way.

Next to the building which houses the displays stand the two remaining walls of the Wesleyan Chapel where the first Women's Rights Convention was held on July 19th and 20th, 1848.

That was just ten days after Elizabeth Cady Stanton and her four friends had their fateful tea party, every bit as important as the one held in Boston Harbor 80 years before. Quickly deciding on a convention, the women immediately contacted friends and advertised in the local newspaper.

Considering the brevity of the notice, the uncertainty of communications and the controversy of the subject matter, the result was astonishing. One farm woman later wrote, "I started out my journey quite alone, but it seemed at each crossroads, my wagon was joined by another, then two more wagons, until finally a perfect flood of us arrived at the appointed place."

Three hundred people attended, mostly women. Many prominent citizens were among them. Frederick Douglass, the escaped slave and already-famous orator, added his prestige to the event.

For the occasion, Elizabeth Cady Stanton and the other four women wrote a fiery paraphrase of the Declaration of Independence called the "Declaration of Sentiments." It said, among other things:

> "We hold these truths to be self-evident: That all men *and women* are created equal."

In listing the ways in which man had long tyrannized women, the document thundered,

> "He has never permitted her to exercise her inalienable right to the elective franchise.
>
> "He has compelled her to submit to laws in the formation of which she had no voice.
>
> "He has withheld from her rights which are given to the most ignorant and degraded men...
>
> "He has made her, if married, civilly dead...
>
> "He has denied her the facilities for obtaining a thorough education, all colleges being closed to her..."

Of those present, 100 signed the document, 68 women and 32 men. One signer was a young girl, Charlotte Woodward. She would be the only one of them alive to cast her first vote in a national election, 72 years later.

The women's movement had begun. Other conventions followed that same year. It was, as it remains, a long and rocky road. Twenty-one years would pass before Wyoming would allow women to vote, the first state to do so. Finally, in 1920, the 19th Ammendment allowed universal women's suffrage. That was only the end of round one.

On this sunny May day, there were many young women at the park. Some had brought their little daughters. More than a few had packed lunches and were sitting in the modest green area by the Chapel.

I thought again of the farm woman, getting up early that morning 145 years ago to do her back-breaking chores, then putting on her best dress, hitching up the horse and heading toward...what? She couldn't know for sure. She only knew it must be done. One more chore. "I started my journey quite alone..."

She is alone no more.

Romance Of The River

September 3rd, 1990

It's all Mark Twain's fault. He had to go and invent the River.

If it weren't for him, we'd just think of it as that big brown ditch that separated various states and carried our accumulated processed waste down to the Gulf of Mexico. An inconvenience to be bridged and walled away. We could turn our backs on it and go about our business.

But no, he had to write about how it spoke to him in a language as clear as any invented by man, how it swept inexorably into the future, sprinkling our history on its banks, how it murmured with dark mystery on a summer night, how it rippled with romance, how its steamboat was as beautiful as a wedding cake with none of the complications.

Because of Mark Twain, we look for Tom Sawyers and Becky Thatchers and Huckleberry Finns in every town perched on an even marginally navigable stream, and are usually able to convince ourselves we have found them.

It's because of Mark Twain that I am sitting in a cabin watching the mighty River carry us on our winding, stately course to the ultimate River City, New Orleans.

Mr. Clemens would recognize and approve our vessel. It is the biggest steamboat ever built. It is beyond question the most luxurious and most comfortable. Whether it is the most beautiful will be argued hotly by proponents of the Delta Queen and other purists who will champion the old Natchez or any of a host of graceful wooden legends festooned with gingerbread, belching black smoke from tall stacks, sending sparks winking into the sky to dance for a moment, then die on the broad surface of the river.

This is the Mississippi Queen.

Mr. Twain would have been astounded by the air-conditioning, the dimensions and the gift shop, but would have been quite familiar with the other amenities. The elegant dining room and the entertainment would ring a bell, and he would be right at home with the crew.

Some say Americans don't know how to treat vacationers. It is said that we are rude and impatient, especially in service positions. If you believe that, you should spend a couple of days on the Mississippi Queen.

I deliberately went all over the boat to see if I could find an employee who was out of sorts or had a surly attitude. Everybody from Captain Shewmaker to an Arkansas roustabout who had been aboard only a few days seemed to be recent graduates of charm school.

This is not to say they were plastic robots with pasted-on smiles. No, these are river people, which means they are thorough going, gold-plated characters, every one. Chief Tom Murphy, Warren from room service, Robert the waiter, Geneva the maid, Phyllis the singer all have their stories.

I was told that the beauty parlor is a fountain of information, so I went there and talked to Barbara. She's from Zanesville and she told us how scared she had been when she joined the crew three years ago. She knew the boat often had celebrity guests and she was terrified she would do or say the wrong thing.

The big day came. Somebody called to say a celebrity was on his way down. Unfortunately, the caller neglected to say who the celebrity was and, to her embarrassment, Barbara didn't recognize him.

Though her hands shook, she avoided doing him actual bodily harm while cutting his hair and finally got up the courage to speak to him.

"Excuse me, sir, I know I should recognize you but your name has slipped my mind."

"Well, I don't know if you should recognize me or not", the man answered. "I'm Lassie's veterinarian."

Barbara has taken care of many celebrities since, including the remarkable Helen Hayes, but Lassie's vet has a special place in her heart.

Our little band of Cincinnatians has toured plantations, battled 100 degree heat in Natchez, sampled exotic delicacies, checked out the last resting place of Huey Pierce Long, eaten ourselves into a stupor and are now headed for the fleshpots of New Orleans with its checkered politics and its fabled French Quarter.

In a pensive mood, sitting on the fantail with a tall drink in my hand, watching the half-moon reflect from the river surface made restless by our paddlewheel, I take out my calculator. Allowing for the river current and recent rainfall, I determine that my Tuesday bathwater from Augusta will meet us at Mile 355, just below Natchez.

Boat trips make me feel romantic. It's all Mark Twain's fault.

Entertainment

IT WAS MAY OF 1961. I was a month early and weighed 8-1/2 pounds. Even before I was born I learned if you're going to make it in this family you better keep it interesting. Tell your joke and get off...That's Entertainment.

The worst crime you could ever do was be a bore. Killing someone at least had flair! In fact, even as I'm writing this introduction, my thoughts swirl. If I don't make these 6 paragraphs quick and witty my Father might edit me or cut it down.

PARANOIA!...Years have gone by. We've grown, we've mellowed with age. He's now a much more patient man than he

George Clooney
Studio City, California

Entertainment

October 12, 1994	The Coat Tale
November 1, 1989	Harry James In Northern Kentucky
November 20, 1991	Sportscaster Vin Scully Is Best
December 9, 1991	Diane Sawyer; Nick Destroys Her Career
July 20, 1990	Jane Powell; Dream Come True: Almost
February 28, 1994	Dinah Shore; So Long
September 15-18, 1989	Tri Staters Write Epitaphs
January 24, 1992	Nick Remembers American Bandstand
September 10, 1990	The "Bistro" And Stars Of The Revolution

The irrepressible John Parker. Augusta, Kentucky, 1987.

The Coat Tale

Wednesday, October 12th, 1994

There was a black and white movie made back in the early 1940s called "Tales of Manhattan." Anybody out there remember it?

It was one of those "star" vehicles in which a studio put everyone on its roster in the film in the hope that the avalanche of top names would bring the customers to the theater.

The studio was Twentieth Century Fox and just take a look at the lineup of stars; Charles Boyer, Rita Hayworth, Henry Fonda, Edward G. Robinson, Ethel Waters, Ginger Rogers, Cesar Romero, Elsa Lanchester, Thomas Mitchell, George Sanders, Paul Robeson and a few more. The writers were no slouches, either. Among those credited were Ben Hecht and Ferenc Molnar.

The device used to advance the plot was a tail coat, which passes
from owner to owner, conveying adventure and misadventure
with each change of possession. The title itself was, of course, a
play on the tail coat, with the "Tales of Manhattan" being
individual anecdotes loosely sewn together.

That tail coat, first seen on American screens in 1942, is
working its mischief still. Let me tell you a story.

In recent weeks, the "Tales of Manhattan" was one of the films
seen on "American Movie Classics", the cable channel for which
I work. Because I introduce dozens of movies every week, it has
been my practice occasionally to employ an appropriate prop to
help explain the background of the stories we're telling. I search
out the props at home in Augusta from rooms full of material
Nina and I have accumulated over the years. Every now and then,
I will also borrow an item or two from a neighbor.

When I saw that "Tales of Manhattan" was on the upcoming
list, I thought it might be fun to take along a swallowtail coat, so
Nina called our friend Elizabeth Parker for help. In addition to
being Augusta's unofficial historian, Elizabeth is the widow of
my outrageous friend, the funeral director John Parker. Before
his death early this year, John was often the subject of these
columns because of his wry wit and his epic practical jokes. He
lives on in legend, now even on national cable.

I was sure John would have had a tail coat and I was right. He
actually had several, so Elizabeth sent one of appropriate size
and I took it with me to New York for the taping.

The segment was uneventful enough. The coat, with its label
"Custom Tailored by the A. Nash Company of Cincinnati, Ohio",
had its brief moment under the lights and that was that.

Or so I thought.

Our producer, Joe Varsalona, a very thoughtful young man,
did not consider it proper to return the coat to Elizabeth unless
AMC had it sent out and dry-cleaned first. Though this meant
we would have to leave it in New York until our return trip in a
couple of weeks, I thought it was the right thing to do, so I agreed.

Last week, the coat and I arrived back at the studio on the
same day. It looked crisp and elegant under the dry cleaner's

plastic wrap. I thought no more about it and went to work in front of the camera.

While in the studio, I became aware of a commotion. Finally, Joe Varsalona broke in over the talk-back. "Nick, can I speak to you for a moment?" I joined him in the dressing room. This was our conversation.

"When you brought that coat from Augusta, Nick, did you bring striped pains with it?"

"No."

"Oh, boy."

"What's the matter?"

"Well, there's this wedding. They're using cutaway coats. They got the outfits dry-cleaned. The cleaners just called. They got mixed up a little. A pair of pants came back with your coat. I guess the pants are an odd size. I guess they need them real bad."

"Whose pants are they?"

"The groom's."

"How soon is the wedding?"

"Forty-five minutes."

"Oh, boy."

There ensued a passage not unlike the hundred or so slapstick scenes we've all watched over the years. In my mind's eye I could see Cary Grant wearing boiled shirt, ascot, vest, cutaway coat, top hat, polished shoes...and no pants. I could even see the old-fashioned garters men used to wear to hold up their socks and the striped boxer shorts.

The wedding was ten miles away, but despite uncertain New York traffic, the pants reportedly arrived on time.

So the "Tales of Manhattan" had one more anecdote to deliver 52 years after everyone involved thought it was edited to the final cut.

John Parker would have been proud.

Harry James

November 1st, 1989

I was going over some of my old notebooks from a few years ago and ran across an incident I had completely forgotten.

Curious, too, because Harry James was a favorite of mine.

In the late '30s through the '40s and into the '50s, Harry James was the first name that came to mind when you thought of the trumpet, and he was in the very first rank of leaders of the successful big bands.

More than any of the others, he was a matinee idol. Handsome, sophisticated and a famous ladies' man, Harry was grist for all the fan magazines and gossip columns.

The records he made just before and during World War II were among the bestselling of all, and still among the most remembered.

Instrumentals such as "Ciri-Biri-Bin", "Velvet Moon", "Two O'Clock Jump" and "James Session" were classics. Perhaps even more memorable were the great vocals Helen Forrest recorded with his band; "I Heard You Cried Last Night" and "It Seems To Me I've Heard That Song Before." Frank Sinatra traveled with Harry James for a while and chipped in with the unforgettable "All or Nothing at All."

Oh, it was quite an era for Harry James, and he capped it off by marrying the premiere pinup girl of World War II, beautiful Betty Grable.

Though both the big band business for Harry and movies for Betty went on a decline in the '50s, they seemed to prosper as a couple. They raced horses, moved away from Los Angeles and surfaced only occasionally for special shows or a short tour.

I hope you have the picture here. Harry James was a giant. In a pantheon of pop culture heroes during his time, his would be a life-sized statue near the front door.

Now, segue to a day just a few years ago. I was anchoring news at Channel 12. There was a small notice in the paper that Harry James would be appearing in Covington. The ad gave an address

I didn't recognize. It was certainly not one of the places you would expect Harry James to be performing.

I decided to go over for an interview. It took me literally 25 minutes to find the place, and I pride myself on knowing our area very well. It was a perfectly respectable and attractive neighborhood tavern.

But that's what it was, a neighborhood tavern. I, and a few other intrepid James fans, stood at the bar and looked quizzically at the man behind it. He smiled and pointed to a door at the back.

I must give credit to the tavern owner. He wanted to upgrade his place, so he bought a house or two next to his tavern, knocked out some walls, brought in a decorator and put together a very fair imitation of a dime-sized ballroom. It was remarkable.

And that's where Harry James was appearing.

Not many of us found it. The house was about a quarter full. The band was playing already and it sounded good. My notes show I was surprised that sitting in the lead trumpet chair was a young woman; she was an excellent player. Harry was not on the stand.

I asked a waitress where he was and she nodded toward a back table.

He sat alone, slumped in his chair. Older, of course, but handsome still. I asked if I could join him and, taking his silence for assent, I sat down.

I told him I was from TV news and his eyes flashed with anger. I knew what he expected. He thought I was a critic and would do the standard 90 seconds on the air about "how the mighty have fallen" and trash him and his band.

He gave me the interview anyway, and it was a good one. He talked with wry affection about his early days with a circus band, and he talked about beautiful Betty who had died, and he told me that Frank Sinatra had left his band without notice, and he added with a twinkle that if Frank would just work off those 14 days at the $75 a week he was paying him at the time, Harry could get off the road and buy a place in Palm Springs.

I asked if he was going to play his trumpet that night, and he nodded. "Later," he said. I asked if he would play "Velvet Moon".

"It's not in the book. Maybe I can fake it with rhythm."

Yes, he could. Yes, indeed. Years fell away. It was the Palladium, the Movies, the Hit Parade. He didn't cheat. He hit the high note at the end like a prophet's dream of Gabriel. I got a lump in my throat as I listened that night, and have one again as I write this.

That's the story I told that evening on the news, and much the same story that I told a few months later when he died.

I couldn't help but notice my interview notes have yellowed and crumpled in just these few short years. Harry's notes never did.

Vin

Wednesday, November 20th, 1991

Broadcasting has given us some wonderful sports reporters over the years. In fact, we have some good ones on the air in Cincinnati right now.

But today, I want to write about the sportscasters who have already reached legendary status. As it happens, a fair number of them have a direct connection with Cincinnati.

Red Barber, of course, has occupied the catbird seat since the 1930s and shows no sign of surrendering it. Oldtimers say his call of Reds' games more than 50 years ago set a standard no one has matched since.

The devotees of Waite Hoyt would argue that. Paraphrasing the noted sports fan William Shakespeare, it not that they love Barber less, but that they love Hoyt more.

Another man with a Cincinnati connection, Al Michaels, carved himself a permanent niche in sports broadcasting history with his matchless call of the championship hockey game in the 1980

Winter Olympics. You'll remember that the underdog American won it all.

Who could forget his "...The impossible dream," (final buzzer goes off), "COMES TRUE!" (Bedlam).

A fellow just a few miles south of us who is planning his retirement, Cawood Ledford of Kentucky, has a strong following and great credentials, as did his predecessor from the Bluegrass state, Claude Sullivan, whose untimely death cut short a career just reaching its peak.

Ageless Jim McKay adds class and tone to whatever he does, but nothing comes close to his moment at the Munich Olympics when the Israeli contingent was massacred by madmen.

I can see his haggard face right now as I type this. "They're gone", he told us. Jim McKay has a special place in the pantheon of sports broadcasters.

Whenever Dick Enberg is announcing football or tennis or whatever, I always stay tuned long enough to hear him say after any good play, "Oh, my!" It makes me smile for the rest of the day.

However, if the chips are down and I have to name a favorite (Cincinnati reporters excepted), it is Vin Scully.

That's a difficult admission for a Reds' fan, considering how long Vin has been associated with the Brooklyn/Los Angeles Dodgers, but the guy has a flair, a command of language and a disdain for cliches which demand attention.

As some of you know, Vin and Johnny Bench were handling the CBS radio chores during the World Series. I thought they were excellent.

During a lull, Johnny was attempting to make the point that his becoming a catcher was not inevitable. Johnny was expanding on his skill at other baseball positions during his high school days and went perhaps one sentence too far when he assured Vin he had won, as I recall, forty games over a few seasons as a pitcher.

Vin asked innocently, "Did you play any boys' teams?" Ouch.

Last week, Vin and several others were cable-casting some jury-rigged "super" golfing event which turned out to be a glorified commercial for a golf club in Kauai, Hawaii.

Vin Scully and the top players added a certain credibility as the camera panned the picture-post-card landscape.

There was a particularly beautiful and nasty hole; number 5, a 219-yard par three. From the tee you had to shoot across a tropical rain forest into a small, isolated green. One of the color men asked Vin how he would play the hole.

"Under an assumed name", responded Scully.

Come to think of it, it's strange that the two quotes I've used are amusing, because that's not really the way I think of his work at all.

Vin Scully is a painter of pictures. He gives you an impeccable call of the event, but he also sets the scene and lends it perspective.

If you're listening to a night baseball game, you'll know if the moon is out and where it is in the sky. You'll know if there's a breeze, and what scents it might be wafting over the stands.

At a tense moment, bottom of the ninth, two out, tying run on third, three and two on the batter, you might be told that a little girl is fast asleep in her father's arms in the fourth row of the grandstand.

Some call it an Irish gift, but many who are Irish don't have it and some who aren't do.

Call it a Scully gift, and we should enjoy it while we can. The sports broadcaster's talent is written on the wind. Here for the moment, then gone into the ether forever. Tape can't do it justice because tape doesn't catch the moment, it embalms it. The very fragility of Scully's poetry may be what occasionally lifts it from craft to art.

They say the Vin stands for Vincent, but I know better. It stands for Vintage.

Diane

Monday, December 9th, 1991

Today, I turn over a new leaf. If I can't beat them, I'm going to join them.

From now on, if you want gossip parading as news, you're going to find it in this corner.

No more of this nonsense about politics or burning issues of the day. Not even sports or Ohio Valley nostalgia. Never again the intermittent attempts at humor.

From this moment on, I'll be a rumor boomer; I'll dish up dirt that'll hurt; I'll sling sleaze with ease; I'll indulge in meandering pandering; I'll headline illiterate alliteration.

To start right at the top, did you hear the one about Diane Sawyer?

Aha! Now I have your attention. This is fun.

Well, I happen to have the inside story on Diane Sawyer and I'm going to spill it all over this page. If there are impressionable children around, don't let them read one word more.

The famous Ms. Sawyer, whose journalistic skills were honed in Louisville, who graced the august "60 Minutes" for a time and who now co-hosts ABC's "Prime Time" with Sam Donaldson, was in our area a few days ago.

True, she didn't stay long, but it was long enough for your correspondent to collect some damning information. If you think I'm going to give it to you right away, then you haven't been watching television news lately. You know we always "tease" the story for 45 minutes before we give it to you. That keeps you watching. Well, I'm doing the same thing because I want you to keep reading for a few more paragraphs before you turn to the grocery ads.

I thought I had a perfect "in" on this story. After all, Ms. Sawyer was coming to this area to interview my sister Rosemary for a future program. What could be better? All I had to do was pump Rosemary after the interview and I'd get some juicy tidbits to launch my new career into raunchy journalism.

I should have known better. Sisters. Big help she was. She gives me a half-hour of how beautiful Diane is and how smart she is and how down-to-earth she is. Bummer.

Fortunately, I didn't have to rely on relatives. Diane Sawyer spent some time with Rosemary in Augusta and in Maysville. They strolled down Market Street together. That was her mistake.

No one has a better network of informants in the Ohio Valley than I do. Within hours, I had the real skinny and it's going to blow the lid off this oh-so-cool-and-collected network correspondent.

I will not name my primary source, except to say that Ms. Sawyer's walk in Maysville resulted in the first-ever interruption of a game of nine-ball in progress at Bush's pool room on Market Street.

Now get a load of this. Diane Sawyer went into Magee's Bakery and ordered two loaves of salt-rising bread. That was only the beginning.

She then ordered a dozen (a *dozen!*) of those little tea-cakes with the boiled icing that require enough sugar to melt a hundred-dollar set of dentures.

Not content with that, she bought a dozen of Magee's special transparent tarts, and you know they have enough eggs in them to provide breakfast at every Bob Evans restaurant in the country. A cornucopia of cholesterol.

Hoping that no one would learn of her lapse, she sneaked out of town with her unmarked bakery boxes. She then sent her crew to Country Jim's in Germantown to buy her — you won't believe this — a country ham! Enough sodium to salinate Lake Superior.

Now that it's over, I must say I take no joy from my exposé. I know that hereafter, every time you see that lovely face filling the screen you will know her for what she is; a depraved sugar, salt and cholesterol freak.

Am I sure of my facts so that I can rebut the inevitable slander suit, you ask? Would you doubt a source who delayed a straight-in on the nine ball to call me with this vital information? I rest my case.

I must close now. I must prepare myself for this new phase of my career. The circulation of this newspaper will now double, and I must ready myself for my new life-style. It will be necessary for me to prepare my Pulitzer and Peabody acceptance remarks.

Poor Diane. She had such a fine career going for a while. I hesitated to destroy her, but I can't continue to base my future plans on the lottery. If I want the big bucks, I'll have to dig for them.

Excuse me. Phil's on the phone.

Jane

July 20th, 1990

You remember Jane Powell, don't you? Wait a minute, I wrote that as if she had passed away, which she most assuredly has not. What I meant was, you remember when Jane Powell was a young MGM singing star, don't you?

For those of you who don't, let me tell you about her. She came out of the great Northwest just at the end of World War II and found her way to Hollywood when she was no more than sixteen. What led her to talent agents was her voice, which was a clear soprano. What got her even more attention was the way she looked on screen.

Barely five feet tall, blonde, slim, with a pert, all-American face, Jane had an engaging way with a camera that allowed her to dominate roles for adolescent females for a few years.

Critics on the two coasts seldom took her seriously, but the MGM brass did because in middle America she sold a lot of tickets.

The early films had no more artistic value than the Henry Aldrich or Andy Hardy series of ten years before, but were just as important as social barometers of their time. Those of us who were "Depression babies" looked at the technicolor opulence of "A Date with Judy", "Song of the Open Road", "Nancy Goes to

Rio" and the others and aspired to better things. Some of us also aspired to Jane Powell.

Hundreds of thousands of teenage boys across the country dreamed of the day they might see Jane in person, or meet her, or (gulp) have a date with her. I suppose Miss Powell was four or five years older than I, just enough to be the "older woman". I saw the age difference as absolutely no barrier to our romance and constructed unlikely encounters and entire conversations in which I dazzled her with my wit and erudition.

To show how time marches on, in a couple of her films one of her supporting cast was Elizabeth Taylor, another MGM actress working her way through the awkward age, just a couple of years younger than Jane.

At the very height of her popularity and just before her first marriage, Jane went on tour and one of her stops was Cincinnati's Albee theater.

I schemed for weeks to save the not inconsiderable sum it was going to take to get in to see her. Even more difficult was dreaming up an excuse for being downtown late on a school night. Grandma would never OK something as frivolous as an opportunity to see the love of my life in person, so I had to invent a school project.

Anyway, the evening in question found me firmly ensconced in the balcony when this tiny blonde vision swept onto the stage in a shimmering white dress which sparkled in the spotlight, and bowled us all over with "It's a Most Unusual Day."

After the show I waited vainly by a back door hoping to catch a close-up glimpse or contrive a meeting. It was much later I found out it wasn't even the stage door that I guarded.

Now segue with me to a time twenty-one years later. Miss Powell has triumphed with "Seven Brides for Seven Brothers" and "Royal Wedding" with Fred Astaire. Her first marriage has failed, and she has remarried.

In the meantime, Nina and I have married and have two small children. It is 1970 and I have just started a talk-variety show on WCPO-TV. That fall, one of our guests is the star of "My Fair Lady" at Kenley Players in Dayton. It is Jane Powell.

The day arrived, and I was more nervous than I have ever been. Normally, I went in to say hello to the guests before the show, but I couldn't bring myself to do so that day.

I gave a starkly simple introduction and she made her entrance. Unchanged, beautiful, gracious, the familiar smile lighting up her face, she took my hand, squeezed it warmly, sat in the chair next to me and looked up expectantly.

A few seconds of silence went by. In broadcasting, silence is death. Her eyes clouded. She shifted uncomfortably in the seat. More seconds ticked by. I was paralyzed. Finally, by a supreme effort, I blurted out "I love you!"

It certainly got her attention. Startled, she shrank back from the madman beside her while the audience gasped.

At last, my broadcast instincts clicked in and the interview went well. So well that Jane and her husband invited Nina and me to a press party in Dayton the next night. That's when it happened.

At the gathering, Jane and her husband drew Nina and me aside. He did the talking. He said that CBS had approached Jane about doing a sit-com. They were willing to underwrite the cost of a pilot and he and Jane had been looking for someone to be her leading man. He thought we looked good together on TV and would I like to come out to California and test for the part?

It all flooded back in an instant. The matinees at the Capitol theater. Seeing each picture multiple times. The phantom dates and the ephemeral good night kisses. Jane Powell's leading man!

Honesty intruded, unbidden and unwelcome. "I've never acted. I'm not an actor. I'm sure I'd waste your time."

Jane and her husband looked at each other. "Oh, that's too bad. Well, good luck with your career." And that was that.

The series didn't get on the air, so I can always fantasize about what might have been. Oddly, I've never regretted it. Sometimes, the worst thing that can happen to adolescent dreams is to have them come true.

Dinah

February 28th, 1994

I was shocked to hear of Dinah Shore's death last Thursday. There was no hint that she had been ill. But, of course, there wouldn't be. If you'll forgive a very old-fashioned word, Dinah was a lady and ladies don't trumpet their terminal illnesses in public.

I first met Miss Shore in the 1970s, but I had known her much longer than that. Her warm, velvety "I'll Be Seeing You" in the 1940s was the quintessential "AWOL Music" of World War II. That's what men in the service called songs that made you want to go Absent Without Leave so you could see your best girl.

That's who Dinah was to so many young men. She was the personification of their Best Girl. Others would be the glamor girls, the sex kittens, the fantasy pinups. Not Dinah. When she came on the radio with that warm Tennessee drawl and said "Hi, fellas", the mental picture was that of a sweet, faithful, loving Girl Next Door, waiting on the porch to greet and comfort the boy who survived unimaginable horrors to come back to her.

Dinah loved to sing and if there were purists who questioned her intonation, none could deny she communicated in song as well as any popular vocalist of her generation.

She achieved her greatest success on the television program that stereotyped her forever. The Dinah Shore program was so wildly popular that anyone alive in the 1950s still has engraved in his or her mind the picture of a bubbly Dinah singing "See the YOU-ess-ay in your CHEV-roh-lay" and throwing us a kiss. It became an easy image to caricature and so, of course, we did.

The problem is, some of us caricatured the person, too. That's unfortunate, because Dinah was more important than that. She meant more to us than we knew.

When I met her, Dinah was hosting her own TV talk show. She was good at it and the program was receiving excellent ratings at that time, particularly in Cincinnati. This was also the time the tabloids were drooling over her romance with Burt Reynolds who was then the emerging male sex symbol, much younger than Dinah.

I was no smarter than anyone else. I smirked and wondered how a young guy could possibly fall for an older woman like Dinah. Then I sat across from Dinah in person. There was a small dinner party at which I was present. I had an extended conversation with her. I interviewed her for television.

In my experience, I had never met a more completely feminine, attractive woman. She did not hide her intelligence. Her sensitivity enveloped you like a warm comforter. Her interest was genuine. Her humor unforced. In the end, I wondered what she could possibly see in Burt Reynolds.

I last spoke to Dinah about three years ago. We had exchanged Christmas cards, but had not really been in touch for more than a decade. She was hosting an interview program for The Nashville Network cable channel. She was going to be talking to my sister Rosemary, whose friend she was and whose work she admired. Still, Dinah wanted something with which to surprise Rosemary. Something that might throw her a mild curve on the air. In short, something that only a brother could supply.

As it happened, Rosemary and Nina and I had been on an Alaskan cruise a short time before. In Valdez, I had bought an outrageous fur hat with ear flaps. That evening on board ship there was a formal dinner. As a gag, I brought the hat and had the photographer shoot each of us wearing it. Rosemary gave the lens a particularly vapid expression which, accompanying the outsize hat, made for a hilarious picture.

It was, however, a picture for family only. Certainly no publication could ever be allowed to get its hands on the photo. No TV show, either.

When Dinah's producer called and asked for something funny with which to surprise Rosemary on the air, I must admit the picture crossed my mind, but I dismissed it out of hand. Not a chance. "I can't think of anything", I said.

Then Dinah got on the phone. That silky, soft voice asked if there weren't something I might have missed. It was all in fun, after all, and you know Rosemary will get a kick out of it.

Well, of course I mailed the picture express. It was a big hit on the show. Rosemary didn't speak to me for a week. I was never able to explain that it was all Dinah's fault.

Well, she pulled it off. She got through life and all the vagaries of American society in the last 60 years without ever really changing her persona or compromising who she was, right to the end. She was a lady.

There was an old song: "Dinah, Is There Anyone Finah?" The answer is no.

Epitaphs I

September 15th-18th, 1989

It seemed like a very simple idea at the time.

In the great American tradition, I would try to get other people to do my work.

There was even a legitimate precedent. Back in the '30s, the Philadelphia Inquirer asked a number of well-known people to write their own epitaphs. The most famous response came from W.C. Fields:

"On the whole, I'd rather be living in Philadelphia."

Well, what Philadelphia could do, so could Cincinnati, I reasoned, and in the process I'd get prominent Cincinnatians to write my column for me. I sent out a couple of dozen requests.

I got back considerably more than I bargained for. I don't mind these celebrities doing my writing for me, but I'm very upset that they do it *better* than I do. It's depressing.

If there were any way to avoid publishing the column I would, but I've already told these people I was going to use their words, so here goes.

There were no rules. They could be serious, outrageous, sentimental or funny. Some were all four, simultaneously.

Look at this from *Mayor Charlie Luken.*

"1951-2058"

"I Now Know; God *Is* a Democrat"

See what I mean?

My friend *Jerry Springer* of Channel 5 shows definite signs that politics is indeed behind him and broadcasting is his life. Or, at least, his epitaph.

"Indeed, here lies Jerry Springer, He forgot to take care of himself. He'll be back in a moment.... well, Maybe not."

Sheriff *Simon Leis* reflected a life of public service when he wrote

"I came... I served."

The great entertainer *Shirley Jester* couldn't decide, so she sent two.

"Someone asked for 'Take Five' and I took them seriously."

OR

"It was time for a break. But this is ridiculous!"

Shirley will be the only one in the marble orchard with 2 headstones.

Except for Bengal coach *Sam Wyche,* who also wrote two great ones.

"Instant Replay; After Further Review, His Life Stands."

OR,

"He treated people differently, But always fairly."

See? This is terrific stuff.

My colleague *David Wecker*, one of the best writers around (I can say that without inflating his ego because he doesn't read the column) characteristically could not be held to one reply. Or two. Or three.

"He distrusted people at first but ultimately warmed to them."

OR,

"Laughed Loudest at His Own Jokes."

OR,

"He left his mark on journalism as well as a number of restroom walls."

OR,

"Took pride in his work, often boasting of the birdcages he had lined."

That will required both sides of the tombstone plus the margins.

Here's WKRC's multi-talented, schizophrenic *Jerry Thomas,* alias Granny, etc.

"At Least I Don't Have To Get Up At 3:30 A.M. Tomorrow!"

The perennial cry of the Morning Man.

Enquirer Editor *George Blake* handled the assignment on two levels. Professional:

"He liked making changes in the newspapers he edited, Always hoping to make them better for their readers. He worked hard for fairness in journalism and in life. Perhaps, most of all, he cared for the underprivileged; needy kids, homeless, hungry. And he helped."

Now, personal, and poetic:

"A flashing wit raised doubt. He often spoke too soon.
From selfsame lips a smile. 'Hey, I'm a friend, it said.'"

Now look at this. I'm out of room and I haven't done Ira Joe Fisher, Post Editor Paul Knue, Gary Burbank, Charlie Mechem and others.

All right. One more column, then we'll let the subject requiescat in pace.

Epitaphs II

September 15th-18th, 1989

"Dear Nicholas,

How good to hear from you. And what cheerful thoughts I've had contemplating my epitaph. Next time I'm in town, maybe you could drop me off at Harry's Big and Tall for some coffin measurements."

Quick now, who wrote that to me?

Seven out of ten of you got it right; *Ira Joe Fisher.* The other three don't watch television.

Here it is, as promised. Epitaphs Revisited. For those who missed the last column, I asked a number of people whose names we know to compose their own epitaphs and not only did a surprising number respond, but they were all very good.

Ira Joe, who is now at WNBC-TV in New York doing the weather, sent me several versions, including

"Doing the weather he lied in life; Now here he lies in death."

But Ira was quick to add "...but I hope...I can escape from weather (as a conversation topic) in death, unless I wind up somewhere that's real hot." So his next choice was whimsical.

"Honesty is what he desired; Honestly he tried.
But Modesty is all he inspired And modestly he died."

Look at this last one from Ira Joe.

"He wanted the mind of Plato, the heart and soul of Socrates.
But his life was more of a tribute to Ol' Mediocrities."

Nothing mediocre about you, Mr. Fisher, in any medium.

The Editor of the Post, *Paul Knue,* apparently reacted to my request in the same way I would have done. He carried the letter around for a couple of weeks, wrote three or four versions that were unsatisfactory, and then, after a family weekend outing, tore them up and started over.

He decided all the earlier paragraphs had emphasized his business, while what really mattered to him was his family and a personal hope to leave things better than he found them. Paul settled on this:

"He cared."

Not bad, Paul.

Congressman *Bill Gradison* contributed the plaintive

"I'd rather be in Cincinnati!"

Wouldn't we all, Congressman, wouldn't we all?

I heard from the irrepressible *Gary Burbank* of WLW Radio. Here is his preferred epitaph;

"X"

That's it. It may require an explanation, so let me give it to you in his own words. "I have a fear of being buried alive. So just before I go over the rainbow to see Dorothy and Toto, I'm going to print 'Buried Treasure' maps that lead to my gravesite, then put a big "X" on my tombstone." That should be quite a party, Gary.

Here's the contribution of the fine broadcaster for the Reds, *Marty Brennaman:*

> "Here lies Marty, he loved his work. Credibility to him was no quirk.
> He said what he thought for all those years, He's proud of that, so shed no tears."

Channel 12's *Rob Braun,* conscious of his family tradition, wants to be remembered as

> "A Man Who Could Fill Big Shoes."

They fit fine, Rob.

Congressman *Jim Bunning* reflected on two major league careers:

> "Here lies the man we called Jim, As a pitcher, he threw 'up and in'.
> In politics, too, the 'brush back' he knew,
> Let's hope at the gates that's no sin."

Now one more.

Charlie Mechem used to head Taft Broadcasting. If something worthwhile or progressive is going on in our part of the world, you can be sure Charlie will be there or thereabouts. I wasn't surprised that he wrote perhaps the most graceful response of them all.

> "Dear God,
> Thanks for letting me visit. I had a wonderful time."

American Bandstand

January 24th, 1992

I watched Dick Clark host a game show on cable a few weeks back. It's now cliché to say how young he looks. Of course, he no longer appears to be the scrub-faced 21-year-old he seemed to remain for a quarter-century or more. But he doesn't look his age, either.

How old is he? I don't know. A bit older than I, but probably not all that much. As I watched him, my thoughts went back to the first time I met him. Well, that's an exaggeration. I didn't actually meet him, then, but I did talk to him on the phone.

It was the summer of 1962, as I recall. Nina and I lived in Lexington, Kentucky. At that time I was hosting a morning radio show, working full-time at a TV station as production director, movie host and weekend news anchor. I taught communications at a business college. I conducted teenage sok hops. And I hosted a teen dance show on television one hour every Saturday afternoon. Only that last one is important to the story.

At the television station, our network affiliation was ABC. At that time, one of ABC's most successful daytime programs was Dick Clark's "American Bandstand".

It then originated in Philadelphia and was on the air every afternoon, Monday through Friday. My memory is that the broadcast time was 4 to 5 P.M.

That summer, either Dick Clark or someone in ABC's promotion department got the idea that when Dick took his two weeks vacation, hosts of similar shows on ABC affiliates all over the country should be brought in to substitute for him.

It was a good idea. Ten hosts from ten cities would mean good cross-promotion during the usual slow days of summer.

Hosts from New York, Chicago, Los Angeles and Detroit were lined up. Other major cities were also contacted. But then they did a strange thing. They called me. At that time, Lexington was the 125th largest city in the nation. Hardly a great promotion vehicle.

It's true that our dance show was very successful, doubling our competition's numbers. Still, I was shocked to get the call. It was Dick Clark himself who asked, and I said yes right away.

There was no nonsense about flying me up or greeting me with a limousine in those days. I was to get up there as best I could, handle my own accommodations, and get back to Lexington on my own. I would receive scale payment as host of a one-hour show in daytime network. I think it was $320.

Our children were both in diapers still, so Nina couldn't go with me. A young University of Kentucky student named Hugh Ward who helped me produce the TV show went along to share the driving chores.

As I recall, we drove straight through and got to the station in Philadelphia about two hours before air-time. The staff briefed me. The show was so tightly formatted that a monkey could have done it, but I didn't know that then, so I was scared. There were several guests, including Jackie de Shannon, not yet famous for her "What the World Needs Now is Love Sweet Love."

I was still quite young, so I was struck in those pre-mini-skirt days at how short the skirts of the young female regular dancers were. One of the girls patiently explained to me that since the studio cameras shot from a high angle downward, hemlines at the normal inch or two about the knee appeared on camera to be down around the ankles. So all the kids hemmed their skirts up to mid-thigh so as not to appear dowdy on TV.

The education of a dance host.

The show went quite smoothly. I received the requisite compliments from the crew, obviously happy I hadn't gone berserk at the thought of being on network.

I'm sure we drove straight home after the show. Our tight budget didn't allow for such fol-de-rol as hotel rooms. Besides, there was the morning radio show to do.

But as I sped back home on the Pennsylvania Turnpike, I thought about the interesting phenomenon that had just occurred.

That same week, my sister Rosemary appeared on the "Garry Moore Show" on CBS. My sister Betty was co-hosting the "Today" show with John Chancellor on NBC. My appearance on Dick Clark's "American Bandstand" on ABC meant that the Clooneys had blanketed the networks in one week.

That thought shortened the drive home considerably.

The Bistro

September 10th, 1990

Nina and I saw Linda Ronstadt at a concert recently. In some ways Miss Ronstadt is the most remarkable figure in popular music, and she's worth a column all by herself. One of these days I'll devote one to her, but this most recent encounter reminded me of something else. The "Bistro" in Columbus, Ohio.

The year was 1968. The United States was in the middle of its nervous breakdown. Vietnam raged. I had been working in Cincinnati radio and television for two years at WLW.

On television, I was the utility man. I was everybody's second banana. For a short time before her retirement, I was one of Ruth Lyons's assistants. After she left, I was Bob Braun's side-kick. Then I was assigned second billing on the Vivienne Della Chiesa afternoon program.

I enjoyed all these jobs very much, but was understandably restless in a subordinate role and waited more or less impatiently for a chance to have a show of my own.

Early in 1968, WKRC offered me an interview program to air at noon. When I told WLW about it, they countered with an offer to do a talk-variety show of my own at their station in Columbus. Since they had given me my first chance on that kind of program, I thought it would be proper to stay with them, so I said "No thanks" to WKRC and took the job at WLW-C.

When I got there I found out some things I didn't know before. The show I was about to take over had chewed up seven hosts in six years. The last, "Spook" Beckman, had been cancelled a few months earlier. Local critics referred to the time period as "Death Valley."

I started my show in April of 1968. Do you remember 1968? I had been on the air less than a week when Martin Luther King, Jr., was assassinated. Six weeks later, Bobby Kennedy was gunned down in Los Angeles. It was the summer of the notorious Democratic National Convention in Mayor Daly's Chicago from which that political party has never recovered.

Not exactly the year to be launching a local fun-and-games TV show, but we bent to the events and often presented serious, issue-oriented programs. One of them dealt with gun control. Columbus was then one of the national headquarters for the National Rifle Association. The resulting letter campaign scared off a number of sponsors and doomed the program.

The NRA needn't have bothered. The show would have failed anyway. I wasn't good enough yet, and the ratings never really took off.

But there were some bright moments. You'll recall those were very interesting times in entertainment with "Laugh-In" and the "Smothers Brothers Comedy Hour." Controversy and protest abounded.

Directly across the street from our television station was a small youth-oriented nightclub called the Bistro which placed itself right at the crest of the new wave by booking all the hot young acts.

Because ours was the only local "live" show, and because we were close to the club, most of them came to guest on our program.

Pat Paulsen brought us his first campaign for president. The First Edition came over, and its leader, Kenny Rogers, told me the reason that they called themselves the First Edition was that they would perform only their own original material. Then one morning Linda Ronstadt strolled into our studio, barefoot and in a tiny mini-dress and proceeded to bowl everyone over with that powerful vocal instrument of hers. The group that had been the Chad Mitchell Trio appeared as Denver, Boyce and Johnson.

One of them, John Denver, did rather well subsequently as a solo artist.

But then we were to have the piéce de resistance. The hottest act in the country was the Smothers Brothers. Their CBS television show was making waves and breaking ratings records coast to coast.

The Bistro wasn't big enough to hold them, but the Ohio State Fair was. Because of our using so many of their friends, we were promised the brothers would guest on our show.

We were set up in a tent on the fairgrounds, and the big day came. Larry Leese, our producer, took the station wagon to go confirm the arrangements. He came back with a long face, and I knew we were in trouble. I didn't know the half of it.

"What happened?" I asked.

"I don't think they're coming. I talked to them, and they said OK, then I got into the station wagon and backed up to turn around. I heard a crunch. I backed over Tommy's guitar. I don't think they're coming."

Actually, they did come, but the accident was just one more symptom. Our TV show whimpered to a halt a few months later. The Bistro didn't last much longer.

But for a few years in a white-hot time, it pulsed and glowed with emerging talent on the plains of central Ohio.

Papa Andrew Clooney in front of his jewelry store in Maysville, Ky. Nick, Betty and Rosemary's grandfather was once Mayor of Maysville. The dog is Kenny. It's the mid-1930s.

Betty, Mother Frances, Rosemary and a very military Nick at Grandma Guilfoyle's farm, Indian Hill, Ohio. The year is 1943.

After a short stint at WLW Radio in Cincinnati, The Clooney Sisters, Rosemary and Betty, went on the road with Tony Pastor's band. That's Tony on the right. It's 1948.

This is Pvt. Nick making the world safe for democracy at Fort Knox, Kentucky. The year is 1955.

Rosemary's husband, actor Jose Ferrer and an equally pensive Nick. The two briefly wrote songs together in 1957.

This is Nina Warren of Perryville, Kentucky, as Nick first saw her. She was "Miss Lexington", 1959.

Nick and Nina married in Lexington in 1959.

Ada Frances came along in 1960, George Timothy in 1961. Here they are in front of the family car in 1964.

Ada and George in 1966, Ft. Mitchell, Ky.

Nick interviews presidential candidate Hubert Humphrey on "The Nick Clooney Show" in Columbus, 1968.

Andrew Clooney and Marie Frances Stone. Dad and Mom. A brief reunion in the 1960s. Rosemary's daughter Maria is in the doorway.

Kid sister Gail Stone. Gail was an actress who then spent time as a talent co-ordinator on Nick's show in Cincinnati in 1973.

Nick and his sister Rosemary watch another performer on the "Nick Clooney Show" on WKRC-TV, Cincinnati, 1973.

Nick interviews President Gerald Ford in the White House for Channel 12 News, 1976.

Denny Janson, Nick, Ira Joe Fisher. This was Cincinnati's leading news team of the 1980s.

Nick and Nina went to California in 1984, where Nick co-anchored news on KNBC-TV. This is Nina at the 1984 Summer Olympics in LA.

Ada and her future husband, Lt. Norman Zeidler, in 1987.

The world's only grandchild. Allison Zeidler, at age two. 1993.

Nina, Nick, Ada, Norman, Rosemary and George. It's Ada's Wedding Day in Augusta, Kentucky. 1987.

Nick hosts the syndicated program "On Trial" in Los Angeles. 1989. Attorney Howard Weitzman is the guest.

Nina still wins the swimsuit competition on our visit to the South Carolina Coast, 1988.

Nina's Dad Jackson Warren, friend Dante DiPaolo, Rosemary, Nick and Nina's Mom Dica Warren at Del Coronado Hotel. San Diego, 1984.

Nina and Nick on a bitterly cold New Year's Day at Shakertown, Kentucky. 1987.

Ada, Nina and Allison in a Rocky Mountain glade above Salt Lake City. 1992.

Sports Director and friend Mike Runge and Nick anchoring KSTU-TV News in Salt Lake City, 1993.

George Clooney, 1995. Photo by Harry Langdon.

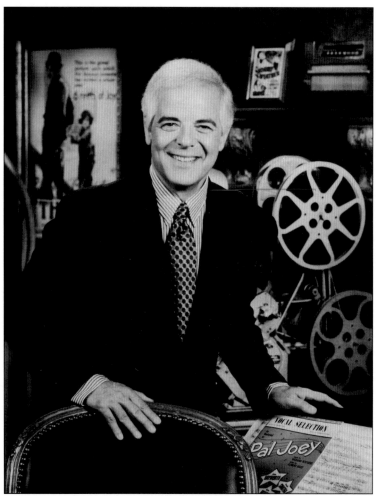

Nick as host for the "American Movie Classics" cable network. 1995.

Broadcasting

For 35 YEARS, I've watched Nick battle every day to find the core of the broadcasting venue in which he was working.

There's no question that his 20 years in news presented the toughest moments. Precisely how do you report the murder of a child without infringing on the family's privacy or exploiting their grief? Unfortunately, that kind of dilemma is common and a mistake in that delicate balance is unforgivable.

On the other hand, in the field of talk and variety, it is only unforgivable to be boring. Nick has never been boring. I've always been amazed at his ability to pull fresh ideas out of his head right there on live television.

Beyond question, Nick's knottiest problems in broadcasting have been off-screen and off-mike. Occasionally, owners or managers attempted to dictate their values or politics through Nick into the homes of viewers. This inevitably touched two of Nick's sacrosanct flashpoints. First, he was angry that any thought they could manipulate him. Second, it violated his moral contract with the viewers, the most important tenet of his professional life. As you can imagine, this made for some lively times for the family, but I think we understood. Eventually.

Communication is Nick's passion, whether it's on radio, television, in the written word or across the breakfast table. To survive long in a career as volatile as communications, one must re-invent himself and Nick has often done that. But he never surrendered that core of integrity we all recognize. And he invested each effort with class.

A broadcaster's best work rides invisible waves into the ether forever, unless the broadcaster writes about it. Nick has written about it.

Nina Clooney
Augusta, Kentucky

Broadcasting

June 21, 1989	Sundays at WFTM
September 5, 1990	Remembering AFN
November 22, 1993	Jim Hagerty (Nicks Early News Days)
October 1, 1993	McAlpin's Radio Show
March 20, 1992	Ira Joe's Long Trip
August 21, 1992	Gene Randall and I — The Odd Couple
September 15, 1993	Edie Magnus Tribute
October 14, 1994	TV News Disclaimer
May 27, 1994	Goodbye, TV News

Nick, the early broadcaster. Note the pipe. Nice accessory in the 1950s.

Sunday Morning

June 21st, 1989

It was quite a responsibility, and I did not take it lightly. I was given my own key, and I — all by myself — was to open the radio station at seven o'clock on Sunday morning.

WFTM, the World's Finest Tobacco Market, the Golden Buckle on the Burley Belt was — and is — a radio station in Maysville, Kentucky and was — and is — located in a tobacco warehouse on Forest Avenue.

I was in high school and a fledgling announcer earning 50¢ an hour and undoubtedly overpaid at that. It didn't occur to me that I was given the Sunday morning shift because no one else would like it. No, sir. Opening a station and being completely responsible for it from 7 A.M. to 1 P.M. was heavy stuff to a teenager; at least it was to this one.

Of course, it would have been a lot better if it could have been any day other than Sunday. Sunday morning had a nasty habit of following Saturday night which in a small town was — and is — the night to have semi-raucous fun. Paying the piper early Sunday morning at a small radio station is paying overtime.

Because, you see, Sunday morning at small radio stations means preachers.

All shapes, all sizes, all denominations. As long as they had the thirty dollars in hand to pay for their thirty minutes, they went on the air. Most of them had to pay in advance, in cash, because of some bad past experiences with station management.

In they would troop, waiting patiently outside the studio door while their predecessors finished up on the air. There would be a mad scramble on the hour and the half-hour while one group crowded out the door and another one pushed its way in. Only thirty seconds was allotted for this changeover operation while I, in a glass-enclosed announcer's booth, closed out the departing preachers program and introduced the one coming up.

They would come from Plummer's Landing and Manchester, from Sardis and Minerva, from Slip-Up and the Kinnikinnick. Most of them would be of the fundamentalist school which subscribes to the theory that the most sincere expression of faith is that repeated at the top of the lungs. There were convincingly sincere.

There would be singers, and the singers would almost always be female, sometimes female and young, occasionally female, young and pretty. I liked that part a lot, and every now and again would share a surreptitious smile with a gingham-clad cutie. It never came to anything because she was encased in her glass prison for the length of the program, and by the time she escaped into the real world, I was encased in mine, announcing the next group.

Those shy smiles were the highlight. There were plenty of lowlights.

Some of the preachers, looking for inspiration, apparently thought they found it in the early signs of dissipation on my teenaged face. Some Sunday mornings, they were right.

I was often preached at, and subtlety was not a virtue prized by radio pastors. They would flail away at me, not ten feet away, protected only by a three-quarter-inch thick pane of glass between us; their faces would be bright red, sweat and sincere spittle would spray in all directions, and my excesses of the night before would emerge in my imagination in stark relief. If I hadn't been lucky enough to indulge in excesses the night before — a frequent failing — I pulled out some old ones from a month or two ago, and if these weren't colorful enough, I made up a few.

I spend many a Sunday morning repenting for sins I hadn't gotten around to yet.

While the preacher caught his breath, the women would sing, accompanied either by guitars they brought with them or by a battered old upright piano which we kept in the studio for that purpose, and which deserved better.

Typically, the half hour program would climb steadily toward a crescendo that peaked after about 25 minutes. That would allow the preacher two minutes or so to decompress, and left him two more minutes to pitch for money.

These pleas were usually rational and modest. The preacher quite honestly said that if they didn't come up with the thirty bucks in the mail by Friday, he wouldn't be on the air next week. It was that simple.

I've often thought of these men and women in the intervening years, and I always think of them with affection and respect. They believed deeply that they had something everyone should hear, and they climbed into their pickup trucks and — along with their marginally talented relatives — went off to the radio station of a Sunday morning to do the Lord's work.

No salary, no marketing analysis, no consultants, no limousines, no banks, no hotels, no networks, none of the trappings that took broadcast religion so far and brought it so low.

I was driving through Maysville on a Sunday morning a few weeks ago and turned on my old station. My heart skipped a beat; the music was tinny, serious, and familiar. I wondered what teenager had opened the station that morning, and I envied him or her.

A little.

This is the tower in Frankfurt where PFC Nick lived while stationed at the American Forces Network. 1955.

AFN

September 5th, 1990

I got a letter from a fellow asking if I wanted to subscribe to a publication which chronicled the comings and goings of the men and women of AFN.

If you were in the service and stationed in Europe anytime from 1945 to the present moment, you'll be familiar with AFN.

The letters stand for "American Forces Network", a subsidiary of the "Armed Forces Radio Service", the umbrella organization which oversaw radio — and eventually television — operation for United States troops stationed all over the world. Including "Good Morning Vietnam."

For much of the time since the Second World War, AFN was the largest network under the jurisdiction of AFRS. That's because our largest permanent contingent of military and civilian personnel outside the United States has been in Germany, and AFN is headquartered in Frankfurt-am-Main.

It was a true network supporting affiliate stations in Kaiserslautern, Munich, Bremerhaven on the Northern coast, Nuremberg, Stuttgart, and Berlin, the "island" city surrounded for forty years by communist East Germany and its occupying Russian forces.

The mission of AFN was simply to provide information and entertainment, American-style, to US citizens who found themselves temporary expatriates in the service of their country in Germany. As it happened, it became a great deal more than that.

I came to AFN by the usual pattern of accidents which marks most of our lives. After basic training I was sent to Fort Dix, New Jersey, along with a few thousand others who looked exactly like me. We boarded troop ships, pitched and rolled our way across the North Atlantic to Bremerhaven where we were bundled into day coaches for the long ride to Zweibrucken, Germany.

This was a replacement depot, and it was here that a battery of specialists determined where you would spend the next 18 months of your life. There were three stages of your interview, but for the most part it was a rubber stamp operation. They looked at your file, checked your primary MOS — military occupation specialty — looked to see if anyone in Germany needed you, and sent you there. If not, they checked your secondary MOS, and sent you there.

As I recall, my primary MOS was clerk and my secondary MOS was combat infantry. In peacetime, the infantry designation held the bleak prospect of spending a year and a half on the Czech border living in a tent and scraping mud off your boots.

Sure enough, my first interviewer said "Sorry, no call for any clerks. Combat infantry." I asked if there were any other choices. He said only if I had some other skills. I told him I'd been a radio announcer for four years. He responded vaguely that there were radio stations in Europe but he didn't know anything about them, and sent me to the next interview. As I walked between the two, I got an idea. When I arrived at the next desk I said, "That fellow told me you were the one to help me change my MOS to radio announcer." "To what?" "Radio announcer." "I never heard of that MOS." He grabbed a huge book and turned the pages while my palms got sweaty. "Well, I'll be darned, there it is. 1563.1." He picked up a pencil and scrawled it on my file. Armed with this shaky authority, I approached the Master Sergeant who would make the final decision.

"These two guys said you'd fix it up to send me to an Army radio station," I exaggerated.

Fortunately, the sergeant didn't throw me out of his office. He asked me about my background, made a couple of calls and sent me off to AFN.

I ended up at the headquarters in a suburb of Frankfurt called Höchst, right on the Main River. At that time, the network occupied a 600-year-old castle, so instead of guarding barbed wire and latrines out in the field, I lived in the tower of a beautiful relic of the Middle Ages.

While AFN was there ostensibly to provide radio for American service people and dependents, the US State Department made a startling discovery. East Europeans listened more avidly to us than they did to Voice of America or Radio Free Europe for the very good reason that they believed the information we were telling our own people was much less likely to be propaganda than that packaged specifically for communist consumption.

We had power to spare — the Frankfurt station alone operated with 150,000 watts — and were heard all over Europe from the British Isles to Poland. Those of us who hosted programs, as

I eventually did, got literally hundreds of letters from Europeans every week, heavy stuff for a 20-year-old PFC.

It was a fascinating eighteen months. In an upcoming column or two, I'll tell you about it.

I'll begin with, "As we sat on the moat wall drinking beer, the Ghost of Höchst Schloss moved slowly toward us..."

I'm anxious to see how that one turns out myself.

Jim Hagerty

November 22nd, 1993

Nina and I were visiting an eastern city of moderate size last week. The city shall remain nameless to protect the blameless.

After taking care of the reason for our visit, we were relaxing in our hotel room and going through a directory trying to decide where to have dinner. Nina snapped on the TV. A local newscast was just beginning its early edition. A young man was reading the news. He was a nice-looking fellow. He approached each subject with a serious demeanor. He read quite well. His face was smooth and earnest. He was, perhaps, 25 years old. He was telling us about NAFTA and the probable stance of the local Congressional delegation.

I found myself distracted from the story by a vague sense of irritation. What was the matter with this picture? What in the world was bothering me?

The answer came flooding in with a suddenness that was startling. Of course. Now I understood with perfect clarity what had been told to me a full generation before.

It was the 1960s. We lived in Lexington, Kentucky. Nina and I had been married just a few years. Both children were tiny. I was working several jobs, all in broadcasting. Morning man at WLAP Radio. Promotion and Production Director at Channel 27. I hosted a teenage dance show on Saturday afternoon and a horror movie late Saturday night. Among all these and other duties, I was also the weekend news anchor. Actually, news, weather and sports anchor Saturday and Sunday.

It was this latter duty in which I took special pride. Peter Grant had been my hero growing up and for that reason doing the news seemed important. I was, perhaps, 27 years old, but on television looked younger.

Our television station was an ABC affiliate. The president of ABC News at the time was James Hagerty, a crusty, no-nonsense former beat reporter and political columnist for the New York Times who had served as press secretary for both Governor Thomas E. Dewey and for President Dwight D. Eisenhower. Now he was trying to put ABC TV News on the map.

Jim Hagerty came to Lexington for a speech at the University of Kentucky, as I recall. He represented our network, so I was selected to pick him up at Bluegrass Field and take him to the Phoenix Hotel. During the drive I, with the temerity of comparative youth, told him I was in the same business as he. I also told him I'd be anchoring the news that night and if he got a chance to watch I'd be glad for his comments. I now shudder at the memory of my overconfidence.

The next day on the ride back to the airport, he didn't bring up the newscast. I did. I asked if he'd watched. He said yes. He didn't say anything else. I persisted. "What did you think?"

"All right", he answered with a sigh, "here goes. Did you write the show?" I nodded yes. "Good. You're an adequate writer. And there's nothing wrong with the way you read the material. But, to tell the truth, you're irritating to watch. My advice is, get out of the business, at least for a few years."

Deflated, I asked what was wrong with me.

"Look, kid, here you are on the screen telling me about rumors of war and problems with the economy and corruption at city hall, and just look at you. You don't look like you ever lost a job, ever missed a mortgage payment, ever had somebody you love die on you. Nothing had marked your face or your eyes yet. You're saying all the right words but you don't have a clue what they mean. I've got the same trouble at the network."

I knew immediately what he was talking about. This was the time of the first incarnation of Peter Jennings, who was just my age. "We've got this kid from Canada. He's terrific. But nobody out there," he waved at some houses we were passing, "believes him. We have to get him off the anchor desk.

"I don't mean to be unkind, but if you want to be the person who tells me what's going on in my world, you've got to go out and live a little. Then come back and try it again. You've got talent, but that's not nearly enough. You've got to feel what the people on the other side of the screen are feeling."

It was bitterly disappointing advice and it angered me. Hagerty was criticizing something I couldn't fix. My age. He was discriminatory and unfair.

He was also right. Peter Jennings left the anchor desk, went out and lived a little, then came back. In a much smaller arena, so did I.

The TV set brought me back to the present. My heart went out to the young man on the screen in front of me. He has talent. But Jim Hagerty was right. He needs years of living before the viewers will believe him. I had *known* it for a long time, because research shows it time and again.

But now, perhaps for the first time, I *understood* it.

McAlpin's

October 1st, 1993

Keeping up with the continuing flap over where Lazarus and McAlpin's Department Stores should be located in downtown Cincinnati has been instructive. Apparently they both covet the same piece of real estate on Fountain Square West. Well, I suppose it's hard to blame them. Who wouldn't covet it, particularly if someone else was paying a substantial part of the development cost?

George and Ada visit Nick on the McAlpins
"Good Morning Show" on WLW. In the
background, Bonnie Lou, Freddy Langdon and
Kenny Price. 1966.

Without addressing the merits of this particular face-off, it has served to remind me how big a part McAlpin's on Fourth Street once played in my life. Indirectly, it is the reason I became a Cincinnati broadcaster.

Let me take you back to the mid-to-late 1960s. In those days, WLW Radio was considered by some in the industry to be an anachronism. Radio was still in the throes of its "Top Forty" or "Top Twenty" format phase with thousands of stations all over the country offering the fast-paced music formula which was a child of the rock music revolution.

WLW was not convinced. The pioneer giant was still offering what was called "block" programming and was considered by the new wave to be hopelessly out of date.

"Block" programming meant producing different kinds of shows throughout the broadcast day for different kinds of audiences, much as television does. At WLW, Dunn and Warner presided in the morning, but the Ruth Lyons "50-50 Club" was simulcast across the noon hour. Richard King's caustic wit would cover the afternoon, but sports would dominate the evening.

This variety was considered a no-no and was in stark contrast to "format" radio which picked a specific audience segment and programmed to it relentlessly, day and night, playing the same hit records, often in the same order, 24 hours a day.

On WLW in 1967, one of the program "blocks" was a show started by Bob Braun and station executives called the "Good Morning Show." It was broadcast live from McAlpin's Tea Room every morning.

This type of program was even by then a dinosaur. The "Breakfast Club" out of Chicago had been the prototype, but was already off the air. The audience was live, the music was live, the commercials were live. The show was a financial success, dinosaur or no, so when it became apparent that Bob Braun's duties would increasingly take him to television as Ruth Lyons moved toward retirement, WLW Radio started looking for a replacement.

That's when I entered the picture. I was working both radio and television in Lexington Kentucky. After an extended negotiation, I came to Cincinnati. Eventually, I took over the show.

I had never done anything like it before. Little wonder. There wasn't anything like it. The audience, mostly women, would write in for tickets far in advance. Those who came to the show knew far more about it than I did and were generous enough to teach me how to be a host.

On most days, music was supplied by the ""Hometowners", consisting of the wonderful entertainers Kenny Price, Buddy Ross, Freddy Langdon and Jay Nees. However, because talent contracts at WLW called for a certain number of hours for each performer to work and not all those hours were used up on "50-50 Club", "The Paul Dixon Show" or other hit television programs, we would one day a week get the whole Cliff Lash Band and there would always be a great singer there to prop me up. Colleen Sharp, Marian Spelman, Bonnie Lou and Ruby Wright all took turns helping me learn how to do my job.

Producer Walt Rehbaum would patiently show me how the contests were run and how to handle our special remote broadcasts from other locations. The engineers, even the sponsors would give me hints on how to deal with certain situations. But by the time I learned, a new general manager had been hired. He was determined to move WLW closer to "format", so the "Good Morning Show", though successful, was doomed. It went off the air.

Now, I can't quite pull out of my memory what the exact configuration of department stores was as I daily trod those 1967 downtown streets. McAlpin's was by no means alone. I'm sure the giant three blocks north was still Shillito's, not yet Lazarus. Rollman's was certainly gone, but Pogue's reigned and the toney Giddings Jenny catered to the carriage trade.

Mabley and Carew occupied the piece of turf now being contested as Fountain Square West.

As I think about it, if the pattern established over the last 25 years continues, no one need worry about which department store wins the battle for that real estate bone. The spot will be occupied by a drive-through yogurt stand and a T-shirt shop.

Ira's First Visit

Friday, March 20th, 1992

Several months back I promised to tell you the story of Ira Joe Fisher's first visit to Channel 12. This seems as good a time as any.

There are probably some newcomers to our area who will need a little background on this remarkable broadcaster. The short description is that he is a television weatherman. The truth is, he became much more than that to most of us.

In all my years in broadcasting, I have never seen anyone who so quickly took a town by storm. Appropriate for a weatherman. Six months after he arrived with his cheerful smile, his infectious laugh, his brilliant command of language and the little cartoons and phrases he wrote backwards on a piece of plexiglass, he had captured us all. He carved out a chunk of Cincinnati television for himself.

But it very nearly didn't happen.

Channel 12 has almost always been blessed with very competent and very popular weather reporters. It certainly is true right now, and it was true back in 1976 when I first joined the news team. Home town boy Mike Fenwick was in charge of the maps and isobars and was doing a very good job. When he went off to another city, we were lucky enough to get a great replacement.

Nick and Ira Joe Fisher long after Ira's fateful train ride from Spokane. 1986.

Steve Deshler came down from Michigan and when he joined us he was just about to come into his own. His style was unique. He had a dry sense of humor and a confident command of his material and he was a hit. So much so that in too short a time he was wooed away by Chicago where, after a few adventures and a stint with CBS in New York, he remains today.

When he left, we had a dilemma. How to replace him? We looked at dozens of tapes from all around the country. One day, program director Mel Smith and news director Bill Crafton called me into an office. They wanted me to see a tape from Spokane, Washington.

In two minutes it was clear that he was the one. Not only were we getting a great weatherman, we were getting an extra name at no additional charge. Ira Joe Fisher. Bill Crafton said he would get Ira to fly out for a meeting. Little did we know.

Ira doesn't fly. Ira doesn't even like to go to the second floor of any building. In spite of, or perhaps because of, a hitch in the Air Force, Ira won't even look at pictures of airplanes unless they are safely tied down on the tarmac.

Still, he wanted to talk to us, so he took an entire week's vacation from his job in eastern Washington state and laboriously strung together a trip to Ohio. I don't remember all the particulars, but it was a monster.

He would board a train in Spokane at 3 o'clock in the morning. He would have a 12 hour layover in Denver, then board another coach for Chicago. There, the train to Cincinnati ran only every other day, so he took an overnight bus, arriving here at 6 A.M. He shaved and shook out his clothes as best he could in the men's room, nursed a cup of coffee for a couple of hours, and got a cab to WKRC-TV at 9 o'clock.

Working for us then was a young woman who did not want to be a newsroom secretary. She wanted to be a reporter, and was impatient with the details of answering phones and greeting visitors. Her impatience was often mistaken for rudeness, with some justification.

News director Bill Crafton didn't know exactly when Ira would arrive, so he took a couple of days off, leaving strict instructions to be called immediately when Ira arrived. That's the part the secretary forgot.

After the three horrible days by train and bus, Ira walked hopefully into our newsroom. He went up to the secretary and said, "Mr. Crafton, please." She didn't look up. "He's not here."

"When will he be in?" "He's on vacation, he won't be back for a week."

Ira's life flashed before his eyes. Now all he had to look forward to was the three long, miserable days back to Spokane. "But, I have an appointment." "Look, buddy, I haven't got time for this. I told you he was on vacation. Call and set up another appointment."

Ira trudged out into the parking lot. Cincinnati seemed a long way from anywhere at that moment. He'd even forgotten to call a cab, but it didn't matter. He didn't have anyplace to go.

By a quirk of fate, I was in early that day. I saw the Chaplinesque figure walking around aimlessly and recognized him from the tape. "Ira?" We went back inside, called the powers that be together, made a deal and the rest, as they say, is history.

Ira Joe is in New York now. That's 19 hours by train.

Gene Randall

Monday, August 24th, 1992

Every time I see Gene Randall reporting on CNN, it brings back a flood of memories.

First of all, I'm reminded what an outstanding reporter and anchor he is. Though CNN used him extensively through both political conventions, I'm always surprised they don't have him on the air much more regularly than they do. He is the best they have.

Many who read this will remember when Gene was a young anchor at WLW-T. It was right at the transition time when Tom Atkins was in the process of replacing Peter Grant as principal anchor. Gene was sort of prince designate at Channel 5 news.

His career was on the sharp upward path. He grew with each broadcast. His interviews were crisp, his delivery straightforward. He was also, as it happened, one of the best-looking young men on television. That didn't hurt. Soon, he married beautiful Carol

Merrill of Maysville in a lovely ceremony that was a major Cincinnati event. Nina and I were there.

However, after five years or so, Gene somehow got crossways of management at Channel 5 and was fired. As I recall, the euphemism was that his contract was not renewed. I know as well as anyone in the country that both amount to the same thing. Gene was out of a job. Some were sure it was because of his activity on behalf of fellow broadcasters in the union. That was, of course, vigorously denied.

This was in the mid-70s, and I had been fired at about the same time from another station. In fact, before many years passed, I had been fired from all three network-affiliate stations in town. Do you suppose they were trying to tell me something?

Anyway, Gene and I, who had been friends since we first met, were pounding the pavement at the same time, looking for work. Some of you will remember that there was a dinner theater back then called "Beef 'n Boards" out near Harrison. The fellow who ran it, Don McPherson, had called me the previous summer to appear in a play and I had done so, very glad to get the work. The run had been a commercial — if not artistic — success, and now Don called again. Would Gene and I like to appear in "Odd Couple"?

Well, if they were foolish enough to pay Gene and me to pretend we were actors, we were certainly foolish enough to do it. Out landlords didn't ask if the rent money was obtained under false pretenses, just that it be on time.

The wonderful British actress Paddy Edwards, who lived in Cincinnati then, was our director. I was hired to be Felix, the neat one. Gene was to be Oscar, the messy one, because he had been reared in the environs of New York City and could manage the accent with ease.

We started rehearsal and from the beginning something was wrong. It became clear we couldn't mess Gene up. No matter what we put on him, no matter how much stubble he grew, no matter how unkempt his clothes or how crumpled his baseball cap, he still looked great. On his worst day, he was sort of a cross between Tom Selleck and George Clooney.

On the other hand, there was no problem at all messing me up. A pull here and a tug there and I looked like an unmade bed. So I suggested we switch roles, and that's what we did.

The reviews Gene got were wonderful and very well deserved. He was terrific. The show was supposed to run five weeks, but we were sold out and they asked if we could extend the run. We could and did to six, then seven, then eight and finally nine weeks. We could have gone even longer, but one of us, I've forgotten which, had committed to another job and had to leave. Still, nearly 30,000 people had paid to see the show, and we were told that compared quite favorably with other successful Cincinnati theater runs.

Gene did another play or two and so did I, but for the most part we went back to our life's work, which was television. The progress was often slow for both of us and took us to many cities.

Then one day, I heard that Gene had been hired as an NBC correspondent and he and Carol were going to Moscow. The Cold War was still hot and it was a plum assignment.

I got a telegram from Poland. It read "Oscar. I'm in Warsaw on my way to Moscow for NBC. It's a long way from Harrison. Hope it's as much fun. Felix."

Felix is still doing important work, and Oscar has his moments, too. But I doubt it's as much fun. For either of them.

Edie

Wednesday, September 15th, 1993

It should be quite a night. Saturday at the Hyatt downtown, there will be a gathering to celebrate — not roast — Edie Magnus.

It's rare in any age that a reporter is singled out for public praise, unless the reporter is retiring and his or her pencil or microphone is safely retiring, too.

But Edie is just getting warmed up. She has already scaled remarkable heights in electronic journalism and most observers, including this one, believe she can go as far as she wants.

And right in the middle of this burgeoning career, her home town wants to throw her a party. How about that? Edie must have some unusual qualities, indeed.

She does. Edie and I worked together in the Channel 12 newsroom for some time. She and Karla Stanley had come to us from WUBE radio. They were both great additions to our newsroom from the beginning.

Edie had quick intelligence, a voracious curiosity and the courage of a lion. She had questions about everything, but mostly about herself. She had a rage to be better. Not better than someone else. Better than she had been yesterday.

She got to our newsroom at just the right time, both for her and for us. We were in the process of coalescing into as solid a working group as I have ever seen. Our skills seemed to complement one another.

We had a very specific philosophy. Many of its elements are — or should be — basic to any news room, but we believed them with a fervor that made them seem new. We would do news, not "Entertainment Tonight." We would be accurate and fair. We would follow truth wherever it led. We would not sensationalize. (In any large city, the truth is quite sensational enough.) We would be skeptical but not cynical. We would ask the hard question. However — and this was important — we would, whenever humanly possible, maintain civility as part of our daily exchanges in the community.

News delineates the stress points in any society. Usually, under stress, civility is the first piece of baggage that is dropped overboard. That's why reporters, as chroniclers of stress, are often seen as rude and insensitive. They've jettisoned their civility in their effort to get the story. We tried to take a different tack. We thought that moments of stress were precisely the crucibles for which civility was designed. If it is lost, there is a danger of lines of communication being shut down and both dialogue and the story being distorted.

Edie caught both the importance and contradiction of this approach. It appealed to her because she is a really decent, thoughtful person. But she also knew that in the clamor of daily events it was not always easy, or even possible, to maintain a courteous demeanor.

The effort was our tightrope, but it was also our hallmark. Edie mastered it. She was as aggressive and energized as any reporter around. If I had something to hide, she would be one of the last people I'd want to see on the front porch. She's relentless.

But in gathering the information and putting the story together, her manner was balanced. You liked Edie when you looked at her. You believed she was doing her best to get at the truth for you.

From those early days to this moment, Edie has never stopped growing. I see her often now on CBS News. She is elegantly coiffed, her wardrobe is impeccable and her makeup perfect. She is quite beautiful. (I suppose if Peter Jennings can be described as "handsome", a reporter can be "beautiful" without loss of credibility.)

But I remember her running into our newsroom with a late-breaking story. Her face would be flushed, her hair windblown, her blouse trailing out of her skirt, shoes scuffed and a run in her stocking. Come to think of it, she was quite beautiful then, too.

Two different venues, but one constant: She had the story cold and it was as right as she could make it.

So now, Cincinnati's Edie Magnus will be at the center of the head table with her husband Saturday night. Former school-teachers, lifelong friends and co-workers will come from far and wide to tell about the Edie they knew. Each will have a slightly different take on her. All will be correct.

And the total will add up to more than the sum of its parts. It didn't take the jobs at ABC and CBS to validate Edie as a reporter or as a person. She was always one-of-a-kind and the fact that she didn't know it only reinforces the point.

Those of us who know Edie will be glad to get a chance Saturday night to say in public what we've been saying in private for a long time: how proud we are of her.

Disclaimer For Newscasts?

Friday, October 14th, 1994

No question about it. In each profession, it's important for everyone involved to find time to distance themselves from the day-to-day grind in order to get a proper perspective on what they are doing and how they are doing it.

This little homily is so apparent it is cliché. But like every cliché, it never becomes true until it happens to you.

For instance, after those many years of anchoring thousands of newscasts from coast to coast, a very simple truth escaped me. I didn't recognize it until I stopped being a part of the process and became a viewer.

We who present the news never clearly tell the people what we're doing on their television screens every night. We believe they know and, of course, they don't know because we don't tell them.

Viewers have every right to assume they are watching a slice of city life, a day reflecting the varied events of their community. Nothing could be further from the truth. The duty of a newscast is to search out the *abnormal* event of any given day. The event may be abnormally good or abnormally bad, but it will not be an ordinary retelling of the day's normal events.

The first ten minutes of any newscast — which is that portion which has the most impact — is nothing more or less than a chronicle of the eccentricities of the city and its environs. Often, it is a cataract of evil tidings. Murders, rapes, robberies, corruption, disease, anger. Are these incidents typical of our city? Of course not. The story of our communities is being told in hundreds of thousands of other homes.

The overwhelming majority of us just get on with life. We send the kids off to school, we go to work, we fix dinner, we go to the movies, we help out at the senior center, we go to church, we call our mothers, we make the house payment.

And watch the news on TV.

Is television news wrong to concentrate on the abnormal events? No. That's the nature of news, at whatever level news is conveyed. When you talk to your friend on the phone, you seldom start off with ordinary events. You start with the extraordinary thing that happened to you. You had a flat tire on the freeway. In your circle of friends and family, that's news, so that's what you tell. Expand that practice to the entire city, or the entire country, or the entire world, and that's what we on television news do.

Our mistake, it seems to me, is not making clear to the viewers what it is we do for a living. Perhaps each newscast should be preceded by a disclaimer: "Warning. The following newscast could be hazardous to your peace of mind. These events are out of the ordinary and in no way constitute a consistent pattern reflective of your neighborhood. They are isolated, unusual incidents and should in no way be considered an indictment of the hardworking, decent people who make up our city."

The result of the misunderstanding between the news producers and the news consumers can be quite serious, indeed. The constant drumbeat of violence, cheating, confrontation and horrors of every description on our television screens lead those who watch to a sullen, fearful and defensive attitude which has evil consequences for society. The impression is that the barbarians are at the gate. We on TV breathlessly convey that message every night.

That's why it is almost impossible to convince people that, for instance, by respected measurements taken from very large samples over a very long period of time, crime is down in the United States. Down, not up.

True, I have seen that information reported on television, but even when this obviously good news was presented, it was couched in terms that were negative. Something like, "Though census figures show that overall crime in this country is down, there are troubling indicators that violence among younger Americans is rising sharply." The story then went on to elaborate on recent examples of the Y-T-M ("Younger-Tougher-Meaner') criminals among us. The good news which, expanded to the full lead and follow-up it deserved, might have begun to reassure the viewer, was buried in an avalanche of pre-teen shootings and stabbings.

Even the financial news turns positive information on its head. A young woman on CNN solemnly told me that unemployment was at a four-year low and that while this might be good news for some, it was really bad news because the effect on interest rates would be deleterious, fueling concern over potential inflation, sometimes a concomitant of full employment.

Wait a minute. Folks going back to work isn't good news? Balance is vital to a story, but accentuating the negative in the name of balance is skewing the news and giving a false impression. There's nothing deliberate about the skewing. It's just part of the process of getting a newscast on the tube. Reporters and producers need to step back and take a look. We need to tell the people what we're doing. Then we need to do it right.

Nick with WGRZ-TV co-anchor and friend Laurie Lisowcki, moments before Nick's last television newscast. 1994.

Goodbye, TV News

Friday, May 27th, 1994

Well, it's been quite a ride, but tonight at 11 o'clock I will anchor my 6,846th - and last - television newscast. For the record, it will be in company with solid news professionals at WGRZ-TV in Buffalo, New York.

We're heading for a great new adventure. More about that in a moment. Nina and I have been in Buffalo only a few months. It's a wonderful city. We travelled here because of one man. His name is Steve Cohen and he was the general manager of this station.

Steve came up through the ranks as a newsman. He became one of the most respected news executives in the legendary CBS

News organization. As a news director and, eventually, general manager of CBS-owned stations he was very successful.

I don't know about your business, but in television I can literally count the number of competent top executives with whom I have worked in 35 years on one hand. There's a good reason for that. For more than a generation, it was impossible to lose money in local television, even if you couldn't pour water from your shoe without having instructions written on the heel. You pushed the network button, sent out a few good local salespeople and routinely turned 30, 40, even 50 percent profit every year. You were usually judged by that profit margin, seldom by the quality of the product you turned out. These two facts of television life bred a decidedly inferior corps of executives.

Which made the good ones, like Steve Cohen, stand out all the more. He is smart and civilized. He keeps a close eye on the bottom line. He also has a wide view of the importance of television, from children's programs to news. He maintains a sense of mission and a sense of humor, along with his sense of community. You won't be surprised that, for a number of years, I had hoped to have a chance to work with him.

Late last fall, he called. He was at WGRZ-TV in Buffalo. The station's ownership was in disarray, but he had undertaken the job of turning its fortunes around anyway. He wanted me to help in news. He was convinced we could swim against the industry's tabloid tide and still win. I was eager to help prove him right.

After a shaky January start on my part, the team Steve assembled jelled. The anchors, reporters, photographers, producers and others were on the same page and had the same focus. The newscast began to look good. Notice was taken in the Buffalo press. Favorable notice. Station profits improved dramatically.

Then, three weeks ago, Steve Cohen was fired. There is no point going into the dreary and complicated ownership politics which resulted in this irrational decision. Suffice to say it is not uncommon in these days of television stations cannibalizing one another and even themselves as the medium becomes more competitive. It is unseemly. I am mortally weary of it all. I asked for and received a release from my obligation here. I will say goodbye to television news tonight.

And now, for me, there is great news. Since last August I had been in touch with my favorite television cable channel, American Movie Classics. For those who don't know, AMC has for ten years been presenting movies of the 1930s, 1940s and 1950s 24 hours a day on cable. Their principal host, Bob Dorian, a friendly and urbane performer, tells interesting tidbits about the actors, directors and writers from the golden age of the silver screen. Often, there are special programs hosted by people such as Ron Howard and Debbie Reynolds and Shirley Jones and Donald O'Connor. There are in-depth interviews with famous actors and directors.

All in all, I think it's a marvelous effort and beginning June 1st, I'm going to be part of it. I haven't been this excited about a new project in years. I'm convinced that motion pictures are an underrated element in the history of the 20th century and I'm happy to be with an enterprise that treats films with respect while not forgetting that they are always supposed to entertain. I'm told my on-air contributions will begin sometime in late June or early July. I can't wait.

In the meantime, at approximately 11:30 tonight, I'll say goodbye to a big part of my life. It has consumed me for many years. I'm grateful for its challenges and its associations. It has demanded my best, which was not always good enough.

I leave the ongoing television news wars to my young friends. I suppose there ought to be some kind of parting thought. All right, for what it's worth: Each battle in each newsroom is important. Don't settle for manipulation, distortion, sensationalism, rumor, prurience, no matter how it is packaged as the "new wave". It is not new. It is as old as Walter Winchell. Settle only for relevance and truth. Then when you walk away from it, as I do tonight, you'll never have to make excuses to your children about what you did for a living.

One more thing. Leave the drama to my movies. They were better at it.

Dr. Henry Kissinger visits Nick at Channel 12 News in 1987. The subject is politics.

Politics

FEW SUBJECTS ARE AS FRAGILE as politics. Issues that burn to the touch during a campaign are ice-cold and forgotten within a year. Still, columns written at the time about the democratic process have interest, it seems to me, as a sort of history-in-progress.

You won't see columns reprinted here about the times I was wrong, such as the piece in the spring of 1992 when I wrote that Bill Clinton was a regional candidate and couldn't win in the fall.

Instead, I'll show you the column that predicted the 1994 Republican sweep of both houses of Congress one year before it happened, the column that predicted the rich and volatile sometime-politician Ross Perot would get back into the 1992 race after abruptly withdrawing and the column pointing out that George Bush was in trouble ten months before the 1992 election.

Hey, it's my book.

Nick.

Politics

Straws

Friday, November 5th, 1993

The results of Tuesday's elections make the job of a columnist relatively easy. We're supposed to predict the future. All right. The immediate future looks great for Republicans. You saw it here first.

Actually, I predict 1994 will be the Republican year in Congressional elections. I don't mean just the usual pick up of 15 to 20 seats by the party out of power. I mean a potential sea change.

In my opinion, the mood is not so much more Republican and less Democrat as it is more change and less status quo. Many pundits thought that 1992 would see the great change in Congress but, except for the significant increase in the number of women, the battle lines have remained relatively the same.

Much was made of the fact that there were more new faces in the 1992 Congress than in any since 1946. What was not emphasized was that much of the change came because of retirements and resignations by incumbents to avoid reforms in the way campaign money could be diverted to private use. In point of fact, not many incumbents were turned out by the voters in 1992.

1994 will be different. The great American public reacts a bit more slowly than experts predict, but the people do react eventually. There is an unrest among us that is born, not of conservative talk shows nor of tabloid exposés, but of an uncertainty of where we are, as a nation, going.

We are headed at warp speed toward a millennial milepost. The year 2000 looms, whether we want it to or not. There is a vague dissatisfaction abroad in the land that finds its manifestation in anger, cynicism and escape. Questions bubble up and boil over.

If this is the greatest country in the world, why doesn't everyone have a job? Why isn't everybody covered by health insurance? Why doesn't government keep its mitts off business?

Why do (insert one; "blacks", "minorities", "men", "whites", "women") get all the breaks? Why doesn't government protect us from heartless business mergers?

In sum, if we're so hot, where are we going?

We have always been a restless people, so this feeling is by no means new. But since the 1960s, our focus has been changing. Instead of finding the devil outside, we've searched for him within. Rules we accepted on faith, we question. We question everything.

At first it was just the "radicals". Then it was the "liberals". Then the "neo-conservatives" had questions of their own. Arguably, this cycle of question-question-question has been good. We've been taking a hard look at everything about ourselves. Nothing has been immune.

It's a tribute to both the stubborn stability and the flexibility of our society that we have survived this torrent of self-examination.

But at some point, the cycle of question-question-question must evolve into a cycle of answer-answer-answer. Our leaders have to stop jockeying for personal power, find the consensus and get on with it.

At the moment our leadership is personified by President Bill Clinton. Is he up to the job? I don't have the faintest idea. Neither do you. You just have an opinion. He certainly has sparked an organized and extremely vocal — occasionally vitriolic — opposition. He has not thus far inspired supporters with anything like the fervor of his detractors. If Republicans can surmount their own internal struggle with the religious right, they can build on this core antipathy.

Only one other president in my lifetime has engendered such a frenzy of anger, contempt, satire and occasional calumny as Bill Clinton. Harry Truman.

Actually, there are a few other political parallels. Truman took on the most controversial, intransigent problems of post-World War II America. At one time or another, he angered every power block in the nation. His popularity numbers were even lower than Clinton's. Because of his early ties to the Pendergast political machine his ethics were questioned. He was the last Democrat president to face a Republican House and Republican Senate. In 1994, Bill Clinton may learn what that feels like.

It's a very long shot indeed, but it's not beyond the reach of the GOP to attain their two-generation dream of majority Congressional power. Without a major economic uptick or some other remarkably positive element, the political change anticipated in 1992 will wash over us in 1994.

Republicans would then have two years — no more — to show the beginnings of real answers. Not questions. Answers. And President Clinton would have two years to run against them, as Harry Truman did in 1948. With surprising results.

One year later, Republicans swept both houses of Congress.

The Perot Factor

Wednesday, August 19th, 1992

Here in the midst of the Republican National Convention, on the very day President Bush will be renominated and his wife Barbara will make the highest-profile speech ever delivered by a first lady, I would like to revisit a recent American political phenomenon.

Ross Perot.

I'm going to ask a question and commend it to your attention. What is Ross Perot up to?

Some time ago, I offered my opinion in this corner that Mr. Perot gave up his run for the presidency for one major reason: it was costing him too much money. Since then, several interviews with Perot insiders seemed to corroborate that view. A "Nightline" program just last week spent two-thirds of its air time interviewing people who said how much the unannounced candidate squealed every time a bill came in.

All right, he has stopped the hemorrhage of his own cash. He is back at his favorite pastime, which is stockpiling greenbacks while he dabbles in things.

Still, there are disturbing indications that he also has something else in mind. He continues to encourage die-hard followers to put his name on the ballot as a candidate for president of the United States. One recent forecast indicated that he might be listed in as many as 42 states by November, perhaps more.

This is the man who said he was undoing his un-campaign as an un-candidate because he thought it would be divisive and to the detriment of the country. The only purpose he could serve, he said, would be to throw the election into the House of Representatives with unmeasurable consequences. Very patriotic. Statesmanlike.

But his name remains on those ballots and there are more every week. What is Ross Perot up to?

He has been asked specifically by reporters if he is going to take his name off the ballots. He responded, "My volunteers put my name on the ballot and only they can take it off." That answer is, putting the best face on it, disingenuous.

In some of those states, all Ross Perot has to do is send a letter to the appropriate state official requesting his name be removed as a candidate. In at least one of those states, he was directly asked by authorities to do so.

He refused.

Just a letter, but Mr. Perot refused to do it and he continues to encourage operatives to get his name listed as a presidential candidate even though he says he is no longer running. What is Ross Perot up to?

Let's imagine one possibility. It is mid-October, perhaps a bit later. George Bush and Bill Clinton are locked in a tight race. They have exhausted themselves on the campaign trail. They have debated. They have explored both the high and the low roads. They have even delved into important issues. They have spent themselves and in the process have clearly defined their differences for the voters. For every stand they took, they made enemies.

Lurking on the sidelines, having expended not a dime of his own money or a drop of his own sweat and having never defined who he is or what he stands for, is Ross Perot. He is on the ballot in 40-plus states.

He proceeds to make whirlwind appearances on the Larry King Show, Phil and Oprah, the Today Show, Good Morning America and a Barbara Walters special. They are free.

He is shocked, he says, by the turn politics has taken and by the weak positions offered by both major candidates. If he had but known how poor the quality of their campaigns would be, he would never have gotten out. He had listened to bad advice from professionals and he had made a mistake.

However, now, at the last minute, he is willing to offer himself as an alternative. The two major candidates had failed. He wants to unify the country and lead it to new sunlit heights. His name is there. Pull the "Perot" lever if you really want change as much as you say you do.

No cost. No sweat. If that isn't his plan, why doesn't he take the opportunity to remove his name from contention when it is offered to him? Why does he encourage continuing efforts to add his name to ballots in additional states?

What is Ross Perot up to?

Ross Perot did re-enter the race.

USSR —
The Best Enemy A Nation Could Ever Have

Wednesday, December 27th, 1989

We're going to have to invent some new enemies and we'd better do it quickly.

In the wink of an eye a whole eastern bloc of nations which only yesterday was giving us the cold stare of the Cold War has disappeared from our "hate" list. Even Russia itself is sending a representative to the arch-enemy NATO, for heaven's sake.

You know what this means, don't you?

It's disaster for several venerable sectors of our economy. Already, those with defense contracts all over the country are looking over their shoulders.

Great Caesar's Ghost, where are they going to sell all those $400 toilet seats? How about the $150 screwdrivers? A switch to the civilian economy is unthinkable.

Homemakers are hard-eyed buyers, not patsies like the Pentagon. They know very well they can get toilet seats for $29.99 and screwdrivers for $1.49 at Sears and get guarantees on both.

The defense contractor is in a cold sweat. After 50 years, peace may actually be breaking out. What a catastrophe! If he can't sell to the government anymore, how is he supposed to make ends meet?

He's supporting a broker, a bookie, 10 family members, a psychiatrist and three full-time lobbyists. Don't those fuzzy-headed idealists dancing on the remains of the Berlin Wall understand anything?

The beach house at Malibu isn't finished yet, not to mention the condo at Park City. This is ridiculous.

They can't actually be asking him to go back to competing in the marketplace instead of schmoozing Washington bureaucrats, can they? Heck, that's no fun.

His daddy told him when he was a little boy that manufacturing something better and cheaper was doing business the hard way. Deal with the government, he said. Promise the fellow you're bargaining with a big-paying job in your company after the negotiating is over. Then strike a deal that gives you a modest 50 per cent profit, after which you overrun the costs by 100 per cent.

Each time you delay the project, take the government watchdog to Florida for golf or to California for the Universal Studio tour.

His daddy used to say, "Yep, son, as long as there's a Soviet Russia and a Warsaw Pact, we'll get our share. Maybe a little more. America is still the land of opportunity." Daddy always was patriotic.

Now the second generation contractor is reduced to watching the phone nervously, terrified that the call he dreads will come, maybe in the middle of the night.

"Hello, this is Uncle Sam. Cancel the toilet seats. We don't need the screwdrivers any more. We declared peace."

A nightmare.

And not just for the contractor.

There is an army of writers simultaneously developing the shakes. They go to fashionable bars to meet equally distraught publishers, producers, directors and actors.

One third of all the movies, one half the "action" TV dramas and one quarter of all popular fiction are now going directly down the tubes.

Already there are rumblings that re-runs of "Hawaii 5-0," "Magnum P-I", the "A-Team" and a dozen other programs are hopelessly outdated because of their inevitable antagonist-of-choice, the commie rat from Hungary or East Germany or Czechoslovakia, all financed by the sinister Russian lurking in the background. Now, those programs look quaint. Almost museum pieces.

Who, for instance, will build and man Tom Clancy's next submarine? It's a sobering thought.

Good Lord, who will "Rocky" fight next? "Rambo" has lost eight late great enemy nations overnight. This is getting serious.

Oh, sure, we get the occasional Khadafi and Noriega, but these guys are small potatoes and everybody knows it. Writers can only build them up so much before the people catch on that they're no more a long-term threat to the United States than a mosquito bite to the behind.

What we need is an enemy with proven staying power to keep all these men and women working, no question about it.

Russia was the best. They don't make 'em like Russia anymore. The Soviets were our enemy longer than anyone else — 40 vintage years — and they were the best kind.

We never really rolled our tanks directly at each other, so we never had to find out if those screwdrivers really worked.

We just kept each other scared to death all the time, which ran up the cost of toilet seats.

Where are you ever going to find another enemy like that?

Bread and Butter

Monday, December 30th, 1991

There is a basic lesson that national leaders never seem to learn. It is as immutable as the turning of the earth. Here it is.

"Strut and fret as much as you want on the world stage, but take care of bread and butter back home."

Cut that out and save it. It fits any country and any era and Mikhail Gorbachev is only the latest victim. George Bush may be the next. Or Boris Yeltsin.

I don't know why these famous people are so surprised when they end up in trouble. Surely there's a political primer somewhere that tells them the facts of life before they get into the public arena. It's as basic as "See Jane run."

We vote our pocketbooks or wallets. Period. We talk about a lot of other things, and occasionally we'll even get riled up on an issue and vote in an individual election for some other reason, but 90% of the time we vote economics. Why don't these fellows know that?

I suppose what happens is that they get all puffed up after the election. They head for the other guy's capital city and have a big dinner with all the pomp and circumstance attendant to such affairs. They have a "summit", or whatever it's being called at the time. They have the illusion that somehow they are now directing great global forces, and won't the people back in Norwood be impressed when they hear what the Queen had to say?

Well, no they won't. Not for long, anyway.

Poor old Woodrow Wilson fell victim to the syndrome. He was certain his League of Nations was at the top of every American's agenda, as it was of his. Wrong. The Republicans knew it and exploited Wilson's lofty rhetoric. They talked "normalcy" and won in a walk.

Winston Churchill was probably the most popular, best-known and most effective world leader of his day. He had been right all along about Adolph Hitler. He rallied his people to the greatest military upset in modern history. He gave words to the highest aspirations of civilization. And at the very moment of his greatest triumph, he was decisively turned out of office. He forgot bread and butter. The British were tired of "blood, toil, tears and sweat." They wanted plentiful food and decent housing.

It wasn't the Iran hostage crisis that made Jimmy Carter a one-term president. It was the oil embargo which resulted in runaway inflation and threatened our savings and futures. Remember candidate Reagan's "Are you better off now than you were four years ago?" Very effective.

Mikhail Gorbachev has been a prophet of freedom for the people of Eastern Europe and the darling of the western democracies, but the folks in Kiev and Volgograd couldn't buy bread or meat in the stores. Exit Gorbachev.

Now Mr. Yeltsin faces the same problem. He has become a world figure and shows some preliminary signs of falling into the same trap as his predecessor. He meets every visiting celebrity and is interviewed on every network. Meantime, after the first of the year, he plans to float the ruble against the world currency, and perhaps simultaneously float his own ambitions off the world stage.

Which brings us to Mr. Bush. Like all these other men, he's smart. He has plenty of experience and access to the nation's best advice.

So why does he get his ox into the same ditch? He had his war with Saddam Hussein and saw his poll numbers go through the roof. Like Winston Churchill's. He declared his "new World Order" and got plaudits from his counterparts around the globe. Like Woodrow Wilson. He's the darling of the internationalists and drawing-room strategists. Like Mikhail Gorbachev.

But he forgot Norwood.

He makes a valid point when he says that this recession is not as deep as the one presided over by Mr. Reagan, but his timing is off. That one was in Mr. Reagan's first year of his first term. This one is lingering into the last year of Mr. Bush's first term. Big difference.

How will he answer the Democrats' inevitable question, "Are you better off now than you were four years ago?"

Bread and butter.

Mr. Bush lost the election ten months later.

John Warner (Congress Declares War)

November 3rd, 1995

I was watching an interview on CNN a couple of nights ago. Senator John Warner of Virginia was being questioned by my old friend Gene Randall.

Senator Warner is a distinguished-looking man of many accomplishments, not the least of which was a brief marriage to the legendary Elizabeth Taylor. He was also Secretary of the Navy for a time.

While obviously a man of strong character, no one can accuse him of having an abundance of intellectual gifts. This was never more apparent than during the brief question-and-answer session between Senator Warner and Gene, who is one of the best "hard news" interviewers in the profession.

The subject was, of course, the Middle East and our involvement there. Senator Warner was lukewarm in his support for a more active role by Congress in our lurch toward war in the Persian Gulf. He seemed perfectly content with the scant attention being paid to the legislators by President Bush as he mounts the most massive military force we as a nation have put together since Vietnam.

Some of this, of course, is simple politics. Senator Warner is a Republican, a leader in the upper chamber, and wants to be seen as supportive of the man who, in addition to being president of us all, is the leader of his political party.

But Senator Warner's unconcern seems to go considerably deeper, and that's what worries me. He might be basing his opinion on misinformation.

He said he had asked Congressional researchers to look up some facts for him, and what they told him was reassuring.

"We have had to take military action more than 200 times in our history. Only 5 times has Congress been required to declare war. There's no need for concern in this matter. The president has been in touch with Congressional leadership every step of the way."

Come now, Senator. The "research" you got from your experts was both misleading and downright wrong. Those 200 times presidents have exercised their prerogatives as commanders-in-chief of our existing military have been small potatoes and you know it. Or you should.

They include marching a regiment into the New England hills to tame some moonshiners, sending a squadron of sailing ships to the Mediterranean to rescue hostages, dispatching a company of Marines to Nicaragua to "protect" American property, sailing a single gunboat up a Chinese river, flying a regiment to the Dominican Republic and shipping another to Lebanon. They were minor incidents, every one. All the 200 together wouldn't add up to the first 12 hours of the battle of Pittsburgh Landing in the Civil War.

No, Senator, it won't wash. Prior to June 1950, this nation never committed substantial resources to combat without a declaration of war.

June 4th, 1812, Congress declared war on Britain. Eventually, we won. May 11th, 1846, Congress declared war on Mexico. We won. April 15th, 1861. Technically, we couldn't declare war because the Union didn't recognize the Confederacy as a nation, but Lincoln said it was an "insurrection" and Congress approved a call for volunteers. The Union prevailed. April 25th, 1898, Congress declared war on Spain. We won. April 5th, 1917, Congress declared war on Germany. December 7th, 1917, Congress declared war on Austria-Hungary. We won. December 8th, 1941, Congress declared war on Japan. December 11th, 1941, Congress declared war on Germany-Italy. We won.

So actually, Senator, Congress declared war 7 times, not 5, and we have won them all.

In 1950, Harry Truman waged war on North Korea. We didn't win. In 1965, Lyndon Johnson waged ware on North Vietnam. We lost.

Panama, Grenada, Lebanon and Libya are all vest-pocket operations which didn't engage the efforts of an entire nation.

400,000 American troops in a desert at the end of a 6,000 mile supply line is war.

Comparing one to the other is either deliberately misleading, or just not well thought-out. I'm sure it's the latter.

Come on, Senator, you and all your colleagues, Democrat and Republican, get in there and do the job you're paid for. The Constitution says only you can make war. Not the president. You. Stop ducking your responsibility.

If Kuwait is worth a war, vote a declaration and let's get on with it. If not, vote it down and bring most of those kids home.

Don't let the president make this decision alone, by default.
It's unconstitutional. It's also, on the record, not very smart.

The ugly mound of mine tailings provide the background for Ruth, Nevada, near the birthplace of Pat Nixon. Picture taken in 1993.

Pat Nixon

Friday, December 31th, 1993

Just a few hours left now in 1993. This was the year Pat Nixon
died. It was also the first year I even remotely felt I knew
anything about her.

Nina and I were on the road again. We came down the
mountain into Ely, Nevada, but we didn't come down very far.
The main drag is still 6,400 feet above sea level. It's called Aultman
Street. About a third of the buildings on it are empty. At 4 o'clock
of a Saturday afternoon, there were six people on one block and
that included Nina and me.

We walked into the Ely Gift Boutique. Two people were inside.
They ran the place. Al Frederick is in his 50s, tall, weathered,
black hair. Donna, his wife, is cheerful and wears a businesslike wig.

"Who's this town famous for?", I asked.

"You mean, besides me?" Al smiled. "This is a company town. Kennecott. All mining. I've lived here all my life. That's unusual. The houses and the people mostly last 20 years, tops. That's it. Kind of disposable. Now, let's see, who famous is from here?"

Donna chimed in. "Pat Nixon's from here."

My ears perked up. The enigmatic wife of the most star-crossed of our presidents? From here?

"Well, not here, really. She's from Ruth, five miles up the road."

Al corrected Donna. "That's not quite right, either. She's from Kimberly. Was right next to Ruth. Kimberly's not there any more. It's just a trash heap. But it used to look just like Ruth."

Pat Ryan Nixon. "Her father was a miner up there, you know. Put a roof over the family's head, anyway. She was still little when they went to Southern California. I was too young to know her. I don't remember her coming back, ever."

Nina and I got in the car and headed for Ruth, five miles away. We talked of Pat Nixon. In the books about her husband's rise and fall, she was invariably a footnote. For instance, in Theodore White's "Breach of Faith", she was mentioned only five times and not once on a matter of substance.

She was always called "a good campaigner" and "a good mother." There was a brief moment in the spotlight when her husband, fighting for his place on Dwight Eisenhower's ticket, referred to her in his "Checkers" speech. Her "good Republican cloth coat" became famous.

We tried to remember if we had heard her speak. Neither of us could recall her voice. But we remembered the words used to describe her during the Watergate crisis and her husband's 1974 resignation. "Stoic". "Disciplined." "Loyal".

A sign led us off the main highway a mile or so and there was Ruth, Nevada. The houses were small, frame and alike, Most were occupied, but some were boarded up and others burned out. There were a few brave flowers in front yards, ornamental sculpture, decorative fences here and there. It was obviously temporary. A company town. What had Al said? The houses and the people usually last only 20 years.

The town's major feature was a huge, yellow mountain of mine tailings, a man-made monstrosity rivalling in size the real mountains ringing the town. We drove around slowly. There was the Commercial Club and the Ruth Club and the DeLeon Brothers Main Store. In front of one of the small square houses three little tow-headed girls looked at us solemnly. One gripped a puppy. One smiled shyly, then looked away.

We asked a man where Kimberly had been. He waved vaguely toward another yellow mine-mountain a few miles away. Over there somewhere.

A little tow-headed Pat Ryan had lived there in a small frame house exactly like one of these. She had played with her temporary friends in their temporary town and, perhaps, made temporary dreams.

I wondered about a little girl whose home town almost immediately after her birth was buried in a pile of mine tailings by the company. Whose house was owned by the company, whose future was shaped by the company and whose family life was in the company's control.

She might learn to be stoic. To keep her feelings to herself.

I looked around at the man-made ugliness in the midst of natural grandeur and, for the first time, felt a rush of warmth for little long-ago Pat Ryan. The miner's daughter who would flee these hills and never look back.

Who would walk the halls of power but would have none, take none. Whose most famous home, a big white house, would prove to be the most temporary and disappointing of all.

1993 swallowed millions of people, some of them famous personalities we thought we knew. Of these, perhaps we knew Nevada's Pat Ryan Nixon least of all.

The admiration is mutual. Nina and granddaughter Allison on the front porch in Augusta, 1994.

Nina

MARRIAGE IS A CONTINUALLY humbling experience, especially if your wife is smart and talented and one of the most beautiful women in the world.

I knew Nina was a good writer, but I didn't know quite how good or I would never have asked her to fill in for me while I took a few days off from the column. She has written maybe a dozen, no more. Among them, one was nominated for a Freedoms Foundation award, one received more reader mail than any I have ever written and one was "borrowed" by a famous young actress to use as her own story on the "Tonight" show.

I love Nina more than anything on the planet, but next time, she can go get her own column.

Nick.

Nina

May 4, 1990	Podiatrist
November 16, 1992	Roy Rogers
November 20, 1992	The Killer Martini
February 1994	Don't Tell Me!

Carew Tower

May 4th, 1990

Carew Tower has been sold and will be renovated. I'm sure the new owners will do something in keeping with its heritage. There is hardly anyone that doesn't have a memory or two connected with this great community centerpiece.

Mine began innocently enough. In 1966, we moved to Cincinnati from Lexington, Kentucky. I began a search for all the support systems a family needs. One was a gynecologist. Wray Jean Braun had thoughtfully put together a list and I chose one in Carew Tower. The appointment day came and I nervously prepared for many firsts: first time driving in a big city, finding a parking place, a sitter, and worst of all, meeting a new doctor. Never mind that I'd had two children, the yearly check-up always traumatized me.

I arrived in the Carew Tower lobby a few minutes early, found a bank of elevators, checked for the doctors' name (something simple like "Greene") found it and went up.

The receptionist was very nice when I said I was there to see "Dr. Greene." She asked if I hadn't made my appointment with their Reading Road office because that was where "Dr. Greene" regularly was on this day. I lamented the problems of coming back another day and she asked if I'd like to see "Greene's" partner who was there and had just had his one o'clock cancel. I jumped at it. Anything to get this over with.

A nurse ushered me into an examining room saying Doctor What-His Name would be in shortly. Now, this is the point where I should have known something was amiss, but try to remember that I was naive, young and consumed with accomplishing this task. I half undressed before I realized the nurse had forgotten to leave me a gown. I didn't want to bother her and perhaps in big cities all they used was this napkin-sized towel lying on the examining table. So I completely undressed and tried vainly to figure where to put the towel for maximum coverage. Finally I hit upon the idea of sitting on the table, pulling my legs up, crossing my ankles and holding the napkin by its two upper corners in front of me like a curtain.

There I sat cold, shivering and scared.

Finally the door opened, and the Doctor entered, reading from a clip board. He looked up, saw me, turned and bolted out the door in one move. I figured he'd forgotten something. A minute later the door slowly opened.

He was pushing a reluctant nurse ahead of him. She stopped. He ran into her and gave her another push. So it went until the two of them stood at the foot of the table with nothing between us but the tiny napkin.

After a long pause, with a strange look he squeaked out, "Mrs. Clooney, just why are you here?"

Being nervous and suffering from a terminal need to explain everything, I began with when I was born. Some time that afternoon I ended my monologue still perched behind my tiny curtain. Neither doctor not nurse seemed able to say anything.

Finally the doctor managed, "Mrs. Clooney, I hate to tell you this. I'm a podiatrist!"

I don't remember getting dressed, out of the building or home. When Nick arrived from work, I was crying hysterically. Knowing where I was going that day he thought I was diagnosed as terminal. When I finally sobbed the whole thing out, he tried manfully not to, but finally convulsed in laughter. Of course that exacerbated my hysteria.

Two years later I, too, finally thought it was funny.

In the mid-eighties, when Nick was anchoring news here, he reported a story I'm sure only I remember. It concerned a national meeting of Podiatrists at Convention Center. All I could picture was hundreds of podiatrists at a cocktail party and someone says,

"Hey did you catch that newsman on Channel 12?"

"The one that's so hot here?"

"Yeah, that's the guy."

"Yeah, why?"

"Let me tell you about his crazy wife!"

Roy Rogers

November 16th, 1992

My age of consummate self-involvement was fifteen. The same year Elvis gyrated "You Ain't Nothin But a Hound Dog" into pop history. I remember distinctly that was also the year my parents intellectual powers sank in the Dead Sea level. My younger brother Jackie was forbidden to speak to me in a public place. Everything in my overflowing wardrobe was referred to as "that old thing". School was attended to see and be seen, to attract and be attracted. Paralyzing embarrassment could overtake me for such a major catastrophe as my slip showing.

This was also the first year Perryville, Kentucky, my hometown, decided to hold a reenactment of the Civil War battle that took place nearby. Big stuff happened, including a parade with a close-by larger town's high school band participating. Before the day was over, adolescent lightning had struck. A visiting trumpet player, I'll call him Alvin, had introduced himself, shared a coke and spent the afternoon at my side. Time was suspended and violins played right up to the very second the bus driver revved the engines to head back to Danville. Alvin and I vowed to bridge the ten miles between our two towns the following Saturday.

After a week of fantisizing that this sixteen-year-old boy would arrive in a golden chariot and whisk me off to what I was sure would be a mixture of "Camelot" and "Some Enchanted Evening", he showed up in his father's well worn Plymouth.

Now I should have started to suspect this was not Cary Grant when he told my worried parents we were going to see a Roy Rogers movie. I should have been even more skeptical when we actually did.

The Kentucky Theater, in Danville, was an undulating sea of kids who were barely old enough to read "Dick and Jane". We were ushered to seats almost dead center. Alvin took my hand and electricity flowed. Roy, Dale, Trigger and Gabby got to the business of setting the West right. As our palms began to sweat,

I noticed a jerking movement from Alvin. Not only did he almost lose my slippery hand, his whole body was bouncing about. Could my ears be deceiving me? Did I hear guffaws from my left? Was he actually joining in the cheers and jeers of a bunch of sticky-fingered urchins? This simply could not be happening to me. What would I tell the other members of the "Gang of Five — Friends Forever" on Monday morning? I studied the audience for contemporaries who might rat. Thankfully we were the only teens there. I would not die after all. I would simply lie.

Now resolute, I attempted to extract my hand from his, just as he squeezed tighter, leaned forward, mouth agape, at one with screen. Roy was chasing an obvious bad guy, dressed in black, riding a black horse. As Roy was gaining, the villain came to a gate, hurriedly dismounted, took his steed through and closed it again. Roy arrived at the same gate moment later. He too dismounted, opened the gate, took Trigger through and was about to close it when Alvin yelled out "Go on Roy! I'll close the gate!"

I was held in the equipoise of a kind of half life. The entire theater hooted and shook with laughter. As they turned to search out the owner of the big voice, I slid down in my chair hoping death would be mercifully quick. It was at that moment that I learned God does not like teenagers. My brother, the worm, yelled from somewhere down front in his tinny soprano "Hi Nina Bruce. You and Alvin enjoying the movie?"

Nina, just before her first Knight in Shining Armor fell off "Trigger."

Last Martini

November 20th, 1992

I know it's not politically correct to tell drinking stories these days, but you shouldn't mind this one because justice is served in the end.

For many of us attempting to grow up during the previous decades, movies shaped most of our ideas. They offered a glimpse of a larger world or relief from the one we lived in. They also taught us the sophistication of drinking "right" and the damnation of drinking "wrong". Of course, after one drink, cranial blight allowed us to believe we were the former when often we were the latter.

Alcohol and I never really cohabitated successfully. More than one drink and I might find myself driving the porcelain bus the next morning. A smarter person would have caught on early and opted for something less painful. For me it took years because I was of the belief that social drinking on the weekend was a natural course of life.

My mind was changed forever on one such social evening several years ago in Augusta, Kentucky. Duane and Jo Holt invited us to dinner and a tour of their beautiful, remodeled home. Remodeling was a community disease then and I too had succumbed. I was remodeling a house on the riverfront. It was not unusual for me to work eight to ten hours and forget to eat, both of which I'd done on the Saturday in question.

"I'll have a martini". I can still hear my voice saying that to Duane. Though a novice at mixing them, he said he'd try. What resulted was the world's largest martini, filling up a highball glass. I knew better of course, but I rationalized that I'd sip it all night and I was, after all, only a three-block walk from home. Off we went on a tour of this enormous house from attic to basement. Finding myself leaning against the arms of the furnace, I realized I'd sipped too much and needed food. Nachos were no competition for the martini, half of which still sloshed in my glass.

My mind took a sideline seat and watched in slow motion as I mouthed diatribes on everything including motherhood. Jo anxiously rushed dinner hoping more substantial food would not only help me but shut me up too, I'm sure.

Now seated at the table, I remembered earlier they'd told us of honeymooning in Sweden and buying their crystal at the Orrefors plant. These beautiful, delicate glasses stood like sentinels beside our place settings, which were on placemats, atop the most highly polished table I'd seen since before my children were born.

Nick and Duane were in a heated conversation about zoning, Jo was the gracious hostess entering and exiting stage left with one delicacy after another. I was wolfing them down like the lions in the final scene of "Quo Vadis?". At last I was full. And getting sleepy. And numb.

If I were to remain erect in my chair, I would have to prop myself up. With great care, I placed each elbow on opposite sides of the placemat, interlocked my thumbs and placed my chin in my hands. Soon, I, the placement and the Orrefors were taking a long slide to my right. I corrected the direction just before we would have fallen off the table into the abyss. The Orrefors swayed like a twig in the wind as we slid back toward Nick, who was ignoring me. Again a correction. Again a slide. This continued for several eternities it seemed, with Jo in the kitchen and Nick and Duane pretending there was no elephant skating on this table. By some miracle, the Orrefors and I did not crash. However, my elbows somehow freed themselves from the confinement of the placemat. This was not a positive development, because they were now on the polished table, able to move in whatever direction they most wanted. They chose direct opposites. My face descended closer and closer to the remains of gourmet Mexican in my plate. Without ever, ever acknowledging my plight or looking in my direction, Nick reached over, grabbed me by the back of the neck, pulled me upright and held me there, not missing a syllable.

Eventually, enough feeling returned to my lips so that I could say goodnight. On the interminable walk home I also said goodbye forever to martinis. I have never regretted the decision. Any drink potent enough to make a ventriloquist's dummy out of a grown woman should be on the EPA's toxic list.

Miss Bruce Morgan at age 95, with Nina's mom, Dica Warren. 1989.

Don't Tell Me

February 1994

A friend of my family's, Miss Bruce Morgan, recently celebrated her hundredth birthday. A few days after that event I visited her. Occasionally her conversation held fragments of the powerful woman I'd known, but mostly it was repetitive and confused.

After about an hour, I told her I needed to leave as it would take me a couple of hours to drive home. She asked how many miles that was. Remembering her confusion and wishing to impress on her my need to get going, I exaggerated. "Oooooooohhhhh a couple of hundred."

She turned to me full face, completely at herself, with a no nonsense demeanor and said "Now don't tell me you can drive a hundred miles in an hour!"

Busted! Held accountable!

"Well, no Ma'am. I can't."

On that long drive home, I reflected on our conversation. It crystallized in my mind as a metaphor for the times in which we are now operating. Confusion seems to reign. Isn't it past time we held ourselves and our institutions accountable?

Don't tell me "the devil made you do it" is a supportable defense in a courtroom!

Don't tell me anyone can view the Rodney King beating and blame the victim!

Don't tell me the thugs who beat Reginald Denny were simply innocents caught up in the atmosphere!

Don't tell me our government, no matter how well intentioned should be in the business of promoting generation after generation of illegitimate children!

Don't tell me you can preach safe sex and then pander to seizing the sexual moment in nearly every commercial outlet going!

Don't tell me downsizing is just part of doing business when workers and middle managers get a few weeks salary as severance and top executives get golden parachutes!

Don't tell me you can't reach a verdict in the Menendez cases! They've already killed their parents, why wouldn't they lie, big time, to save their necks?

Don't tell me Lorena Bobbitt was insane! She was taking revenge.

Don't tell me radio, television, print and movies can hold themselves blameless in the violence quotient by calling it freedom of speech!

Don't tell me yellow sheet, sensational, pulp papers are acceptable as journalism!

Don't tell me responsible journalism is not in grave danger of being destroyed by papers and programs that pay sources, with the highest fees going to the person willing to make the most outrageous statements regardless of the truth.

Don't tell me athletes, actors, politicians and high visibility people from all walks of life are not role models! There is no choice here. It comes with the territory. Along with the glory, money, hard work and ego strokes comes the responsibility.

Don't tell me Tonya Harding isn't responsible for the attack on Nancy Kerrigan!

Don't tell me any of this is "Not my job"! We must hold ourselves both individually and as a society responsible and accountable for those influences that affect us and particularly our children.

We must allow common sense to come up for air.

These are only a few of mine, courtesy of Miss Bruce Morgan. I'm sure you can add many more.

A great Ohio Valley neighborhood; Maysville, Kentucky, where Rosemary, Betty and Nick were born. Painting by Steve White.

Neighborhoods

WHEN WE WERE KIDS, my sisters Rosemary, Betty and I moved around a lot. Our parents' troubled marriage and the nation's troubled economy were two of the major reasons for our itinerant status. As one uncle said, "we moved when the rent came due."

As a result, we went to many schools in many neighborhoods. My own tally was fourteen different sets of classmates by the end of high school. At the time, the benefits of this blur of change were distinctly disguised. Still, there were some. We got to know a number of neighborhoods from the inside out, the way no commuter from the suburbs will ever know them.

Even today, all I need do to conjure up the precise feeling of how it was — and how it has changed — is to park my car and walk the familiar streets again.

Sometimes, I do.

Nick.

Neighborhoods

October 13, 1989	Cincinnati's "Corners" are gone
June 7, 1991	Maysville H.S. Closing (The Music Man)
April 3, 1989	Chasing The Ghosts of Newport
April 4, 1990	Walking Around Newtown
July 2, 1990	One-Elephant Circus in Augusta
September 13, 1989	Over-The-Rhine: Monument To Survivors
November 20, 1989	Changes in Cincinnati's East End
January 10, 1990	The Maysville Women
October 18, 1989	John Parker; Augusta Should Warn Visitors

In Search of Corners

October 13th, 1989

Pardon me, but I seem to have mislaid seven or eight Corners. Have you seen them? I can't find them anywhere.

I woke up one day last week and realized they were gone. I don't know what in the world I did with them. I got in the car and drove to the places they used to be, but there was no sign of them. How could I have lost something as large as a Corner?

Even the Daddy of them all, Peebles Corner, has vanished without a trace. Peebles Corner was a big deal, and I mean Big. The Paramount and the Orpheum theaters rivaled the best of the downtown movie houses, and there were scores of stores and restaurants of all descriptions. Streetcars and automobiles competed noisily and cheerfully for attention at the intersection and noon found the sidewalks so packed you could hardly move. A shopping trip to Peebles Corner may not have been exactly the same as a shopping trip downtown, but the difference was marginal.

Now it's done. I searched Gilbert Avenue from one end to the other and even asked a few passersby, but they couldn't help me.

Alarmed, I drove to Central Parkway and headed north. If someone had snatched Peebles Corner, what about...?

I made a left turn, went over the short viaduct and there it was. Or rather, there it wasn't.

Knowlton's Corner.

That wonderful bustling, noisy, bewildering focus of five or six streets has disappeared, too. Oh, the streets are there all right, but where are the hundreds of people and the scores of businesses? Where could they have gone?

This is getting serious. If Knowlton's Corner and Peebles Corner are no longer there, what hope is there for the smaller, satellite Corners that used to be important gathering places in my youth?

By now I didn't have much hope, but having come this far I was determined to take a look.

DeSales Corner. The big, beautiful church still dominates Woodburn Avenue, but I counted only five people on the street. Five! On a Saturday afternoon a while back, there would have been five per square foot.

I tried one more. This one was a friendly neighborhood Corner where a kid with a dime in his pocket and a hole in the knee of his pants could go for a little excitement. Hewitt's Corner. Two drugstores, a dime store, a barber shop, a tiny restaurant where the smell of sizzling hamburgers and onions assailed your nostrils when a paying customer opened the door as you walked by, and the Ritz theater showing double features of Hollywood's best fresh from their first runs at the big movie palaces downtown.

There's nothing left of Hewitt's Corner that is recognizable. A couple of young people I talked to didn't even know this quiet little area ever had a name. I had found the same thing at Knowlton's Corner and even Peebles Corner, if you can believe it.

On the way home I was sorting it out, trying to trace what happened, when I realized I was sitting in what happened, steering it toward home.

The automobile.

It took us farther from central locations, it replaced public transportation, it shortened heretofore unbridgeable distances, it created suburbs, and it killed the Corners. The Corners, tightly boxed in, starved for space, had no room for our automobiles, so we abandoned them and invented shopping areas that would accommodate our cars.

I remember when I was a little boy reading a newspaper story that America had reached a milestone; we had one car for every five people. All of the United States could ride at once, and there was nothing like it anywhere else in the world. Now that number is one car for every two of us, and that fact shapes much of our lives, doesn't it?

The Shopping Mall was created to pay tribute to our passion for the personal freedom a motor car can give us. Tri-County,

Florence, Kenwood, Forest Fair, Eastgate, Northgate and all the others exist solely because of the automobile.

I had found the Corners. They had been spirited away and deposited in erstwhile cornfields ringing the city.

We consumers who used to be Cornered are now Malled.

It's called progress.

The Moment

Friday, June 7th, 1991

Those who write for a living have an almost mystic faith in the power of words. They have to, because words are their stock in trade. With enough hard work or talent, a precise word or phrase can be found to describe any moment, any person, any incident. At least that's the theory.

But it's not true. There are occasions when words are quite simply inadequate. They can give the bare bones, the simple facts of an event, but fail utterly to convey the real feelings or give a sense of how those involved were affected.

Three times in one weekend I ran into that brick wall, and three times I tried to write about these moments. No dice. Let me give you the bare bones.

There was a band concert.

A baby came to visit.

An aging man sang a song he wrote.

Those are the facts. They all occurred on one day, a Saturday in June. Now if I identify the band, the baby and the man, my reporting job is finished. And yet, I wouldn't really have told you anything at all, because the importance comes not from the facts, but from the way those facts touched people, and that is what is so difficult to write.

I'll try again. There was this band concert, see. Officials decided to shut down the high school in the small town of Maysville, Kentucky, and since it had been a centerpiece of the community for more than one hundred years, they couldn't just put a padlock on it and walk away, so they had a homecoming weekend. It turned out to be quite a wing-ding. Hundreds of former students came from virtually every state in the Union to say goodbye. The town was crawling with people of all ages, shapes and sizes in white-and-gold T shirts catching up on a few decades worth of gossip.

Perhaps the biggest of a dozen or so planned events was the Alumni Band concert on Saturday afternoon. For six weeks, upwards of a hundred former members of Maysville High's concert band limbered up unaccustomed fingers, lips and lungs and, with help from some recent band directors, rehearsed themselves into some semblance of musical respectability.

Then, the night before the performance, the Big Man arrived.

John K. Farris. For about thirty years, Mr. Farris had directed the fortunes of the Maysville High School Band. There had never been anyone like him before. With his trim mustache and goatee, he led the local musicians to triumph after triumph at state competitions. "Superior" ratings became the standard and "Excellent" a cause for concern. His recitals and concerts were packed. His musical discipline was legendary. Twenty years ago he retired, and shortly thereafter moved to Florida. Now, for one brief shining moment, he was back.

Someone found his old band uniform and fixed it up. White with a gold stripe down the pants. He put it on as he said hello to his former students at rehearsal. Just one rehearsal with Mr. Farris, that was all.

By 1 o'clock Saturday, I had no idea how many of us were jammed into the auditorium, but it was a couple hundred more than would fit. The temperature hovered in the mid-90s. Everyone was talking 60 miles an hour, including the hundred musicians on the stage.

Until John K. Farris strode out from the wings, erect, carrying his nearly 80 years with grace and dignity. He bowed to the audience, stamped his foot on the podium, a signal which brought the musicians of all ages and stations in life to immediate attention as if they were still high school sophomores. He raised his baton and their instruments snapped to position as one.

Incredibly, they were great. The years fell away. Lawyers, doctors, business people, travel agents, teachers, whatever, they were Maysville High School musicians again with all of life still in front of them and everything still possible. For fifty minutes it lasted, rousing song after rousing song, each evoking a huge ovation from the sweating crowd.

Then Mr. Farris paused a little longer than usual. When he finally raised his baton once more, the orchestra followed him again, but slowly, softly. The first four notes told us what it was; Auld Lang Syne. For the first time in my life, a montage rolled before my eyes, just like the movies. Ball games, graduations, classrooms, teachers, a jumble of young faces whose haircuts and clothes proclaimed a hodge-podge of fashion from before the turn of the century to this spring.

"We'll take a cup of kindness yet..." Mr. Farris didn't allow it to end with a sharp bar line. He softened it, faded it, whispered it, so that those of us listening strained to hear. Was it over? Weren't they still playing? Wasn't there just the faintest hint of the old Scots melody still floating on the heavy air? Wasn't it going still, just a bit longer?

Then we realized we were listening to silence. It was over, all of it. The school, the band, the day. Yes, and Mr. Farris, too. He had just managed to capture all of it in one song and say goodbye to and for it all. His face was red. It was time for him to return to Florida, his uniform to go back to some local closet, and the musicians back to real life. They had combined for a small miracle, and the moment would never come again.

Go try to write about that. Then there was the baby and the song. You had to be there.

Newport

April 3rd, 1989

Friday night, 8 P.M., Monmouth Street, Newport.

For any long-time Cincinnatian, that conjures up images that beat against each other with an ambivalence that no other part of the tri-state can generate.

Sex, gambling, booze, a sort of tawdry glamour, a place where young men of a certain age came to scatter a few wild oats; a rite of passage.

Violence, too. Cincinnati's one regular contact with "the mob" and "the rackets", The Purple Gang, the Syndicate, contract killings, turf wars. There was a kind of perverse pride in having our very own "Sin City".

Actually, what we now remember as Newport wasn't all Newport. Some of the most famous gambling and entertainment palaces were scattered elsewhere over Northern Kentucky; the Latin Quarter in Wilder, the Lookout House out on Dixie Highway, the Beverly Hills in Southgate. No matter, we called them all "Newport".

There was reason enough. Newport had much more than its share of attractions. The Yorkshire and the 633 Club on York Street; dozens of bars and strip joints. The track announcer's call of horse races from all over the country was heard on loudspeakers outside grocery stores and specialty shops; for the convenience of sportsmen in the area, it was said. Right.

The late Ralph Mussman, a Newport native, sports star, teacher, mayor, city manager and city commissioner at his death, once told me he was nearly thirty years old before he knew off-track betting was illegal.

Now it's Friday night in Newport, 1989. I've already trudged north the length of York Street. The Yorkshire; wasn't it there? Yes. Now it's "Transitions", dedicated to helping those who battle substance abuse. A gentle irony. A long walk, ten blocks. No clubs, two bars, one family restaurant, one funeral parlor, six boarded-up buildings. So much for York Street.

Now one block east, and I'm on Monmouth. Plenty of bars and strip (dance?) joints here; "Talk of the Town", "Dillinger's", "Kit Kat Club", and right where the "Silver Slipper" used to be is the "Brass" Whatever ("Mule" is the euphemism for family newspapers). I walked in. The club holds 300, there are about 50 there; very few couples. A parade of surprisingly attractive young women make their way to the stage to ritually remove elaborate costumes. It is oddly sedate. Was this the stuff of my adolescent dreams? Or is it just that adolescence is such a distant memory?

No, it's more than that. There is something familiar about the women's dance; son of a gun if they aren't almost exactly the same as those I saw on an early morning television exercise program, and I think those women were at least as scantily-clad.

Back outside, I head south. A stop at Peluso's grocery store is the most fun so far; it hasn't changed in 30 years. Back on the street, a pretty young girl tells me I spoke at her school when she was in the 6th grade, and then hurries away leaving a trail of powerful perfume; a ten year old boy named Earl shines my shoes and tells me business was better back when he was a kid.

All right now, where is it? I ask a policeman but he doesn't know. He's too young. I've come here looking for a specific club, the one-time king of Newport clubs. Name entertainers, good dinners, swank furnishings, gambling for high rollers. When I was fourteen, I put on my eighth-grade graduation suit and in company with two older men (they were sixteen), went to the Glenn Rendezvous. Class. We were seated immediately. Were we asked for I.D.'s? Be serious. The comedian was Billy Vines, and nothing had ever been so funny before and nothing since. I nursed a weak bourbon and coke all night. We did have dinner which was ambrosia. Underdressed showgirls (particularly one) were so heart-stoppingly beautiful that I have always believed my voice changed between the first and second shows.

Now, where the heck was the Glenn Rendezvous? A stop in a very pleasant neighborhood bar (Barb'z) sorts it out. Right across the street, between 9th and 10th on Monmouth, next to a club now called the Mousetrap.

It's a parking lot. The beautiful Glenn Rendezvous is a parking lot. It could be a metaphor for old Newport.

Note the term "old" Newport. It's important that nostalgia not distort reality here. This was also a place of degradation, rampant corruption and sudden death, make no mistake.

Don't weep for "old" Newport. Look at it today. It is, at last, on the move. If you find the city disheveled and unattractive, it's because you're looking in the wrong place. York and Monmouth are not the center of gravity anymore, even at night. The clubs will remain for a while, museum pieces. They are doomed and they know it; there time has gone.

If you want to find Newport now, look at Monroe Street and the whole Mansion Hill area; check out other neighborhoods where clean-up and gentrification are taking hold. At the turn of the century some of Greater Cincinnati's most desirable housing will be here. If you're looking for nightlife, go to Newport's riverbank; but I don't have to tell you that, do I? Thousands flock regularly to "Steamboat Row" for the food, the fun and the view, and they don't have to dodge the occasional surly gunsel that peppered the old downtown experience.

Don't weep for the days of Sleep Out Louie and Screw Andrews and the bedeviled George Ratterman and the legendary April Flowers.

The emerging Newport will be better.

Newtown Revisited

April 4th, 1990

Rain was threatening when I parked my car and started to walk the length of Newtown's Main Street for the first time since Harry Truman was in the White House.

When first I saw Newtown it was a mere child, 155 years old. Now here it is all grown up at 198 and getting ready for its 200th birthday in 1992.

For those who haven't been there, Newtown is a modest community east of Cincinnati on Highway 32, not far from the Little Miami River whose caprices have stunted its growth. When approaching from the east, your first landmark is, as it has been for half a century, a driving range. That's where I started my sentimental stroll.

The driving range has had a severe case of growth. Now there's a batting cage and miniature golf and a pro-shop and I don't know what all. But standing on one of the tees, the view is the same. Bottom land, as far as you can see. Every couple of years when the spring rains came, we'd watch that long, flat expanse of fields warily as the Little Miami began to creep towards us. How far would it come this time? That low spot would fill first, then that one over there, then the whole plain would be a shallow brown lake edging in our direction, teasing Main Street, threatening to cut us off and invade our basements.

I saw a man old enough to have seen a few of these rites of spring and asked if water has gotten into the village recently.

"You mean into the houses? No, it must have been 10 years or more. 1978, maybe."

I walked up Main Street. Tommy Arnold lived over there. He was one of my two best friends. Wait a minute, these street numbers are all wrong. 6613? Where'd the other 6600 come from? They used to start with 1 and go from there. For instance, we lived at number 32, right over there, bought with Uncle George's GI Bill money. Now it's 6708, and it's Moore and Sons Funeral Home. Oh well, they've kept the house looking nice, anyway.

And the frame house right across the street. A beautiful young girl lived over there, maybe a year or two older than I. I could hardly wait for the first warm day of spring when she'd get into her shorts and sit in the side yard to read and catch a few rays. I would think of any dumb excuse at all to casually walk by 10 or 20 times, or plop myself down on our front porch so I could look at her. I'd have a dozen mental conversations with her. I'd even rehearse opening lines.

"Sure got warm early this year didn't it?" or the more daring "You certainly look great in those shorts." I knew I'd never have courage enough for the second one, but I thought I might manage the first.

But days went by, and though I walked past her often enough to be charged rent, I couldn't bring myself to speak.

One afternoon Tommy Arnold, my other best friend Angelo Bianchi and I were tossing baseball in our side yard. Angelo overthrew me, or I muffed the catch, and the ball went bouncing across the street. Intent on getting it before it was lost, I didn't notice it had landed at the feet of my dream girl. I grabbed the baseball, then my eyes panned slowly up like a movie camera, all the way up those lovely bare legs, then to the pretty face framed in dark hair. She smiled at me.

Caught off guard, I decided in a split second to go for broke. "Boy, it sure got shorts early this year, didn't it?" I blurted. She was stunned into silence. Indeed, it's hard to think of a response to that, even now.

I ran blindly back to the safety of my yard, and never dared to look at her face-or legs-again.

The house is still there. I didn't see the beautiful girl.

More businesses than there used to be. Two old brick homes are now "C.C. Motors". Then there's a "Body Shop". Across the street, that was always a tavern. Used to be "Fehr's", now it's "Murphy's". This is "Pool Care, Inc.", but when I lived here it was a "Dot" food store. The drug store's gone, now it's "Dale's TV Sales and Service".

I'm at the corner of Church and Main, and over there where it used to be the "Paramount Cafe" it's now the whimsically named "Newtown Yacht Club." Inside, a convivial bunch is lifting a glass against the noon chill. In a flurry of friendly conversation, they fill me in on comings and goings. Across the street at the Sohio station, I strike oil. Mike Arnold runs it with his son, Chuck. Mike is my friend Tom's cousin! Tom is in Sacramento and has five daughters, he says. Angelo runs a business out on Beechmont and he's doing fine. Mike's on the committee for Newtown's bicentennial, and he's going to keep me up to date. Great. It's a good town with nice people.

It started to rain as I headed back for my car. How about that. Tommy has 5 daughters. You don't suppose he married that pretty girl across the street, do you? Nah.

The Circus

July 2nd, 1990

All right, so it's only a one-elephant circus. But she is a very nice elephant. Her name is Paula.

I suppose I never got the hang of circuses when I was a kid and now I know why.

I started at the top. The Big Top. Somebody in the family drove us to Cincinnati when I was very little and before I had seen any circus at all, I saw the Barnum and Bailey, Clyde Beatty, Biggest Whopping, Three Ring Greatest Show on the Planet. There were death-defying leaps and Emmet Kelly clowns and man-eating tigers and it was all going on at once in those three huge rings, and now I know I was a victim of overkill.

I never told the adults who took me, but I was disappointed. It was too much and it was disjointed and it was loud and I was too far away and, all-in-all, I'd rather have spent my time playing sandlot baseball or reading a good book.

I should have started with the Fisher Brothers Circus. Now
I know what all the shouting was about.

For the first time in thirty years, the circus came to Augusta.
I mean actually *to* Augusta, in town, down at the ball park on
Second Street where our son played center field for the Augusta
Panthers.

It was the prettiest day of the spring and I went down to watch
them set up. I had read about one of these smaller outfits in an
interesting book called "Under the Trapeze" by Cincinnatian
Robert McKay and I was curious about the folks who work for
a circus that comes to a town of 1,500 people, does two shows,
then packs up and goes to another small town the next night.

The first person I ran into was Rich Atencio, very young, quite
handsome and as gregarious as a politician.

"Oh, yes, two shows, 6 and 8, 90 minutes of family
entertainment." He is the concession manager.

"148 days this summer. No days off, unless there's a bad storm
or the town cancels us. 148 days in a row. All one-nighters.
Tomorrow night it'll be — let's see — Falmouth; then ah, is there
a Warsaw?" I assured him there was. "Right, Warsaw."

The tent was already up, a cheerful blue and white stripe
spattered with mud from being rolled and unrolled on
waterlogged Ohio Valley fields.

"I guess there are 40 of us altogether. At least half of us are
performers, but we all do more than one job." Rich smiles and
goes about his business.

I really started to get into the fun of it. I watched the tiny
midway go up and the animals turned out to munch in the
erstwhile outfield.

That night, I came to the second show. There was
a respectable crowd; maybe 250 of us, mostly kids, and we were
ready to have a good time.

There aren't any Fisher Brothers anymore, but I stood next to
one of two Fisher sisters, mature ladies who are daughters of the
founders. One takes tickets, the other runs a stand where she
sells souvenirs, some of which she made over the winter.

"That's my grandson", she says, pointing to the casually-dressed ringmaster, "Mel Ray Silverlake, that's his name." A calliope gives an arpeggio and we begin.

"Laadies and Geeentlemen! Jane Randall and the educated horse...

"Aaand nooow, the lovely Jackle-Ann will juggle...

"Aaand nooow, to amaze you, the astounding Queen Ivory.." This, as it turns out, is elephant Paula's stage name. She comes out proudly bearing placards for Farmers Liberty Bank and Kelsch's Market. I'm starting to have a very good time.

"The daring and beautiful Miss Priscilla..." She *is* daring and beautiful, a neophyte trapeze artist swinging 15 or 20 feet in the air. A Fisher sister confides, "That's Priscilla Reeves. She's only 13. She's going to be good."

Suddenly, the lights go out. Miss Priscilla has just arched her back and hooked her pretty legs around the bar for a somersault when we're all plunged into semi-darkness, only the dimming twilight filtering in through the tent doors providing any illumination at all.

The 13-year-old daredevil went right on with her act, in the "show-must-go-on" tradition that was probably born in circuses several millennia ago.

Margarita and her doves perform. They are a hit. So is "Troy from Texas" who is really from Chicago. He does rope tricks just like Will Rogers used to do, but he doesn't have any of Will's one-liners yet. A Japanese lady hung by her hair while having tea. The clowns were all female. There were dogs and ponies.

The Augusta audience was warm and receptive, seeming to understand they were just as much a part of the show as any of the performers. When Paula-alias-Queen Ivory came out for the big finish, I was sorry it was over.

A little late in life, I discovered that I liked circuses, so long as they were the right size. I wonder where they are tonight? Probably just a short drive away...

The Rhine Is Over

September 13th, 1989

I recognized two sounds right away. A baby and a speeding police car, both wailing.

I was at the heart of things, Liberty and Vine, the Overest and Rhinest of Over-The-Rhine. A long time ago, this was the center of my universe.

I went to church right over there and went to school right over here, most of the 7th grade and part of the 8th.

I earned money by delivering pamphlets and flyers all up and down Vine, Walnut, all the way over to Sycamore. I got to know it very well.

Bingo was the second most popular drug of choice — a distant runner-up to booze — and I was in the middle of that, too.

As a 7th grader I was picked to call the bingo games, and this was no small responsibility. Women packed the church hall, and they were serious. Winning a $50 cover-all could make a big difference for a whole month to families living on the edge of disaster, and these chilly-eyed players brooked no nonsense from the 13-year-old pretender intoning "...under the B, the number 9..." into his very first microphone. I learned the value — indeed the necessity — of accuracy early on.

For a century, Over-The-Rhine had been the entryway for newcomers to Cincinnati. The Germans and the Irish paused there on their way to assimilation. Appalachians, heeding the lure of bright lights and a living wage, came by families and struggled with the unimagined complexities of big city life.

In their turn, blacks who were short on wherewithal and long on need found their way to this deteriorating collection of buildings just north of downtown and have added their alternating layers of hope and despair.

I drive through the area all the time, but except for brief visits to specific locations for news stories, I haven't walked these streets since the 8th grade. It's time I did.

Some of the sounds and smells are familiar, but none of the business names strike a bell. There are not as many families. Still a lot of bars, and still doing a good business, even at 2 in the afternoon. Some of the customers look as though they've been on the same stool since back when I was calling bingo.

Where was Kiefer's? I think it was the first restaurant I ever went to, and I was plenty impressed. Was it 13th and Vine? An old man says yes, it was right there, pointing to a boarded-up building.

There are a lot of those, more than before. More burned-out buildings left to fall down, too.

More storefront monuments to hope: "The Bread of Life Ministries", "Living Word Love Center".

One of our long-ago avenues of escape is blocked. The Empire Theater, never the Albee, is now nothing at all except a marquee and a lot of boards. No enveloping, democratic Saturday afternoon darkness which for a few hours allowed you to be anyone at all, anywhere at all, as the bigger-than-life images on the screen transported you to another way of life. I don't think TV is an adequate substitute for that.

Here's a little concrete park that wasn't there before. A few people on the benches. What's it called? One man answers, "I call it the Waterhole." Why? "In the jungle, the Waterhole is where local inhabitants come at night to drink." Oh.

I'm there for hours, walking up to Five Points, over McMicken, down Walnut. I talk to dozens of people, and what they tell me is familiar. Inadequate services, absentee owners, no jobs, crime and violence, father has skipped, youngest girl is pregnant. Years fall away. It's the same plaintive litany I heard as a thirteen-year-old delivering pamphlets to these same doorways.

Now I'm back in front of St. Francis Seraph, the site of Cincinnati's first Catholic church. Four stubborn trees survive to cast a welcome shadow. A man sleeps against the locked door of the church; some ancient hope of Sanctuary?

Among the many things that are different, and worse, one thing is clearly the same. Central Parkway is still wider than the ocean. It's the guarded border to a foreign country. South of it lies downtown and Success, handsome men, beautiful women, scrubbed and secure children. It is a land of mortgages and new cars, dinner out and money for college. It is a land where people listen when you talk.

Those north of the Parkway are still the waifs, pressing their noses against the toy store window at Christmas.

I wanted to tell them all something. I wanted them to know they could cross the Parkway, that thousands of us had done it. I wanted to tell them to forget my suit and my self-satisfied gray hair and my paid-for car. I had walked these same streets, had the same fears and hopes, and the same anger, too. You can get out of here, I wanted to say, and not just feet first or in cuffs. Don't give in to the anger, use it, focus it.

Oh, there was a lot more I wanted to say, but no one was paying much attention.

After taking the summer off, bingo was starting up again tonight.

The East End

November 20th, 1989

It was twilight on Eastern Avenue. There was a sharp, cruel chill in the air. It would be a cold night.

Coming toward me on the chipped sidewalk was a little girl, maybe six or seven years old. She was pumping a rattletrap bicycle, oblivious to anyone or anything, concentrating on keeping her balance. Her nose was running. She wore a thin summer dress. She was barefoot.

I turned up the collar of my coat and shivered against the 35 degree river chill as the little girl barreled past me, face and arms and legs red in the raw breeze she created as she pedaled her bicycle toward the setting sun.

I wanted to throw her my coat, but she was too young and quick and I was too old and slow and she was gone.

This was my second day of trudging this old street from sparkling new Sawyer Point on one end to the 5000 block on the other.

It had been a long time.

Years ago when I was not a lot bigger than the little girl who had just driven me off the sidewalk, I had routinely walked Eastern Avenue, its whole length, with some friends, all of us intent on going downtown where the action was. Usually the action ended up being a syrupy coke at Fountain Drugs on Government Square, but it was enough for us. Then we'd walk home, having put our bus fare to much better use with a shared caramel apple.

I went to school at Our Lady of Loretto, way out in the 4900 block. I think it had been a city building at one time, but now it was all-purpose; church upstairs, school downstairs. Only a hundred feet east was another church, Presbyterian, whose preacher and custodian all the children got to know and like very well. We were made ecumenical by proximity.

Just beyond that was a playground where Mary Ann Scheve whistled a rock 30 feet or so catching me squarely on the head, putting an end to whatever smart-aleck remark I was making at the time.

It scared her to tears. She thought she'd killed me. So did I. My bandaged head got a modicum of respect for a few days, but not nearly as much respect as Mary Ann Scheve's arm.

Now it's 1989 and I'm standing in front of the same playground, reaching up and feeling the tiny scar on my head, a vestige of a tiny drama played out on this tiny field so long ago.

The playground is still a playground but the Presbyterian church is no longer a church. The building is still the same, actually more attractive than it was. It's now T.A. Gleason Environmental and Geotechnical Services, if you please.

Our Lady of Loretto is still a church but no longer a school. The firehouse that was behind us is now Bentley-Meisner Plan Design and is, again, more attractive than it was.

But most of Eastern Avenue is, as it was then, an anomaly. It remains an entryway to or an exit from the wider community, mostly for Appalachians.

Ramshackle or vacant or boarded-up or burned-out houses stand next to neat, painstakingly painted, defiantly landscaped homes, little scattered pockets of pride.

It is a community molded by poverty, floods, hard luck and hard times. But it is far from inert. There is a groundswell of movement, efforts to change things for the better.

I walk into the East End Community Learning Center. Working on narrow margins, a group is teaching adults to read. 50 people, ranging in age from 18 to 60 are raising their sights and broadening their horizons. It is a brave effort; a ripple trying to become a wave.

Two doors away, there is another kind of ripple.

The East End Tavern. The sign says "since 1887" and I'm assured that at one time it was a combination tavern, hotel and one of the city's first Kroger stores. There are pictures to prove it.

Now it's a very attractive, very friendly cafe. Popular, too, with rock and roll music on the weekend and a young clientele. I would venture to say that not one of the customers was from Eastern Avenue. It is *in* the East End, but not *of* it.

Someday, perhaps soon, there will be a lot of that. Eastern Avenue will become "hot". Parts of it already are.

Pressures will coalesce. Some will toil to improve the community from within. Some will strive to improve the community from without. The spirit on one hand, the wherewithal on the other. Both are needed.

And the people of the East End remain on the razor's edge, uncertain where these inexorable forces are taking them and what it all will mean.

The East End is not yet taking a firm hold on its own bootstraps, but it's not gentrified yet, either.

It's still the little girl trying to keep her balance on a hand-me-down bike, riding barefoot in the cold toward a setting sun.

Maysville Water

January 10th, 1990

It must be something in the water in Maysville, Kentucky. Some microbe or molecule that anticipated, preceded and supersedes the Women's Movement.

The truth is, the women of Maysville have never in my memory felt themselves to be the inferiors of anyone and have gone about quietly proving it for generations. Well, not always quietly.

Your know about Maysville. It's a pretty little city 60 miles upriver from Cincinnati and a few years its senior.

What brings to mind the subject of Maysville and its women is the retirement of Harriett Cartmell from the office of mayor of that community.

The city will of course go on and prosper in the upcoming years, but something very important and certainly unique will be gone from the face it shows the world.

Attractive, articulate, peripatetic, opinionated and indomitable, Harriett Cartmell is one of a kind. She became internationally famous a few years ago when she stated publicly what many people had long been saying privately: Marijuana should be legalized and regulated, just like tobacco. It was already the state's biggest cash crop, she said, so the Commonwealth and the city ought to get something out of it.

Folks were not used to hearing such controversial opinions uttered by public servants and the feathers hit the fan. On the one hand, she was featured with a huge picture in "People" magazine. On the other hand, she was pilloried by many of her neighbors who thought she had lost her moral equilibrium.

It must have been lonely out on that limb, but she never backed down. She couldn't. Her mother wouldn't have liked it. Her mother, Rebekah Hord, had also been mayor of Maysville, and was plenty controversial herself.

I haven't researched it, but surely this is the only mother and daughter who were ever chief executives of a substantial community. I've always thought that spoke well not just for the dynamic women themselves, but for the people of the city, too. Long before it was fashionable to do so, Maysvillians left gender out as a determining factor in choosing their municipal leaders. They didn't make a big deal about it, they just did it.

Not just in politics, either. When I was growing up, Maysville had two daily newspapers. One of them, the Independent, was run by a very independent woman, Martha Comer. Never a shrinking violet, Martha found an ever-strengthening voice in the public affairs of the state and carried on the newspaper tradition of her family right up to the present day. She's still a consultant and a daily contributor to the paper.

Politics and journalism having been spoken for, another wave of Maysville women decided to try the entertainment field. From their perspective, it didn't seem so crowded. Rosemary and Betty Clooney began their public careers singing on street corners to attract a crowd for their grandfather who was running for mayor. He won.

That seemed easy enough, so they tried the stage at what is now the Opera House Theater on Second Street, where there used to be amateur shows. They won those, too.

As most in the Cincinnati area know, Rosemary and Betty went on to national and international singing careers, but carried a large chunk of their home town with them wherever they went. When it became necessary for Rosemary to incorporate, she didn't think twice before naming it the Maysville Corporation.

Nina and I were having dinner recently with Harriett Cartmell. At the same restaurant were other outspoken, attractive Maysville women; Dorothy Wood, Hula Duke and many more. Interspersed with them was a younger generation, every bit as outspoken as these trailblazers. On the way home Nina and I talked about it, puzzled over it, and finally decided it must be the water.

It's not that talent has missed Maysville men. Stanley Reed became a Justice of the Supreme Court of the United States. Ted Berry became the first black mayor of Cincinnati and has had a distinguished career in public life.

It's just that these particular microbes and molecules in Maysville's water seem more even-handed than elsewhere and allow those who quaff it to recognize ability wherever they find it. Maybe the city should bottle it.

Parker

October 18th, 1989

I have been told that every city in the United States has its own John Parker, but I do not believe it.

If that were so, the nation would be in chaos, ungovernable, a helpless, rudderless wreck, confused and bewildered.

John Parker lives in Augusta, Kentucky. We should put up a sign to that effect at the city limit.

He is outrageous, incorrigible, unbelievable, and the fact that he is among the funniest men on the planet does not excuse him.

He is a funeral director, which may explain a lot.

My wife, who is admittedly a little gullible, was attempting to run an antique and junk shop in our little town a while back and John, with characteristic generosity, would come by each day, buy a coke out of the machine, sit down and share his vast fund of knowledge with Nina for an hour or so.

On one of these days, she had bought a load of junk from a farmer in the midst of which was the disreputable remnant of a worn-out saddle. It was missing nearly all the elements which once made it viable. She had put a price of five dollars on it and had thrown it into a corner.

John was shocked.

"Good Lord, Nina, that's a Satterfield!"

"What's a Satterfield?"

"What's a Satterfield?! William Satterfield, the inventor of the cavalry saddle, was born in Augusta. He's an internationally famous man. One of his originals, like that one, is priceless."

Nina, seeing the bedraggled collection of dusty leather strands in an entirely new light, brought it out from its ignoble corner, cleaned it, polished it, and put it on the front counter along with a sign she carefully lettered announcing it was an "Original Satterfield." She wrestled with the meaning of "priceless", finally settled on $150 as being close enough, and waited for the rush.

Within a week she sold it.

Parker, all innocence, then told Nina he had no idea she would swallow such a whopper, and bought another coke by way of expiation.

It took Nina a month to find the people she had sold the "Satterfield" to and to give them back their money. By then they had told the story far and wide at dinners and cocktail parties. Satterfield is now better known in the Ohio Valley than the poor anonymous man who actually *did* invent the cavalry saddle, whoever he was.

It was Parker who started the famous Augusta Duck Races which flourished for a while on Bracken Creek and were featured on public television. People came from miles around to bet on ducks whose sense of direction deserted them when they hit the water. Most of them immediately went south, which is where a number of guests suggested Parker should go, too. The only winners were Rotary Club charities.

Parker owned a horse named Beulah who, thank heaven, had considerably more sense than he. On some pretext or other, he asked me to ride in a buggy pulled by Beulah in downtown Cincinnati at the height of noon-time traffic to gain attention for some visionary scheme of his.

To show how smart I am, I did it. Remember, Beulah was a small-town horse, not used to the hustle and bustle around Fountain Square. She often bolted when she was supposed to stop, and vice-versa. Parker who was allegedly driving, had no more control over Beulah than William Satterfield, and besides, Parker wasn't too sure where he was going, either.

After terrorizing Fifth Street and us for a few minutes and drawing increasing interest from the Cincinnati Police Division,

Beulah quite sensibly stopped and refused to go any further. Parker was chastened for nearly an hour.

But soon it was time to buy a car which for Parker is not a business deal, it is a pageant. He comes to Cincinnati and gets a room for three days. He then proceeds to frustrate every car dealership in the tri-state with his outlandish demands and endless negotiations.

After 72 hours, he happily drives home his new bargain station wagon, leaving behind a trail of shattered auto salesmen; broken men and women seeking therapy and new careers.

We who know him all agree that his wife Elizabeth is a shoo-in for sainthood on the first ballot, and we all fear that his son Johnny is showing definite signs of the family malady.

This is merely a friendly warning. Do not buy anything new or used from John Parker of Augusta. Considering the business he's in, it might be wise to leave instructions in your will, too.

Often in quiet moments, memories crowd the present. Not all the memories are good, but all are insistent.

I Remember

ONE OF THE FIRST THINGS a columnist must do is to conquer his or her journalistic aversion to the first person singular pronoun. No longer is it possible to hide behind the editorial "we". If the opinion is yours, you must take the heat for it. If the story is yours, you must answer for the facts.

If the memory is yours, it is seldom yours alone. Others share it so you'd best check the dates and places, no matter how sure you are. Memory is capricious, a poltergeist loose in your brain.

Only after poring over an almanac, a dozen old letters and several yellowing newspapers can you dare to commit to print, "Did I ever tell you about the time..."

Nick.

I Remember

Andy Hardy Syndrome

Monday, February 3rd, 1992

Do kids still "put on shows" for their peers, or their elders, or doting relatives, or anyone who will sit still long enough to watch or listen?

I always called it the "Andy Hardy Syndrome" based on those dozen or so films starring Mickey Rooney and Judy Garland in which Mickey at some point would inevitably burst out with, "I know what we'll do, we'll get old man Bixley's barn and we'll put on a show! We'll invite the bigwigs from Broadway, and then they'll just have to give us a chance!"

I was a bit too young to see those black-and-white epics in first run, but when they came around again in neighborhood theaters in the '50s, or on early television, I watched every one of them. I related to them, too.

My sisters Rosemary and Betty and I were always "putting on a show", and we weren't alone. Our uncles and aunts would have special pieces they would perform at the drop of a hat, too, and many of our friends had the same ritual at their homes.

Just after dinner at family gatherings, Great-Aunt So and So would say, almost on cue, "Why doesn't Little Miss Such and Such do her song? I always enjoy it so." With a little coaxing, Little Miss Such and Such would stand in the middle of the living room, surrounded by admiring family, and do her best Shirley Temple imitation.

That would be followed by a succession of other performers, each doing his or her specialty, or, perhaps, something cooked up just for the occasion.

On a given Sunday in Maysville, 10-year-old Rosemary might be heard to sing "Old Covered Bridge", 7-year-old Betty would follow with "My Reverie", and I would warble "Lights Out, Sweetheart." Then Rosemary and Betty would do a couple of socko duets, and we'd come to our big finish: two trio numbers for Rosemary, Betty and me which had been produced and choreographed by Uncle George. "Oh, Look at Me Now" and "The Sheik of Araby." This last one was quite racy, because Rosemary and Betty would sing the chorus and I — knee-high to the coffee table — would interrupt after each phrase with the pithy "Without no pants on!" Ungrammatical, but effective, because it always brought the house down.

The rage to perform didn't end at the family circle. It seemed somebody was always putting on a show somewhere.

I remember when I was a senior at St. Patrick's High School in Maysville, we needed money for some class project, so several of us decided to, of course "put on a show."

This time we were a little more ambitious and went to the manager of our town's largest theater, the Russell, and asked if we could have some time between the showings of his current feature film to put on our version of a "Hollywood Premiere". The manager's name was Ben Tureman, and he was a courageous young man, because he agreed.

I believe my job was to write the show and be the master of ceremonies, and we arbitrarily designated students from our tiny school to impersonate various movie stars. They were to be driven to the door, make a grand entrance, go up on stage for a brief interview or performance, then exit gracefully.

We worked hard on it. The girls found some very glamorous get-ups and the boys honed their comedy routines. The big night came and my memory is that we drew one heck of a crowd. Of course, it may have been the feature film, but we were sure they were there to see us, and were properly nervous about it.

Jim Joe Gallenstein and Mike Guilfoyle were Martin and Lewis, and they were funny. Louisa Dwyer was the talented one of us, so she portrayed the then-popular soprano Lucille Norman and sang to warm applause. I think red-haired Ida Means was Lucille Ball. Bill Ryan must have been Tony Curtis. I believe Jeannie Germann was Elizabeth Taylor, only prettier. Everyone had a part, everyone did what he or she could to make it work, and my memory is that we had a good time and pulled it off pretty well.

All of this was quite as spontaneous as it sounds, and it was not unique. We organized at least two more shows during my short time there, and that was in addition to any formalized class plays or musical presentations.

Perhaps that's still going on in families and neighborhoods everywhere and I'm just not as aware of it as I used to be.

If not, a generation is missing out on plenty of fun and a useful stockpile of experience and memories. Maybe we should break out those Andy Hardy movies.

Puttin' On The Ritz

Wednesday, February 10th, 1993

In the interest of journalistic integrity, it is necessary for me to issue a "clarification." I have learned to use the word "clarification" instead of "retraction" because "retraction" is very harsh and makes it sound as if I had made a mistake which, of course, I did, but using "retraction" makes me feel bad, so this is a "clarification."

In a recent column decrying the closing down of the Mariemont Theater, I wrote that my first "date" had been there and that Carol Robinson, with whom I shared the 7th grade at St. Gertrude's school in Madeira had been the victim.

However, I was reminded by a relative that I actually had a "date" several years earlier. Or at least I thought I did. It's an incident I had done my best to put out of my mind.

This was at the time when we lived at 1936 Fairfax Avenue which we thought was in the Cincinnati suburb of Walnut Hills but have since been told is actually in Evanston. Anyway, I was about to enter the second grade at Hoffman School, so I guess I was seven years old.

World War II was raging and it was the central fact of our lives. There were scrap drives and bond drives and there was the beginning of rationing. All radios, including our floor model Zenith, kept us up-to-date on the ebb and flow of the fortunes of the Allies.

The movie newsreels did the same thing and most of the feature films had war themes as well. If we had been good all week, my sisters Rosemary, Betty and I would usually be allowed to go up to the Ritz Theater at nearby Hewitt's Corner on Saturday. On very special occasions, we might even be allowed to make the much longer walk to the glitter and glitz of Peebles Corner where the posh Paramount and Orpheum Theaters presided. We knew that young Tyrone Power had once been an usher there and now his star-quality face often filled those very same silver screens.

Anyway, the War, the Radio and the Movies dominated our lives. After seeing many movie musicals and listening to radio shows, I decided I was a songwriter. It is good to set your goals early. My first effort was patriotic and, in the manner of children everywhere, blood-curdling. It went like this:

"Our Army, Navy and Marines, Are on the job, no matter what it means.
Death or freedom, slave or freed, Killed in action, or Bleed."

You sort of have to hear the music to get the whole effect. Still, I was sure I had caught the essence of the time and I had high hopes for my song. Rosemary and Betty would sing it with almost no encouragement at all. Rosemary still will, worse luck.

At the very moment I was settling on my life's work, I felt the first stirrings of romance as well. One block up on the other side of the street lived the Most Beautiful Girl in the World. Her name is lost to the mists of history, but she was the absolute image of one of the great stars of the moment, the sultry Dorothy Lamour.

I seized any excuse to walk by her house in hopes she would be on the porch. She never was. Admittedly, the romance had a few imperfections. First, she was 13 and I was seven. Second, she didn't even know I was in the same city, or care. Third, she didn't know I was a great songwriter, even though I hummed "Our Army, Navy, Etc." every time I passed her house.

Uncle George came to the rescue. He had joined the Army Air Force and was working at Wright Aeronautical while waiting for a spot to open up in an Air Cadet class so he could learn to be a pilot.

He found out about my forlorn hope and offered to try to fix me up. I was terrified, but after a few weeks, I agreed. The appointed Saturday came. Uncle George and my sisters dandied me up. I had enough money for both tickets and for two candy bars, with an extra dime for emergencies.

"Dorothy" was waiting for me in front of her house. She was even more beautiful close up, though she did pop her gum distressingly. We walked to the Ritz. I said not one word, though my mind was working furiously for appropriate and clever phrases. I had obviously used them all up in song writing.

Curiously, each time we crossed a street, "Dorothy" would take my hand. It was more than I had dreamed of. At the box office, I clearly remember reaching up to hand over the admission and the click of the tickets coming out of the machine. At the candy counter, I got Walnettoes and I think "Dorothy" got Milk Duds. I pointed, at my choice, still not saying a word.

The walk home was in summer twilight. At her house, I shook her hand, not looking up. I hadn't uttered a syllable. On the walk to my house I was so mortified I wanted to join "Our Army, Navy, Etc." myself and never see Fairfax Avenue again.

It was many years before I found out Uncle George had given "Dorothy" a whole dollar to babysit for me that day! All right, so maybe it wasn't much at first dates go, but a great songwriter has to start somewhere.

This is Grandma Ada Guilfoyle, who raised Nick and his sisters Rosemary and Betty. She also made washdays memorable.

Washday

Monday, June 29th, 1992

Here's another washday.

I suppose that's a bygone term. I'll bet a majority of you reading this do not automatically equate Monday with washday, or even have any notion what I'm writing about.

Washday was one of the eternal verities. It was a pillar of the week, something to be counted on. Saturday was a trip downtown and maybe a visit to the movies for Chapter 23 of the

Flash Gordon serial. Sunday was church in the morning and a family meal in the afternoon.

Monday was washday. That was the day you stayed out of the way of the lady of the house. I had a friend in Maysville who used to tell me he got "a whuppin' every washday." It probably was not an exaggeration.

And no wonder. I expect washday is what gave Monday a bad name in the first place. My two sisters and I lived with Grandma Guilfoyle and by the time we came along, technology had begun lending a hand with washday, but it was still the hardest kind of manual labor.

First of all, families were bigger. By the time the extended family was added, it was not at all unusual to have seven or eight people living in the house at one time. There was also more physical work being done. One man might be working at the meat plant, another on a farm, another on a construction project. A woman would spend hard hours in a family garden. And kids were, well, kids. There was just more dirt. Many of us heated with coal or wood which added more of what we now call "particulate matter" to the mix.

There were few fabric blends. Dirt that got into cotton or wool required a great deal of coaxing to get out.

Aunt Ann had contributed a Maytag wringer washer to the family by the time my memory of this weekly ritual began. I can't even conceive of what it was like only a few years before.

As it was, washday was work dawn to dusk. Grandma would have all the dirty clothes in various piles by the time I got up.

The Maytag would already have begun its intricate dance, spinning back and forth, beating linens into submission and at the same time inching its way across the floor in its exertion.

By then, Grandma would have taken a big bar of P&G soap and sliced it into the washing machine. Nothing fancy. Few suds. Workmanlike.

In the meantime, she took the really dirty trousers and shirts and started scrubbing them on the washboard which was slanted into a big galvanized metal tub.

There were two more of these. One was for rinsing and another for some mysterious process called "blueing". After Grandma had scrubbed her fingers nearly raw on the washboard, even those stubborn clothes were ready for the washing machine.

This mechanical marvel had that wonder of wonders, a wringer. It was exotic because it had the fascination of danger. A gear could make it go forward or backward. Good thing. A relative had become instantly famous by getting her hand caught in there and only "reverse" saved her from an even more serious injury.

No dryer, of course. Grandma marched dozens of times out to the clothesline and applied scores of clothespins and propped the lines up with half a dozen clothes poles.

Unless the weather turned foul. Then there were garments on clothes horses all throughout the house.

Some big items, such as chenille bed spreads, couldn't go through the wringer. Grandma wrestled those water-heavy monsters and squeezed them by hand. I swear, she got them drier than the machine.

That wasn't all, of course. There were the "delicate" things for the young women of the house which required individual and special attention.

In my preschool days, I watched all this from a safe distance. Grandma was understandably short-tempered during and after this process, especially considering there was still dinner to fix when she finished the wash.

On the few occasions I attempted to help, Grandma quite properly told me no. The combination of hot water, chemicals, electricity and that formidable wringer was no place for a kid.

No place for a lady, either, but that's where ladies were, coast-to-coast, every Monday for generations. Thank God, for most, technology has changed all of that. For many, washday has become wash hour and can be done any day at all.

And Monday has lost its most potent nickname.

C.B. and Me

Wednesday, April 13th, 1994

I was watching the American Movie Classics channel recently when they showed a film of Cecil B. DeMille promoting one of his own movies. He often used to do that on "trailers" that were used in theaters instead of previews. In addition to his celebrity as a director of epic films, DeMille was a well-known radio personality, introducing "Radio Theater" productions every week from coast to coast. His voice was better known than his face.

His voice is certainly what I remember from my one encounter with him. It was an unforgettable moment and, except for the ending, might have made a pretty fair Hollywood script itself.

My sister Rosemary was making a film on the Paramount lot. I was 19 and had been in radio for nearly three years. It was one of those awkward moments. I had done something they used to call "volunteer for the draft." The idea was to get one's military obligation over with, but not have to enlist for a full three years. Instead, young males asked the draft board to put their names at the top of the list. That way, they'd go up with the next call, but only have to serve two years, the standard draftee term. Miss Alma Potts at the Maysville Selective Service Board put my name at the top, but told me there was no call-up from our region that month. So, I twiddled my thumbs.

At this point, Rosemary and Mom called and invited me to come out to spend a week or two in California. It sounded like a good idea, so off I went.

One day, our kid sister Gail and I were visiting Rosemary on the lot. We were sitting in Rosemary's dressing room bungalow while she did fittings or something. Gail was about eight years old. We decided to take a walk around the lot. I think we hoped we would see a parade of movie stars.

In those days the lot was very busy. I was holding Gail's hand so she wouldn't get run over. A huge black limousine pulled up beside us. The back window as rolled down and a face appeared. It was immediately familiar to me as that of Henry Wilcoxon, a star of many epics in the 1930s and 40s. He asked my name. Then he asked if I was under contract at Paramount. I said no.

He then said, "Mr. DeMille", and gestured to the other person in the back seat, "thinks that you walking with that little girl made for a charming tableau. He would like you to read for him." I didn't know what that meant, but I said "sure." He gave me a card for the Paramount casting director and told me to contact him.

When we got back to the bungalow, Rosemary was there. It was only then that I began to realize what a big deal this was. She said something like "What! Cecil B. DeMille wants you to read for him?!" She was so nervous *I* began to get nervous.

I went to the casting director who gave me a date — I believe it was the very next day — and a script. The script was from the movie "Golden Boy" which, I think, had been the first starring part for William Holden. The scene was on a park bench, a conversation between the boy and his girlfriend. I no longer remember any of the script except one line. The boy was to look up and say, "Look at that sky. Boy! What a sky."

I had no notion what a "reading" was. Since I came from radio, I assumed I was to literally "read" the script. In some cases, I later discovered, that is true. In this case it was not.

On the appointed day, I was ushered into a brightly-lighted room where there were two chairs. On one wall there was a window. It was dark behind the glass, but I knew that's where Mr. DeMille was. Watching.

A pretty young red-haired actress was there. She was at least as nervous as I. She, however, had known enough to commit the script to memory. A disembodied voice over a speaker told us to begin. We did. We were asked to repeat the scene three times. By the second time, I had it memorized, too.

Then there was a wait of a half-hour or so. I was summoned to the darkened room. Still no lights there, except for the spill from the other room. Perhaps five people occupied theater seats. Mr. Wilcoxon asked me to sit down. He started to speak, but was interrupted by the man in the back. The faint light only sculptured his face, but his voice was unmistakable. I had heard it many times on the radio. Cecil B. DeMille.

"Mr. Clooney, you present us with a dilemma. We like the way you look and we like the way that you sound. However, we do not like the two together.

"You look like a 20-year-old boy. But you sound like a 40-year-old man. No matter how often we looked at your scene we could not reconcile the difference. The only remedy of which we can think is the maturing process. Come talk to us in five years."

I mumbled something incoherent and backed out of the room. I was none the worse for the experience and had, after all, been rejected by one of the most famous movie makers of all time.

It may be only a small brush with film history, but it is all mine.

The Old Man

Monday, June 14th, 1993

There is an old man I know. He lives alone. He has been retired for maybe twelve years. He sold the house when his wife died about ten years ago. He has a one-bedroom apartment now. It is crowded with furniture meant for bigger rooms and with a lifetime accumulation of memories, mostly pictures.

His two children live very far away on the west coast. Their jobs took them there. They call when they can.

Every morning is a challenge for the old man. There is very little about him that doesn't hurt. Looked at in one way, he reflects, old age is a gathering of small hurts. He no sooner gets used to one than another pops up.

He doesn't think of the pain as a tragedy, but as a nuisance. It slows him down, saps his energy, forces him into a dozen tiny compromises.

Each simple act has its own ritual. Getting out of bed, step one. Push up on the right elbow, the left one won't hold his weight. Step two. Put both hands under the right knee, lift it over the side of the bed. Sit there for a minute, work out the stiffness. By the time the knee will support him, the feeling will have come back to his feet.

Early in the morning, he needs the walker. Only then, and only inside the apartment. As he makes his slow and painful way to the bathroom, he thinks of actor Tim Conway and his interpretation of an old man making his stately way across the stage. The memory makes him smile. He knows he looks like that every morning.

Some days, shaving is a problem. When the arthritis flares in his fingers it is literally too painful to grip the handle and guide the blade over the familiar furrows of his face. Those days, he has to shave left-handed. The tiny cuts which result aren't what bother him. There are little tufts of beard he misses and he wants to look neat.

He remembers how little he thought about bathtubs when he was young. They were just there. He filled them up, got into them, scrubbed clean, got out, toweled off and went on his way.

Now he knows what a shiny white trap a bathtub really is. It is slippery. It is hard. It can be mortally dangerous. His bath is another daily adventure.

He makes up his bed and goes to the closet. He has three suits. Each is good quality. Each was in fashion 20 years ago. He lays out one of them.

His breakfast is coffee and toast with strawberry jam. He hesitates about the butter, shrugs and spreads it on. He washes the dishes and puts them away.

Getting dressed takes the better part of an hour. He has left a Windsor knot in all three of his ties so he can put them on easily. His black shoes are slip-ons, but the brown ones which go with today's suit are lace-up. It requires five minutes to get them on and loosely tied.

His Social Security check came yesterday. It covered the rent. It will cover his major trip to the grocery tomorrow. It will pay for the supplemental insurance premium. He is grateful for it.

But to take care of his part of other medical bills, utilities and, much more important, to buy things for his granddaughter, he has to dip into his savings from the sale of the house. His account is now under $9,000. He knows his mortality is in a race with his solvency. He calculates it with daily and cool precision.

He dresses up each day and goes out to buy a newspaper. He doesn't take his walker. He has a handsome cane his wife gave him. He leans on it heavily. Just as he used to lean on her, he remembers.

He doesn't get all the way across the street before the light changes anymore. When did that happen? He's straining harder now than he ever did to beat the throw to second when he was a kid.

A kid. There's a knot of kids in the middle of the next block. They're not talking, just standing there, smoking. They appear surly. Did he look that ominous to old men back when he was their age? He begins to sweat. What's left of the Social Security money feels heavy and conspicuous in his wallet. There's no one else on the street. He's on his own.

He puts his chin up as he goes by and looks at them. He says good morning. They whisper among one another. Then they laugh, loudly. A Tim Conway joke? Maybe. Oh, well. "Sticks and stones..."

When he gets back home with the paper, he is wringing wet. Six blocks, round trip. He had to stop three times to give his nerve endings a rest and let the pain subside. Three times. Not bad.

Years ago in Italy, during the war, they gave him a Bronze Star for going about six blocks under fire with a message. What a breeze that was, he thinks. A stroll in the park.

No Bronze Stars for old age. He opens the paper. There's a piece in it by a young reporter about the affluent older generation. He smiles grimly.

Nessie

Friday, March 15th, 1991

How do you feel about monsters and goblins and things that go bump in the night?

This comes to mind because of the cumulative effect of those endless commercials on television which urge us to buy various series of books and videos which will give us the real scoop on the "para-normal". "Secrets of the Unknown". "Mysteries of the Ages". "The Truth About the Bermuda Triangle", and so on.

I suppose you'll have to write me down as a skeptic. I always found the isosceles triangle more mysterious then the one around Bermuda, but I did make one foray into the mists of mythology. Or is that mysts of mithology? Anyway, I went looking for Nessie, the famous Loch Ness Monster.

As I've noted before, I spent part of my military obligation with the American Forces Network in Frankfurt, Germany, and after I had been there a few months, the Features Department instituted a series of radio programs call "Invitation to Europe". This was the brainchild of Alan Landsburg who was, like me, a PFC at the time, but later went to international fame as a writer, television producer and successful filmmaker.

His idea was to travel around Europe, dig up interesting stories from various regions and turn them into broadcasts which would help American forces decide where to spend some of their leave time. Bullfights in Spain, sunshine on the Riviera, the wines of Bordeaux, winter sports in the Alps, a weekend in Paris and, well, you get the idea.

Do you know what? The Army actually bought it. Go figure. Alan and a friend went to several of the locations with their portable tape recorders, interviewed a few people and stayed several days on TDY (temporary duty) which meant Uncle Sam picked up the tab.

My connection with all of this was that Alan asked me to be the narrator. For the most part, my work was done in the studio, so I didn't get to go on many exotic trips.

However, my friend Cy Nitzberg and I were planning to take some leave time and go the British Isles. There was a flap in the press at that time about the Loch Ness Monster, so I suggested we take a tape recorder, go to Scotland while on leave, and if we got anything usable for a show, the Army might reimburse our expenses and, even more important, chalk the whole trip up to TDY rather than leave time. Off we went. A surprisingly long and cold train ride from London brought us to the town of Inverness in Scotland at about 2 o'clock in the morning. We had made no arrangements for a hotel and in those days the only ones available literally locked their doors at 10 P.M. Nothing would rouse them. We spent the remainder of the night on a bench outside, waiting for the dawn.

Which, incidentally, revealed a lovely little city intersected by the clear and beautiful River Ness connecting directly with the famous Loch which was our target.

We spent several days exploring the area, and hours at a time on "monster watch" from locations we were told were most advantageous to catch a glimpse of Nessie.

We talked to perhaps a dozen people and through the pleasant burr of their accents were able to piece together the view of the locals. Three had seen the monster, though they didn't think of it as such. They believed it to be a family of giant eels which had mutated because of the great depth of the freshwater Loch. All who had not personally seen it still believed there was something in the lake, though they would prefer reporters to stop pestering them about it. They told us of one man, a diver from London, who had been hired recently to salvage a boat which had sunk. After a few minutes underwater, he pulled the emergency rope, was hauled up, shaken and wild-eyed. He spoke to no one, would answer no questions, packed his gear and went back to London. They had his name and address, which we dutifully copied.

Frankly, since we were 20 years old, Cy and I were more interested in the happy coincidence which brought a girls' drill team from Iowa State University to our hotel at the same time we were there. There were called the "Highlanders" or something, which was the excuse for their trip to Scotland, and we stayed up until all hours singing and telling stories and flirting. One elderly vacationing English couple confided they had not stayed up that late since the Blitz. Next morning we watched our new college friends rehearse, smartly turned out in their colorful kilts. In those pre-miniskirt days, the sight of so many beautiful feminine knees was dazzling, indeed, and drove thoughts of Nessie quite out of our heads.

Still, we had enough material for a show, but we needed a big finish. When we got back to London, I took a cab to the address of the diver. I knocked at the door. The man who responded had a shock of white hair. Diving gear was visible in the hallway.

I said, "Good morning, I'm from the American Forces Network, and I was told you might have seen something in Loch Ness while making a commercial dive there."

A very strange look came into his eyes. He made a high, whimpering sound and then slammed the door in my face. I tried again, but he wouldn't respond. As I walked away, I tried to remember where I had seen that look before. Then it came to me, and I stopped in my tracks. Of course.

It was terror.

1940s Literate

Wednesday, January 27th, 1993

I've decided that if you're going to get all you should out of this column, you simply have to take some tests. This will be the first of five quizzes I will conduct within the next several months.

I will call them the "Decades Testing", or the "DTs" for short. These carefully crafted tests have taken me years to perfect. The one you will take today is called "1940s Literacy." The subsequent installments will be called "1950s Literacy", "1960s Literacy", "1970s Literacy" and, against the evidence, "1980s Literacy."

The scoring will vary on each. Today, you get one point for every correct answer. If you are in your 60s or above, you get no bonus points because you should know all this stuff anyway. If you are in your 50s, you get one bonus point because, hey, you were just a little kid then. If you're in your 40s, two bonus points, 30s, three bonus points, 20s, four bonus points. Teenagers get six bonus points just for taking the test.

We'll start you off easy.

What was a P-38?

What was "Meatless Tuesday"?

Who was Gabriel Heatter?

What was a "one-button roll"?

Who sponsored the "Hit Parade" on radio?

What was a "ruptured duck"?

What was the "bazooka" named after?

What did bobby-soxers keep their bobby sox up with?

What was an "A" sticker?

Who was The Voice?

The Look?

The Body?

What was a "coffin nail"?

When Clark Gable came back from the service, his first movie had the slogan "Gable's Back and (Somebody's) Got Him." Who was (Somebody)?

Who was Phil Spitalny?

What got vulcanized?

After the war, what were women's longer skirts called?

Who hosted radio's "Blind Date"?

What was the 52-20 Club?

Who was Vice-President when the war started?

What was the most popular weekly magazine?

What are Marvels?

What piece of clothing got a Windsor?

Who was the most popular pin-up?

Okay, that was too easy, but how about who sang "It Seems to Me I've Heart That Song Before"?

Who was Colin Kelly?

How much was a pay phone call?

A regular stamp?

Who was head of the United Mine Workers?

What was a "slave bracelet"?

Who were the Dinning Sisters?

Where did the word "jeep" come from?

Who built it?

What name was scrawled everywhere American Troops went?

What was a "retread" when it wasn't a tire?

Who flew the Spruce Goose?

How did the SeaBees get their name?

Fill in the slogan, "There's a (blank) in your future."

What was the cartoon name for a soldier who never got anything right?

On what hill did the Marines raise the famous flag?

Who was the one-armed major league baseball player?

Who signed off his program "with lotions of love"?

"Omaha" was one American beach at Normandy. What was the other?

Where are the stars at night big and bright?

What major ship capsized at its moorings in New York harbor?

What's a snood?

What did you get for red tokens?

All right, I've run dry. That's 47 questions. Send me your answers, but I should get them by next Wednesday because this is my version of a snap quiz and you shouldn't have time to look all these up. Oh, yes, don't tell me how old you are, just how many bonus points you get. I know it's the same thing, but it feels better, doesn't it?

What do winners get? They get to win, that's what they get. All answers a week from Friday, How 1940s literate are you?

1940s Literate II

Friday, February 3rd, 1993

Hold it, hold it. The mail's still coming in, but I promised I'd grade your papers today, so here come the answers to your Literacy Test.

A P-38 was a twin-boomed fighter plane. All of you got that right, but Joe Breslin of Maysville says it was also a can-opener. I don't know whether to take his word for it or not.

"Meatless Tuesday", a voluntary plan to save meat in World War II.

Gabriel Heatter was the radio commentator who said "Ah, there's good news tonight." Every one of you knew that.

But not this. The "one button roll" was a double-breasted men's suit designed to fasten only the bottom button. It had large lapels.

Lucky Strike sponsored radio's Hit Parade.

The "ruptured duck" was a pin given to discharged veterans.

The "bazooka" was named after radio comic Bob Burns's musical instrument, which Gordon Sandberg writes was made of two gas pipes and a whiskey funnel!

Trick Question, so everybody got it right. Girls used *anything* to keep their bobby-sox up; gum, nail polish, rubber bands, glue. Some rolled them down, some let them sag. The best answer came from Regina Villier. What held up bobby-sox? "Bobby-pins."

The "A" sticker meant three gallons of gas a week.

"The Voice" was Frank Sinatra. All but five of you got that one.

"The Look" was Lauren Bacall. Half of you got that.

"The Body" was Marie McDonald. Only Dan Armstrong of Cincinnati got that.

"Coffin nails" were cigarettes. See, we knew it back then, too.

"Gable's Back and *Garson's* Got Him." Greer Garson.

Phil Spitalny headed an "All-Girl Orchestra."

Tires got vulcanized. Two of you said "soldiers."

Long skirts after the war were called "The New Look."

This one stumped everybody except Eadie Bently of Fort Thomas. The host of radio's "Blind Date" was Arlene Francis.

The "52-20 Club" was a readjustment allowance for veterans. 20 dollars a week for a year.

Henry Wallace was vice-president when the war started in 1941.

The most popular magazine of the 1940s was "Life."

"Marvels" were inexpensive cigarettes.

The "Windsor" was a knot in a man's tie.

Betty Grable was the favorite pin-up. Almost everyone got that right.

But I was surprised that only B. Gray of Cincinnati knew that Helen Forrest sang "It Seems to Me I've Heard That Song Before" with the Harry James Orchestra.

Colin Kelly was a pilot killed shortly after Pear Harbor and was arguably our first high-profile World War II hero.

A phone call was a nickel. A stamp was 3¢.

He of the thundering eyebrows, John L. Lewis, headed the Mine Workers. This was another one everybody got right.

"Slave bracelets" were worn by some women on their ankles.

The Dinning Sisters were a big hit on the National Barn Dance radio program.

The "jeep" was named after its military designation, the "G.P.", or "general purpose" vehicle. With a boost from a Popeye cartoon character, "G.P." became "jeep".

It was built by Willys-Overland in Toledo.

From Tulagi to Bastogne, "Kilroy Was Here."

A "retread" was a person who returned to service after discharge.

Howard Hughes flew the Spruce Goose, The "Seabees" got their name because of the first letters of naval Construction Battalions. The C-Bs.

"There's a *Ford* in your future" was the slogan, but I liked one of your guesses. "There's a *Woman* in your future." The cartoon character who never got anything right was "The Sad Sack." The famous flag-raising was on Mt. Suribachi on Iwo Jima.

The one-armed ballplayer was Pete Gray who patrolled the outfield and got 51 hits for the St. Louis Browns in 1945. Walter

Winchell signed off "with lotions of love" and it was Jergens Lotion, of course. The American Beach at Normandy other than "Omaha" was "Utah". The stars at night are big and bright "Deep In the Heart of Texas." It was the "Normandie" that capsized in New York harbor. A "snood" was a fancy hair net for women. Red tokens were used in meat rationing.

There. Out of 47 questions, plus bonus points, the average score was 26. Not bad. The best score of those I received before deadline was Dan Armstrong who got a 38, so he gets to win.

This was fun. In March, we'll test your 1950s Literacy.

1950s Literacy

Friday, March 26th, 1993

Here's your long-awaited test for "1950s Literacy". You did so well on the "1940s Literacy" test we gave you last month that you have raised my expectations.

Remember, you get one point for each correct answer. This is a pop quiz, so no fair looking things up in the encyclopedia, but there's no rule against working together if you want to.

Bonus points. If you were born in the 1920s or 1930s you get none, because you should have the best chance of knowing these. Born before 1920, one bonus point. Born in the 1940s, one bonus point because you were pretty young. Born in the 1950s, two bonus points. Born in the 1960s, three bonus points. If you're any younger than that, I'll give you five extra points just for signing your name. Get out your pencil. The one with the eraser.

1. What was a "poodle skirt"?
2. Who was "Maggio"?
3. Who sang "Oh Happy Day"? (Not to be confused with the "Oh Happy Day" of the 1970s)
4. What was Florence Chadwick famous for?
5. What was a "beatnik"?
6. Who was "Tail Gunner Joe"?

7. Who was the male star of the movie "The High and the Mighty?"

8. Who beat Sugar Ray Robinson in oppressive heat at Yankee Stadium for the light-heavyweight championship of the world?

9. Who played the villain in "Rear Window"?

10. Who was Sharon Ritchie?

11. What priest was a TV star?

12. Who said "Old soldiers never die, they just fade away..."?

13. Who sang "Thunder Road"?

14. Who said "just the facts, ma'am."?

15. Who sang "Don't Forbid Me"?

16. What Russian Leader denounced Josef Stalin?

17. What famous luxury liner was struck by another passenger ship and sank with the loss of 50 lives? (A bonus point if you can name the other ship.)

18. Name the heavyweight boxing champ who retired undefeated.

19. What was a "purple passion"?

20. What was Adlai Stevenson's famous remark when defeated by Dwight Eisenhower for the presidency in 1952?

21. Who wrote "On the Beach"?

22. What American Secretary of State won the Nobel Peace Prize?

23. Whose hit record was "Tequila"?

24. The Russians launched the first man-made orbiter, "Sputnik", in 1957. A few months later, the United States launched one. What was it called?

25. Who was Alvin?

26. What states were added to the Union?

27. What was controversial about the play "Tea and Sympathy"?

28. What was the significance of Panmunjom?

29. What was the Kefauver Committee?

30. Describe a Nash Metropolitan.

31. What all-time great entertainer died shortly after performing for the troops in Korea?

32. What was Johnny Ray's greatest hit?
33. Who pitched a perfect game in the World Series?
34. What Kentucky siblings sang "All I Have to Do is Dream"?
35. What was "payola"?
36. What was "Brown vs. the Board of Education"?
37. Who was "Borned on a Mountaintop in Tennessee"?
38. Who was the Reds' most successful second baseman in the 1950s?
39. What was Elvis Presley's first million-seller?
40. What Eastern European country rebelled against Soviet domination and was brutally repressed?
41. Who sang the hit "Sixteen Tons"?
42. What was memorable about the "$64,000 Question"?
43. Where was "Right Here, in River City"?
44. Who sang "Come on-a My House", "Half as Much", "Mixed Emotions", "Botch-a-Me", "Hey There", "This Ole House", "Mambo Italiano" and "Tenderly". If you get this one wrong, I deduct 43 points.

If your letters or cards are postmarked by a week from today they'll make my arbitrary deadline. Then I'll let you know how you did.

1950s Literacy: The Answers

Wednesday, April 14th, 1993

I have all the entries that were postmarked by the deadline, April 2nd, so here come the answers for our "1950s Literacy Test".

1. A "poodle skirt" was a circular skirt with a poodle applique. Some were made of felt, so there aren't many around anymore.
2. Maggio was the doomed character in "From Here to Eternity." Frank Sinatra portrayed him in the movie.
3. "Oh Happy Day" was the only known hit of Don Howard, 1953.

4. Florence Chadwick was the first woman to swim the English Channel in both directions.

5. A "beatnik" was a counterculture character. Many of you called beatniks "1950s hippies".

6. "Tail-Gunner Joe" was the nickname of Senator Joseph McCarthy, who earned a few other nicknames in the 1950s.

7. John Wayne was the star of "The High and the Mighty". Can you whistle the theme?

8. Joey Maxim defeated Sugar Ray Robinson who was attempting to win the light-heavyweight title in Yankee Stadium. It was over 100 degrees.

9. The villain in "Rear Window" was Raymond Burr.

10. Sharon Ritchie. This question stumped all but four of you. She was "Miss America, 1956", a pretty blond from Colorado. She was not, as Dave Gibbons of Mayslick, Kentucky, insisted, an old girlfriend of mine.

11. Fulton J. Sheen was the priest who as a TV star gave Uncle Miltie fits.

12. General Douglas MacArthur quoted a line from the song "Old soldiers never die, they just fade away..." after he was fired by President Truman.

13. Robert Mitchum, the star of the movie, sang "Thunder Road".

14. Jack Webb as Joe Friday wanted "just the facts, ma'am."

15. Pat Boone, white bucks and all, sang "Don't Forbid Me."

16. Nikita Kruschev denounced Josef Stalin in 1956, much to our shock.

17. The "Andrea Doria" sank with a loss of 50 lives after a collision with the "Stockholm". If you named the second ship, you got a bonus point.

18. Rocky Marciano retired as undefeated heavyweight champ.

19. The "purple passion" was grape juice mixed with virtually any clear alcohol.

20. After his first defeat, Adlai Stevenson paraphrased Abe Lincoln, "I'm too big to cry, but it hurts too much to laugh."

21. Nevil Shute wrote the brilliant doomsday novel "On The Beach."
22. George C. Marshall, the Secretary of State who spent much of his childhood in Augusta, Kentucky, won the Nobel Peace Prize.
23. "Tequila" was a big hit for "The Champs."
24. America's answer to "Sputnik" was "Explorer I."
25. Alvin was the most famous of David Seville's "Chipmunks."
26. Alaska and then Hawaii were added the Union.
27. The most controversial theme of "Tea and Sympathy" was homosexuality.
28. Panmunjom was the site of the frustrating Korean peace talks.
29. The Kefauver Committee was convened to explore organized crime in the United States. Estes Kefauver rode it to a vice-presidential nomination.
30. A Nash Metropolitan was a tiny two-seat car with the spare tire mounted on the rear.
31. Just a few weeks after returning from entertaining troops in Korea, the legendary entertainer Al Jolson died.
32. Johnny Ray's greatest hit was "Cry."
33. Don Larsen pitched a perfect game for the New York Yankees in the World Series of 1956.
34. The Everly Brothers sang "All I Have to Do Is Dream."
35. "Payola" was money given by record companies to some disc jockeys for air play.
36. "Brown vs Board of Education" was the Supreme Court ruling that ended racial discrimination in our schools.
37. Davey Crockett was "borned on a mountaintop in Tennessee."
38. Johnny Temple was the Reds' premier second baseman in the 1950s.
39. Elvis's first million-seller was "Heartbreak Hotel."
40. Hungary rebelled against Russia in 1956.
41. Tennessee Ernie Ford had the big hit "16 Tons."
42. Some contestants on "$64,000 Question" had the answers in advance.

43.   "Right Here in River City" was in Meredith's Willson's beloved Iowa.

44.   Hey There. If you blew this one, I would have no Mixed Emotions. I would not invite you to Come on-a My House to Mambo Italiano. I would order you out of This Ole House and flunk you. Fortunately, every one of you said Rosemary Clooney. Good guess.

The average of all who wrote was 21. With the bonus of #17 and excluding age bonuses, the best possible score was 45. Milton Held of Cincinnati got 44! Impossible! But he wasn't alone. Pete Householder of Warsaw, Kentucky got a 40 and so did Tom Louis, Athletic Director at Seton High. Margaretann Bachmeyer of Walton got a 39, Dusty Rhodes had a 38 and James and Ruth Hampton of Covington scored 37. You folks are awesome! When I recover, I'll organize one for the 1960s.

Taps For Cincinnati

April 15th, 1989

Tapping telephones in Cincinnati? Somebody has to be kidding. That's like tapping white bread and tapioca. We haven't had anybody worth tapping since Boss Cox went to that Great Political Machine in the Sky.

It's all a joke, right? Who could possibly stay awake long enough to listen to an entire phone conversation with Walter Beckjord or Bill Keating or Ted Berry? Or, for that matter, Nick Clooney?

Don't get me wrong. I'm not insensitive to the distinction of being on the list of (alleged) victims, and I do appreciate being included; I'm just not sure of where to send the thank you note. Of course, it does give you a sort of creepy feeling, like someone peeking in your window at night. In fact, to paraphrase Mark Twain, if it wasn't for the honor of the thing, I wouldn't like it at all.

No, the more I think of it, the more I'm sure it's a hoax. Al Schottelkotte had twelve kids; when do you think he was ever *on* the phone? Si Leis hasn't completed one entire sentence since he majored in Tortured Syntax with me back at old St. X High on Sycamore; whoever was listening to him would have thought he was talking in code.

They've got it all wrong. These weren't phone taps. Cincinnati was just a little slower than the rest of the world to get off the "party-line" system. Everybody was just comfortably eavesdropping on everybody else, like in the old days when our telephone prefixes were LOcust and JEfferson and MAin instead of numbers and we shared our phones with other families whom we got to know better than we wanted to.

Phone taps? Naw! Those are for Washington D.C. and Moscow where the stakes are high.

What deep conspiracies had to be penetrated in Cincinnati? The imminent invasion of the dangerous Flying Pigs? The life and death struggle over soap in the Fountain? The formula for Skyline Chili? (Well, that might be worth a tap or two.)

We're forming a club of the (alleged) tap targets. We'll meet in some convenient TAProom; we'll call the meeting to order with the playing of TAPS; for entertainment we'll watch the Cincinnati Police TAPdance around the charges.

We have most club offices filled; Ken Blackwell for President (we had to or he wouldn't join), Carl Lindner for Treasurer (close race with Jerry Springer), Carl Rubin for Legal Advisor (Timothy Hogan filed a formal protest), and John Smale as Investments Counselor (edged out Marvin Warner). Since no one at Cincinnati Bell was (allegedly) tapped, we made their spokesman Kyle Hill an honorary member and unanimously elected him Recorder.

We planned to ask three member of Police Intelligence (we voted that a contradiction in terms in this case) to be our Entertainment Committee, but some club members were afraid that if we did there would be no liquid refreshments at our meetings. All three had taken the fifth.

I'm all tapped out.

The Airport

Wednesday, June 8th, 1994

I am writing this from somewhere within the bowels of the Greater Cincinnati and Don't Forget Northern Kentucky Because We're Sensitive About It International Airport.

I have no idea where I am. I'm dropping this note on a moving sidewalk in the hope that a professional guide will find it and send a rescue party. I'm short of food and water. Each fast-food kiosk I have passed in the last day or so has said "Open In June, 1994". I thought this *was* June of 1994, but my sense the moment has probably been skewed by my hard time on...

...Concourse B.

I write the name in awe. I was afraid to commit it to paper for a while, fearful of stirring the anger of the Concourse gods, but nothing matters anymore. I have already eaten my boarding pass.

I think now of the irony. What a warm spot we who have lived in the tri-state for a long time have had for this place. We've watched it from its modest beginnings as the Boone County Airport to the Greater Cincinnati Airport, and now this.

The airport grew as the area grew. Delta named it a "hub" and the expansion has seemed to have jets of its own. Soon it was an international airport.

Of course, each increment of growth brought problems as well as conveniences. We would no sooner learn a new parking pattern than another one would take its place. Instead of a friendly walk across the street to pick up a rental car there was a bus ride which toured a substantial part of Northern Kentucky before depositing us at our vehicles.

We didn't really mind. Just growing pains, we thought. Everything soon would be straightened out, we thought. How childish that optimism seems now as I nibble a decorative plant. I remembered how each addition meant we had to walk a little farther. Just a little farther, we thought. No big deal.

All of that was before Concourse B.

I should have suspected something when the man who helped with my luggage gave me my receipt and said, "All set, Mr. Clooney. Everything's fine. Except it's Gate B-2. I'm sorry."

Sorry? Why sorry? I never heard anyone say "sorry" about a gate selection before. Now, of course, when it is too late, I understand.

I started my walk with my usual carry-on typewriter. Past the ticket counters. Around the turn with the little zoo animals telling that the construction was all to serve us better. Then through the metal detectors which now go off if your shoelace tips are metal instead of plastic.

The first row of gates is familiar, comfortable. Just a few hundred yard. Even the next, Concourse A is one we've gotten used to, though we always seem to be assigned to gate A-10, never A-2. That's an extra quarter-mile, easy. Still, there's the moving sidewalk which works most of the time. We've done it all often.

But now I was required to find "B-2". I was a bit bewildered, so I asked a Delta official for directions. "Oh, my. B-2. That's around the corner, down the escalator, through the tunnel, up the other escalator, past the international gate and...I'm afraid it's something of a walk."

That was four days ago. I think. I have walked until my shoes look like those of Adlai Stevenson. My right arm has lengthened more than two inches just carrying my typewriter. Many less hardy travellers have fallen by the wayside. But as I struggled on, I had one great hope to sustain me. When — if — I ever arrived at Concourse B, at least my gate would be one of the first. B-2. There was that minimum light at the end of this tunnel.

After what seemed an interminable time, I saw the escalator. Up, up, we remaining stubborn crusaders went. We were nearing, we thought, our goal. Past the international gate. Past more closed kiosks. There, in the distance, I thought I saw it. Wasn't that a line of gates? Yes! It was! Didn't they say "B"? Yes! They did! There, the first one, what was the number? "B-1", right? No! It was "B-10"! Oh, cruel hoax. On this Concourse, the designer started with the higher numbers first. May he eat airline omelets forever. I've crawled to B-8 now, but I'm clearly out of steam. Some passing official-looking person answered my cry for help by saying something about a "people mover" coming soon.

Alas, too late for me. If a Good Samaritan finds this note, please send airline peanuts and a Complimentary Beverage Of My Choice to Gate B-7. Quickly. I can take pride in only one thing. I appear to be the only passenger who has made it this far down Concourse B. Like many true pioneers, I will probably never receive proper credit for this accomplishment.

I'm scratching my initials in the floor tile near B-6. Perhaps Neil Armstrong could go farther. I cannot.

Travellers beware. There is the Gobi Desert. There is frozen Siberia. There is the Donner Pass. And there is now Concourse B.

Holidays

FIRST, LET'S ESTABLISH that this is *not* a paid personal announcement...it comes from the heart. I've long admired Nick and Nina Clooney. They're pretty special people, down-to-earth folks who have a keen eye for observing the majesty, the goodness, and the foibles of humankind. Throughout Nick's long and varied career in media he has unfailingly delivered honesty, professionalism, and care. My God, how rare these commodities are today. When we find them how dear they are and how much they need to be embraced.

Having said that, I was asked to submit one of Nick's columns as a personal favorite of mine. When the December 26th issue of The Cincinnati Post hit the stands I read it and flipped, immediately, to "Clooney's Corner" and chuckled...repeatedly. I've recommended this particular column as *required reading* to no less than 43 friends and colleagues so far. There isn't anything particularly wise or prescient about this column but it neatly and accurately sums up the peculiar "Christmas Presents Dance" regularly executed by men and women all over the world. I loved it. I even have it cut out and placed under the glass top of my desk. Read it...it'll make your day (maybe even your week or year). Thanks, Nick and Nina! You do good work!

Dr. Jim King
Director of Radio
Xavier University

Holidays

In Between

Monday, December 26th, 1994

Beware. Today begins that most dreaded week on the calendar: the notorious "Week Between The Holidays". The big day is over and a new year looms. That's enough to depress anyone all by itself. Now add to that the kids are out of school and the bills for Christmas are beginning to come in and you have a formula for disaster.

Let us dwell for a moment on what we remember from "Weeks Between The Holidays" past. The first highlight is, of course, the clean-up from Christmas. It was on some other memorable December 26th that we learned just how stubbornly egg nog stains cling to a deep pile carpet. And how about the ever-popular cranberry sauce on the lace tablecloth?

Of course, that doesn't hold a candle to the candle drippings on the polished sideboard. And the turkey gravy that mysteriously appeared on the wallpaper in the dining room, just about table high.

And speaking of high, how about the uncle who had one beer too many and tripped over the little red wagon, landing on the lower branches of the Christmas tree, breaking three ornaments including your favorite that had been on every tree since 1951?

Ah, the holiday season.

There are fragments of those Christmas tree ornaments plus bits of wrapping paper and ribbons you will not find until Mothers Day. Still, you give the cleanup your best shot and move on to the next highlight of this infamous week.

Leftovers.

Isn't it amazing how something can taste so good on Sunday and taste so bad by Wednesday? It took official warnings by the Centers For Disease Control and the Surgeon General to convince our home cooks that dressing left out for any time at all can prove fatal if eaten. Heaven knows how we survived in years past when we choked down three-day-old dressing along with our three-day-old bread and three-day-old pre-sweetened iced tea, but we did.

Still, convincing the family to dispose of leftover dressing does nothing about the leftover turkey, ham, green beans, yams, fruit salad, even leftover mashed potatoes, for crying out loud. Leftovers, Day Two is not bad. Leftovers, Day Five, is a nightmare.

Finally, we get to the real reason the "Week Between The Holidays" was invented.

To take back our Christmas presents.

Today begins a stampede unrivalled by any period except the day after Thanksgiving, but this time we're not shopping, we're exchanging. Clerks in stores all over the tri-state awaited the arrival of this morning's onslaught with fear and trembling. Those stores which remain closed today only put off the inevitable by 24 hours.

We know that women often complain that men are difficult to buy for and seldom seem pleased with their gifts. That is probably true, but it is also true, in my experience, that men usually accept the gifts, put them in a drawer or in the garage and get on with their lives.

Speaking now from one male's point of view, let me state the obvious; women are very easy to buy for. If there are young men who don't understand the drill, here it is. Go into any store anywhere. Buy the first thing you see. Have it wrapped and put it under the tree. Your wife or girlfriend will open it and not like it. She will then take it back and exchange it for what she really wanted in the first place.

Oh, yes, you can ask for hints, you can spend weeks combing specialty shops for absolutely sure-fire perfect gift, but you will be wrong. Every time. No exceptions.

Pay attention. I'm trying to save you time and grief. Some of you will say the obvious answer is gift certificates. Bite your tongue! Too cold and impersonal. What about simply asking your partner what she wants? Insensitive clod! You have excised all spontaneity and your personal input from the process.

How well I remember buying a dress for Nina early in our marriage. I never made that mistake again. Then I foolishly thought I had it all figured out. Practical gifts. She's a sensible young woman. I bought her two new tires for her car for Christmas. I barely survived the chill of that particular "Week Between The Holidays".

Now, the years have brought understanding. The gifts one buys for Christmas are only surrogates, stand-ins for the real thing. Your loved one will open the present, smile indulgently, thank you profusely and immediately begin the complicated calculus which lets her know what she can get for it in the barter bazaar that takes place between Christmas Day and New Year's Eve.

There you have it. I think we have combined all the necessary ingredients. The clean-up, which will not be complete until about June 1st. Leftovers, most of which you will consume by Saturday, but the rest of which will go into the freezer for future soups and stews. And the exchange frenzy, the real hallmark of any successful "Week Between The Holidays".

I leave you with one final thought. This is only Monday.

Ohio Valley Christmas Legend

December 22nd, 1989

This is a Christmas story.

The radio announcer was perplexed. He had undertaken a task that was proving to be just slightly beyond his capacity.

He was to write a short Christmas anecdote, one each day, between the first and twenty-fourth of December. The first ten had flowed off his pen easily. Eleven through fifteen had required two trips to the library. Sixteen through twenty-one were tough. They consisted of rehashed family memories and all of them were stretched pretty thin.

He wasn't worried about numbers twenty-three and twenty-four. They would pretty much write themselves. Nobody had ever

Winter on the Ohio River from the Augusta, Kentucky riverbank.

topped the baby/parents /angel/shepherds/manger/wisemen/ star story yet, and he was not about to try.

But one day was sticking out like a sore thumb. December 22nd. He was out of ideas. He had used everything he had ever heard or read about Christmas in the first twenty-one days and that empty page sitting in front of him yawned like an antarctic snowscape. Staring at it didn't seem to help much, but he stared anyway until little black dots began to dance around the edges. If those little spots would just connect up into words, maybe he could knock off this script in time to finish up his shopping after all.

Nope. They remained just spots. He closed his eyes and they were still there. Maybe if he just put his head down on the desk for a moment...

...the phone jolted him awake. How long had he slept? He shook his head to clear it as he picked up the phone. The voice on the other end was old, almost a caricature of old.

"Are you the fellow doing the Christmas stories?" Yes. "I haven't heard the Ohio Valley Christmas legend yet." He didn't want the old man to discover his ignorance. At least, not right away. Which legend was he referring to?

The old man started talking, and this is the story he told.

A long time ago, a packet boat started for Cincinnati from Pittsburgh on a clear, cold December 23rd. It was a sleek, lovely steamboat and was loaded down with freight and a full complement of passengers, all scheduled to arrive in Cincinnati by Christmas morning.

Now it was just after 5 on the afternoon of Christmas Eve. The river looked like a pane of dark glass laid gently down between the hills of Kentucky and the fields of Ohio. The only thing disturbing its surface was the lone steamboat, and it was in a hurry.

Sparks flew from its stacks as it rushed down the Ohio racing Christmas morning.

Darkness was just falling, but the Captain wasn't concerned. There wasn't a cloud in the sky and there would be enough light from the moon and stars for him to recognize every feature of a river he knew like the back of his hand.

The passengers gathered in the dining room and had just begun an impromptu session of caroling as their boat rushed past Maysville, off to the left. They were making good time, aided by the current, as Ripley loomed on the right. They finished dinner as tiny Higginsport came and went, and began singing a few more Christmas favorites as they saw the lights winking on in Augusta on the Kentucky riverbank to their left.

They had just started "It Came Upon a Midnight Clear", the notes echoing across the smooth surface of the river, when they were stunned by the most feared of riverboat disasters.

A boiler blew up.

Almost immediately, much of the boat was enveloped in flames. In a instant the Captain, who was at the wheel, brought the boat hard over, jamming it against the nearby Ohio shore, holding it there as flames licked about the pilothouse.

The bow remained against the bank while the stern swung around. It was enough time. Just enough. The passengers were able to scramble ashore over the bow through the shallows.

One young girl fell into deep water. A cabin boy dove in after her, pulling her to safety. She made it, but before he could grasp the waiting hands, he was swept away into the black river.

A steward who had made it safely to shore thought he heard a cry and ran back into the flames to help. He didn't come back.

The Captain who courageously held the boat against the bank remained at his post, the flames roaring around him.

It was a Christmas miracle. In spite of the explosion, everyone survived except the three crew members.

An interesting story, said the old man on the telephone, but what raised it to the realm of legend is what follows. The name of the gallant cabin boy was Caleb R. Noel. The steward who gave his life was L. Mark Holliday. The brave Captain who died to save everyone was the famous riverboat pilot Billy Christmas. The boat which burned to the waterline was named for the Pennsylvania town where its owner was born: The Bethlehem Star.

The silence on the telephone stretched uncomfortably, and the announcer realized the old man was finished.

"Wait a minute. When was this? Who are you?" But the phone went dead in his hand. He stared at it for a moment, then wrote down what he had heard.

The next morning he spent two hours at the library trying to verify the incident. No luck. Had he dreamed it all? Should he air the story?

Then he realized he hadn't tried the final test the old man described. The proof.

Stand on the riverbank just west of the little community of Chilo, Ohio, one hour after dark on Christmas Eve. Look out over the river. Soon you'll hear the faint echo of long-ago voices singing "It Came Upon a Midnight Clear." And if the night is cloudless, you'll see the silhouette of three men standing together, motionless.

Three men, listening.

The Fourth

July 4th, 1990

Well, it's my big day. How do I look?

Yes, I know my birthday was a couple of weeks ago, but I've reached the age when I'd just as soon forget about birthdays, if you know what I mean. And plenty of you know what I mean.

No, this is my red-letter day. I sure hope it's nice weather, at least part of the time. I think we all feel better and look better if there's sunshine, a big blue sky with a puffy white cloud or two and a gentle breeze rustling through the trees. My friends always told me that a light breeze was very becoming to me. Not one of those gales that comes whipping through Chicago or Cleveland, for heaven's sake. It's hard to retain your dignity when you're holding onto a pole for dear life.

Dignity is very important to me at my age.

Well, let's see, what have we got? There's the parade and the cookout and the softball game. What, no speech? I know I used to complain about them a lot, but you know, I sort of miss them. Some of those men and women made pretty good speeches.

Every time I listened to them, I'd think about Mom. She would have been so proud.

You heard about the scandal, I suppose? No, no it's all right. I appreciate your tact, but I can talk about it now. I admit I was pretty upset when it first came out.

Can you imagine those people saying she was not my real Mother? Don't they think I have any feelings at all? Dusty, musty old researchers, I wish they'd keep their opinions to themselves, and make no mistake, those are nothing but opinions. Don't they think I'd know my own Mother?

All those days and weeks sewing, cutting, snipping, worrying, washing, ironing, just to make sure I'd look nice. Who'd do that except a Mother? She deserves her great reputation and I'm proud of her. Whatever I look like today I owe to Betsy Ross. What a woman.

But let me get back to my first question. How do I look?
I mean, *really*. I'm going to tell you something I never told
anyone.

I don't like the way I look now nearly as much as I did when
I was a kid. You remember when I used to wear my stars
in a circle? No, of course you don't, you were too young, but
maybe you've seen pictures? Now, I don't like to brag, but I was
really something to see when I was young. Let me tell you, I turned
a head or two. Some of the older crowd sat up and took notice
when I came around.

The Union Jack — you'd never believe how pompous he was
then — tried to ignore me. We had some real donneybrooks, he
and I, but we're the best of pals these days. Time marches on.

So many of the old crowd gone now. The Fleur-de-Lis went
early. That ugly swastika didn't last long, but it was too long, wasn't
it? That was the only colleague I ever really hated.

I suppose we ought to talk about the big controversy,
shouldn't we?

In one way, I'm sorry to see it. I've got such good friends on
both sides of this argument. I know they're throwing verbal rocks
at each other, but how can I be angry at men and women who
have done such wonderful things while I fluttered in the breeze
above them?

The man who struggled day and night to get his family through
the depression. The woman who raised her children alone and
got every one of them through school. The man who lost his
best friend and most of his innocence in the thunder and
violence of war. The woman who battled scorn and deep
prejudice to bring dignity and fairness for her sex to the
workplace. There are men and women who did all these things
and more who find themselves on either side of this debate, and
that's fine. What worries me most is our countrymen
questioning each other's motives.

The people who want the flag-burning amendment enacted
are my friends. They are not insincere boobs who are wrapping
themselves in me to win elections or make points at the VFW.
They're outraged that anyone would desecrate me because they

believe it's an attack on everything I've stood for. They're good people.

The folks against the amendment are my friends, too. They're worried that the good result of protecting me would be accomplished by the bad means of chipping away at the Constitution. They're not soft on me, they're just strong on the Bill of Rights, and I can't argue with that. They're good people, too.

Secretly, I suppose that I'm flattered that an old codger such as I can still stir passions as deeply held as these among my friends after all these years. Like all senior citizens, the thing I fear most is indifference, and it appears we're a long way from that.

As far as the handful of kids that started all of this, well, maybe I shouldn't say it but, until they grow up, I'd rather they burn me than salute me.

Wait a minute. Here comes a breeze. Let's stretch it out now. Fifty stars, thirteen stripes, crisp red, white and blue.

How do I look?

Christmas 1961

Friday, December 25th, 1992

This Christmas tree is definitely odd. It has gaps here and there, like a five-year-old boy with a couple of teeth missing. It needs help.

All of our Christmas tree lights and the ornaments we have accumulated year by year are back at our real home in Kentucky. Work decrees that we must be away from Augusta today, but Nina decrees that we will not be without a Christmas tree.

So there it stands. Or leans. It's got a couple of strings of tiny white twinkle lights and Nina has worked some wonders with ribbons instead of ornaments. Last night when I got home from work it looked quite beautiful, really.

Nina and Ada Frances on Christmas morning.

This harsh morning light is less kind to it, as it is to all things and all people except Nina. She seems as immune to the cruelty of morning light as she is to the vagaries of time.

This four-foot tree sitting on a three-foot table has no such immunity. Still, it has character. It clearly knows it has a great burden of tradition to uphold. It must represent all the combined memories the two of us have of Christmas Trees Past.

The pinnacle of them all was Christmas Tree 1961. In Christmas Tree Heaven, old '61 is undoubtedly at this very moment holding court over various cedars and pines assembled, sipping eggsap and saying, "You call yourself Christmas trees? Why, when I was a seedling, you wouldn't even have been candidates for composition board. Let me tell you, in my day, you had to have strength and color and scent and a perfect figure, just like mine, to make the grade. Did I ever tell you about

December of 1961 in Lexington, Kentucky, down in the United States..."

It was December 24th, a Sunday night. Our new president hadn't been in office a year yet. The Bay of Pigs was behind us. The Missiles of October were a year away so we didn't know yet how fragile everything, including Christmas, really was.

Nina and I lived in a small rented house on the Richmond Road. Our son George had been born just the previous May, so this Christmas wouldn't mean much to him beyond eating the bright wrapping paper.

For our daughter Ada, it would be a different story. She was 19 months old, very precocious and talked a blue streak. This would be her first real Christmas.

For some reason I no longer understand or remember, Santa Claus in that fateful year made one of the dumbest decisions in the long history of Yuletide celebrations. He decided that on Christmas Eve, he would bring not only the presents, but the tree and all the decorations as well. Mrs. Claus had serious reservations, but Santa was so certain that his method would add to the joy of the occasion and squeals of delight from the little girl of the house that he insisted.

When Ada and George went to bed on the evening of December 24th there was not a candle, not a stocking, not a bough of holly to be seen anywhere. Ada knew the real story of Christmas, of course. She also had been told that Santa would come in the night and that, if she had been good, there might be presents. That was all she knew.

Downstairs, Santa already had second thoughts about his great plan. Mrs. Claus had no doubts at all that old St. Nick had finally bitten off more than either one of them could chew.

There were toys to be assembled, stockings to be hung, presents to be wrapped, candy to be made. In came the tree. It was a beauty, all right, eight feet tall, nearly that wide and heavy as a barrel of anvils. Santa invented a few new words while getting it to stand up in the corner. Strings of lights took an hour to untangle. Ornaments new and old were hung and icicles thrown on the limbs with abandon. A battered star dating back to when I was Ada's age went at the top.

The dawn and the Clauses were in a tight race and it was by no means certain who would win. Santa was sweating buckets and Mrs. Claus was rushing to each trouble spot in turn.

Just before six, Nina heard two little feet hit the floor. She went upstairs while I checked Santa's handiwork. He had made it, by a whisker.

Ada came down the steps. Nina had her left hand. With her right she grabbed each spindle of the stairway as she descended. She could see only the glow from the room until she got to the bottom step. Then, there it was. Just last night, this had been her familiar living room. This morning it was a wonderland of lights and toys and marvelous smells. Ada's eyes, already huge, became saucers. Her little mouth fell open. She uttered not one sound. Her tiny right hand went to her heart as if to hold it in. Her knees gave way and she sat down hard on the bottom step. Christmas washed over her for the first time in waves of carols and colors.

Nina and I squeezed back a tear or two. Somewhere I was sure I heard Santa saying, "I told you this was a great idea..."

Yes, this year's little tree has a lot to live up to. But you know, now that I look at it again, it has a certain rugged charm.

I'm wondering about a tree 1500 miles away, and another little girl with big eyes who is having her first real Christmas today, just as her mother did a wink of time ago.

Merry Christmas, Allison.

Columbus Day

Monday, October 12th, 1992

"All right, students, take out your blue books and.."

"Miss Jordan?"

"Yes, John?"

"Didn't this used to be a national holiday? Didn't schools and banks and everything used to close?"

"What do you mean, John? Who told you that? What are you talking about?"

"Well, I was up in the attic and I found Mom's old history book and in one chapter they had this story about a man named Col..."

"Don't say it!"

"...umbus."

"John! Never curse in this classroom. Once more and you go to the principal."

"But Miss Jordan, all I said was Col.."

"Stop!"

"...umbus. I think his first name was Curtis or Christopher or.."

"His first name was Plague, that's what it was. I'm so disappointed in you, John. If you knew how hard all the best minds have worked for a generation to stamp out the last vestige of the memory of that awful name so that you and other young people would not be contaminated by it...I think I'm going to be physically ill."

"I'm sorry, Miss Jordan. Really. I'll never say it again. Boy, did that old book have it wrong. Oh, it said he made plenty of mistakes, but it also said he was brave and smart."

"He was an abomination. He was the worst of the worst. There is nothing bad enough to say about him. He infected two continents with the horrors of war and disease and the cult of western materialism. All the most terrible things on earth, as we have told you, are the result of Euroculture, which he inflicted on paradise. It spread like a cancer over this idyllic wonderland and destroyed the world's greatest hope."

"I'm glad you set me straight, Miss Jordan. You wouldn't believe the propaganda in that book. It did tell about the disease the sailors brought, all right, and the brutality of some of the newcomers. But I didn't know how pure the people already here were."

"God's pristine children. Innocent and giving, trusting and generous."

"Do you know they had the nerve to say that the first boatloads of men from Europe got along really well with the natives..."

"Indigenous people."

"Sorry. With the indigenous people and when they returned to Spain they left 30 fellows to build a town, but when they got back all 30 had been butchered by the, er, indigenous people."

"Lies. Nonsense. No one knows what happened and that account was written by corrupt westerners."

"Yes, ma'am, I see your point."

"They were sweet, gentle souls who treated men and women equally, venerated their elderly, ate only vegetables and left the land as they found it."

"Yes ma'am. How do we know that?"

"Why there are dozens of accounts written at the time."

"By corrupt westerners?"

"I'm beginning to worry about you, John."

"I won't speak about it any more because I'm afraid some of this stuff would really freak you out. I mean, it says a few years later when the corrupt western invaders contacted the Aztec culture..."

"The highest expression of human accomplishment to that moment."

"Yes, ma'am. The book said they had slaves, a despotic monarch, human sacrifice, murder of old and disabled and endless wars, conquering weaker people in all directions. It said they gathered gold and jewels for the aristocracy which, if I didn't know better, would sound an awful lot like western materialism to me..."

"Childlike wonder at the beauty of the colors."

"I see. But you know, Miss Jordan, after I read that old book I was lying in the attic trying to imagine what it must have been like back then. Sure, some smart people *thought* the world was round, but nobody alive then *knew* it was when those guys got in their little boats.

"Do you suppose their hearts were in their throats when they went past the point any sailors had ever gone? Did they feel like Alan Shepard or Yuri Gagarin or John Glenn or Neil Armstrong must have felt?

"They bumped into a new world they didn't even imagine was there. They found a people who had greatness and frailty, just as they had, but whose technology lagged.

"The indigenous people would never be the same, nor would the westerners. A country would eventually emerge from that clash and combination of cultures. It would be something new. The ideas born of that melding would catch fire and sear back across oceans and continents until, centuries later, it would light up the world.

"I know I'm wrong, Miss Jordan, but it almost seems that the seed of it all was planted, however accidentally, on this day 500 years ago by this fellow Col.."

"Don't say it!"

"...umbus."

A New York Christmas

December 24th, 1990

It's a warm, nostalgic time of year, and this, specifically, is the most wonderful day of the season. Christmas Eve, when anticipation hits its pinnacle, when the great day is still ahead of us, when anything is still possible.

After the sun goes down, each of us will find a moment to conjure up memories of a favorite Christmas past. I, for instance, will undoubtedly be touched by the memory of our family's traditional TV Game Show Christmas.

Did I see you wince? You mean you've never experienced a TV Game Show Christmas? Well, perhaps I'd better enlighten you.

The year was 1974. In August I had been asked by someone at ABC Television to host a pilot for a game show. Since I had only two other jobs at the time, it sounded like a good idea to me, so off to New York we went.

The show was the darndest thing I've ever seen. "The Money Maze". The producers had constructed this huge, life-size maze, taking up every inch of space in the largest studio ABC had in New York City.

The idea was that a couple would come to the show and answer a few on-camera questions I would pose. If they were successful, one member of the team would go down into the maze, the other would remain with me in a sort of crow's nest where he or she would try to direct the partner down below toward various pillars of light located throughout the maze. When the contestant reached the pillar, he or she would push a button to light it up, then go on to the next. If they lit up all the pillars, they got $10,000, or in some cases, more.

There was an audience in elevated bleachers on the three sides, looking down into the maze watching this hapless contestant trying to get through the torture chamber by voice command alone. After each game, the configuration of the maze was changed. Amazingly, many were successful and took home the cash.

I didn't think anything would come of the pilot, but we had a good time in New York and then returned to the real world; Cincinnati and our TV talk show, radio show and dinner theater appearances.

In November, much to my surprise, the producers called to say that ABC had picked up the show and it would go on the air just after the first of next year.

The whole family was excited, but our emotions got mixed in a hurry when the network called back and said they wanted the show to start early. In fact, they wanted it to premiere the week before

Christmas, which meant I'd have to go to New York about the middle of December and stay there until after New Year's Day.

You see, here's the way it works. When you really begin a daily network show, it takes time to work out the bugs during the early tapings. At first, it might take a whole day to do one show. After a while, it gets easier, and when you're really rolling, you do all rehearsals and prep one day, then tape all five shows the next.

But to start with, I was going to be married to that studio night and day. Including Christmas.

Our house is just like yours; this is a very special time. I'd never been away from Nina and the kids at Christmas. What to do?

Easy. They went with me. We drove to New York right through a snow storm as I remember and then got two rooms at the Park Sheraton Hotel just a couple of blocks from where I was taping.

In the few hours I wasn't working, we did every tourist thing you can do in the Big Apple, going from Wall Street to the crown of the Statue of Liberty to the Garment District and everything in between. We had a good time,

Then came Christmas Eve, this very day 16 years ago. As the sun went down, the kids were looking out the hotel window at the busy, unfamiliar city. The touring was over and they seemed, understandably, a little blue.

Nina went across the street to a flower shop and bought a perfect little Christmas tree, about a foot tall. Then we quickly got some extra gifts, wrapped them and hid them in the same place with the others we had brought with us.

After supper, we took Ada and George to the Christmas pageant at Radio City Music Hall, a brilliant show of music and color and movement that fills the whole stage. On the way back, we stopped at St. Patrick's Cathedral, and finally on to the hotel.

While the kids slept, we put the presents around our Lilliputian tree and on Christmas morning when they opened them, the laughter and fun proved again that this holiday is, indeed, a moveable feast.

The game show lasted only ten months. Our Game Show Christmas will last forever.

And so will this one. Merry Christmas, everyone.

The Fourth

Monday, July 5th, 1993

I just finished rereading the Declaration of Independence. I try to do that once a year, usually right around the Fourth of July.

This year, I concentrated on the men who signed the document 217 years ago. It's very hard now to imagine what they were like, though they were at the height of their powers just three full lifetimes ago.

I pulled out a list of their names and ages and occupations and home towns. There were 56 in all, if my list is correct. One was a manufacturer. Just one. He was an "iron master". Not much manufacturing back then.

Here's another difference between 1776 and 1993. Thirteen of the signers were farmers. That's almost a quarter of the total. Whatever else those men were, they were considerably closer to the land than we are.

Only nine were businessmen. That runs counter to the current conventional wisdom that business is the repository of all the common sense in the Republic and that no one can possibly govern who hasn't met a payroll, but there it is. Someone forgot to tell the Founding Fathers.

Four were physicians. One a surveyor. Four listed their occupation as "politician" or "public servant". I wonder how many of today's politicians would list their occupation as "politican"? The word has obviously degenerated over the years.

One was a clergyman. He was also a college president, so our eventual commitment to the separation of church and state was not compromised early on.

Twenty-three of the signers were lawyers. That's almost twice as many as any other occupation and should provide at least a partial antidote to the current tidal wave of lawyer-bashing.

All 56 of these men, including the lawyers, deserve our gratitude and our careful study. They were on the cutting edge of a political system that has swept the world. They had courage.

There was no guarantee that they wouldn't spend the rest of their lives in jail or, worse yet, be hanged from the nearest tree.

The average age of those present was 44. What do you suppose was going through the minds of the two youngest men in this august group, Thomas Lynch and Edward Rutledge, both 26 and both from South Carolina? How must they have felt as they looked across that stifling room and, perhaps, caught the eye of the oldest man there, 71-year-old Benjamin Franklin, already the greatest man in the colonies?

As he put his pen to that historic paper, his fellow Pennsylvanian John Morton, a 52-year-old surveyor, had just one year to live.

That got me to thinking. I found that six of those who signed the Declaration did not live to see how it all turned out. Morton was the first. Next was Phillip Livingston, a New York merchant who died in 1778 at age 62.

1779 was a tough year for the fortunes of the fledgling Republic and for the signers of the Declaration. Lawyer George Ross of Pennsylvania died at 49. Merchant Joseph Hewes of North Carolina died at the same age. Farmer John Hart of New Jersey was 62 when he died.

And remember youngest-signer Thomas Lynch of South Carolina? He didn't get much older. He died in 1779 at age 30.

Their last view of the United Colonies was not a hopeful one. George Washington and his ragtag army were about to spend a worse winter than they had the year before at Valley Forge. Major defeats loomed in the south. The treachery of Benedict Arnold was still a year away. What was to become the world's greatest democracy was still decidedly a work-in-progress when these men breathed their last.

The incredible victory at Yorktown was two years away. The peace treaty that validated our independence which they had so bravely declared was four years in the future.

But I like to think they never doubted for a moment. I hope they believed all would come right at the end.

I suppose that's the reason I haul out the old Declaration of Independence once a year. It seems to me there's a compact between those long-ago men and every American who has followed them. In spite of their personal flaws and individual prejudices, these 56 men set in motion a force which would eventually widen the boundaries of human freedom beyond anything seen on the surface of the earth. In the cause of self-evident truths and unalienable rights, all Americans, men and women, black and white, believer and atheist, rich and poor, young and old, all of us are, it seems to me, required once again to "mutually pledge our Lives, our Fortunes, and our Sacred honor."

I hope you had a great Fourth.

Christmas Eve, 1993

Friday, December 24th, 1993

All in all, it was a most satisfying night. It was snowing gently. The drive home from downtown Cincinnati was pleasant, with pockets of cheery holiday lights dotting the dark Kentucky hills.

For the first time in the 1993 season, I felt the Christmas spirit. At a gathering I had just left, 14 men had raised their voices in some of the most beautiful of yuletide songs. "Lo, How A Rose Ere Blooming" was echoing through my head as the miles slipped by.

The newest addition to our family, "Spags", the formerly homeless mutt who adopted Nina and me in September, danced a greeting as I opened the door. She was pantomiming two messages. First, she was glad to see me. Second, it was a little past our usual time for her late night walk.

It only took a second to snap on her leash and head back out into the night. Spags has taught me a great deal more about the little river town where we live than I ever knew before. I now know every house. That's because we take a slightly different route on each walk. There's a good reason for that, especially at night. You see, we leave a wake of barking watchdogs wherever we go, and I think it's wise to spread that honor around.

It was just after 11 o'clock now and the snow was coming down a little more heavily, blanketing the lawns and roofs as we walked. Spags was not used to snow and she tiptoed through it gingerly, snapping suspiciously at the snowflakes as they fell.

Most of the homes we passed were battened down for the night, but their Christmas lights blinked cheerfully. Some families were watching the late news. Some listened to music. Some were reading books or newspapers. Some were already asleep. All seemed warm and peaceful and safe.

When we got down to the river, a towboat was grinding it's way upstream. I wondered if the crew members had finished their Christmas shopping. As the waves slapped against the bank, I took inventory of my own list. Still a few gifts yet to buy in the brief time left.

By now the snow had turned the little dog's black hair white, much as time and a life in broadcasting had already done mine. We headed home. I was still thinking about gifts, but not quite in the same way as before.

The 200-year-old row houses we were passing got me to thinking about the men and women whose complicated trajectory had combined to result in my being at this spot on the planet. I wondered how they would view the gifts life had to offer in 1993.

In a few minutes, I would walk into our house. Every room would be warm. Every room. All day. All night. Just a wink of time ago, there were Clooneys in Kilkenny who huddled around a peat fire against the damp cold of an Irish winter. What would they think of the gift of perpetual warmth?

A few more blocks now and I'll flip a button and the room will be flooded with the light of midday. No ghosts can lurk in any corner. The Koch family of southern Germany was not rich, but 200 years ago, had Mother and Father Koch possessed all the accumulated wealth of Europe, they could not do what I can do with the flick of my finger.

After I get into my pajamas, I'll push another little button and a picture will appear like magic on the front of a box ten feet away. The picture will come from a city across an ocean. The Farrows of England and the Vandens of France 300 Christmases ago were only beginning to dream of crossing that same ocean in a storm-tossed wooden ship to find a new life. What would they think of my magic box?

They seem so far away, so different, these forebears of mine. What did they take for a cold? What music did they like? What tasted good to them? What made them laugh? Did they have a little black dog who shook the snow from her back? I know so little about them.

But on this, of all nights, a measure of understanding can take shape through the mist of the generations that separate us. Tonight, at least, we are more alike than we are different. The human heart cannot have changed so much.

After all, the Clooneys and the Guilfoyles and the Farrows and the Kochs and the Vandens told the same story we'll tell on this Christmas Eve. They spoke of a frightened young couple, hungry and homeless. They sang of stars and shepherds.

And of a baby. A baby whose timeless magic overwhelms even the wonders of central heating against the winter, lights that defeat darkness and a marvelous electric picture box.

Merry Christmas, everyone.

The Tree

Wednesday, December 21st, 1994

This thing weighs a ton. We'll never get it into the house. This was a dumb idea. The worst idea of the whole Christmas season. Whose dumb idea was this? Oh, yeah. Well.... It wasn't as though we really wanted a live Christmas tree. We didn't have any choice. All right, so we waited a little late to get our tree this year, but who would have thought there wouldn't be any left? Not one cut Christmas tree to be found in Augusta. Almost a whole week before the big day and not one left in all of Maysville, either. You know those lots, packed every year with trees of all shapes and sizes? All yawning empty this year. Just some broken branches, piles of needles and an occasional forlorn pine wreath to mark where the forest of cut evergreens had been. None at Kroger, either, or Clyde's or Bestway.

Across the bridge to Aberdeen. Nina and her Mom checked to the right. I scanned the left. Nothing. Until, "I think I see some trees over there." We looked where Nina was indicating. Sure enough, I could see some trees neatly lined up, too.

But as we drove up, my heart sank. These trees all had the telltale burlap sack wrapped around the base. They were the dreaded live trees. Oh, no, anything but that.

Once, in a fit of environmental virtue, the family had decided we would buy only live Christmas trees from then on. Immediately after each New Year's Day, we would plant them in our yard as living mementoes of our holiday celebration.

That great idea lasted one year and it was very nearly one year too many. We bought a modest-sized tree and I confidently reached down to pick it up and put it in the car. It would not move. It was as heavy as a pool table. By the time I wrestled it into the car I was speaking an octave higher. My exertions in subsequently dragging it into the house have become the stuff of family legend. It remained in the living room until the vernal equinox was upon us, at which time Nina — unreasonably, I thought — demanded its removal.

Now, 25 years later, was there to be a replay? Say it ain't so.

"Look, don't you have any cut trees?" I asked the nursery man.

"Oh, no, they've all been gone for several days. In fact, I haven't seen any cut trees anywhere since Saturday. They went fast this year."

Tell me about it. I walked around the nursery, eyeing each tree with suspicion. I've always wanted big trees. No dinky bushes for our family. But this time I must admit I was being drawn to a group of tiny spruces over in the corner all by themselves. Very pretty. And they probably didn't weigh more than 200 pounds each.

"We'll take one of those."

"No, you won't. They're all sold. Just waiting to be picked up. Everything here has been sold. Don't you see those red tags on them? Wait a minute. I guess there's one over there still for sale. Half-price, too." He was indicating a good-sized tree off to his right.

"Norwegian spruce. It's a beauty, isn't it?"

All I could see was that much of Norway apparently came with the spruce. It was attached to the biggest ball of dirt and roots in the entire nursery.

Still, it appeared this was the last tree for sale within a 30-mile radius, so we took it. The nursery man had a special dolly to haul it to the car. It took three of us five minutes to inch it up into the trunk.

We had a silent ride home. I don't know what Nina and Dica were thinking about, but I was trying to remember who in Augusta might have a fork-lift. If we put some boards on the front porch steps for a ramp and took off the door frame, we could probably drive it right into the living room.

But first, we'd have to get it out of the trunk. Darkness had fallen, so the neighbors wouldn't see my exertions. Good. We got every tool in the place to use as levers. Finally, I climbed into the trunk myself. I was getting stubborn about it. Maybe I'd never get it into the living room, but I would darn well get it out of the car. Centimeter by centimeter I worked it up to the edge of the trunk. Then I let it drop. The thud was measured at 4.3 on the Richter scale in Golden, Colorado.

The tree is now on the strip of grass between the curb and the sidewalk. My vote is to leave it there. It is canted at an attractive 45 degree angle and should be quite a neighborhood conversation piece. Nina says she will get a couple of boys from the high school to bring it in tomorrow. Right. They'd better bring their dads and a sumo wrestler, too.

Another thing. Once in the living room, this tree stays. It will be a Valentine's tree, an Easter tree, a Fourth of July tree, Labor Day tree, a Thanksgiving tree and a Christmas tree again.

In fact, we are introducing to the Ohio Valley, the first-ever indoor Tree for All Seasons.